CAMBRIDGE
UNIVERSITY PRESS

CAMBRIDGE ENGLISH
Language Assessment
Part of the University of Cambridge

Cambridge English

EMPOWER

PRE-INTERMEDIATE

Student's Book

B1

Adrian Doff, Craig Thaine
Herbert Puchta, Jeff Stranks, Peter Lewis-Jones
with Graham Burton

Lesson and objective		Grammar	Vocabulary	Pronunciation	Everyday English
Unit 1 Communicating					
Getting started	Talk about sharing things on your phone				
1A	Ask and answer personal questions	Question forms	Common adjectives	Syllables and word stress Sentence stress	
1B	Talk about how people communicate	Present simple and present continuous	Adverbs	Long and short vowels	
1C	Greet people and end conversations			Sentence stress	Greeting people; Ending a conversation
1D	Write a personal email				
Review and extension	More practice		WORDPOWER *like*		
Unit 2 Travel and Tourism					
Getting started	Talk about holiday activities				
2A	Talk about past holidays	Past simple	Tourism	*-ed* endings	
2B	Describe difficult journeys	Past continuous	Travel collocations	Sentence stress: vowel sounds	
2C	Ask for information in a public place			Joining words	Asking for information in a public place
2D	Write a travel blog				
Review and extension	More practice		WORDPOWER *off*		
Unit 3 Money					
Getting started	Talk about shopping				
3A	Talk about experiences of generosity	Present perfect or past simple	*make* / *do* / *give* collocations		
3B	Talk about spending and saving money	Present perfect with *just*, *already* and *yet*	Money	Sound and spelling: /dʒ/ and /j/	
3C	Talk to people in shops			Sentence stress	Talking to people in shops; Paying at the till
3D	Write an update email				
Review and extension	More practice		WORDPOWER *just*		
Unit 4 Social Life					
Getting started	Talk about weddings				
4A	Talk about your plans for celebrations	Present continuous and *going to*	Clothes and appearance	Sound and spelling: *going to*	
4B	Plan a day out in a city	*will* / *won't* / *shall*	Adjectives: places	Sound and spelling: *want* and *won't*	
4C	Make social arrangements			Sentence stress	Making arrangements
4D	Write and reply to invitations				
Review and extension	More practice		WORDPOWER *look*		
Unit 5 Work					
Getting started	Talk about people at work				
5A	Talk about what people do at work	*must* / *have to* / *can*	Work	Word stress	
5B	Talk about your future career	*will* and *might* for predictions	Jobs	Sound and spelling: /ʃ/	
5C	Make offers and suggestions			Sentence stress: vowel sounds	Offers and suggestions
5D	Write a job application				
Review and extension	More practice		WORDPOWER *job* and *work*		
Unit 6 Problems and Advice					
Getting started	Talk about being afraid				
6A	Give advice on common problems	*should* / *shouldn't*; imperatives	Verbs with dependent prepositions	Sound and spelling: /uː/ and /ʊ/	
6B	Describe extreme experiences	Uses of *to* + infinitive	*-ed* / *-ing* adjectives	*-ed* endings Word stress	
6C	Ask for and give advice			Main stress	Asking for and giving advice
6D	Write an email giving advice				
Review and extension	More practice		WORDPOWER verb + *to*		

Lesson and objective		Grammar	Vocabulary	Pronunciation	Everyday English
Unit 7 Changes					
Getting started Talk about different generations					
7A	Talk about life-changing events	Comparatives and superlatives	Life events with *get*		
7B	Describe changes in lifestyle	*used to / didn't use to*	Health and fitness collocations	Sound and spelling: *used to / didn't use to*	
7C	Talk to the doctor		Health problems and treatments	Tones for asking questions	Describing symptoms; Doctors' questions
7D	Write a blog about an achievement				
Review and extension More practice			WORDPOWER *change*		
Unit 8 Culture					
Getting started Talk about a painting					
8A	Talk about art, music and literature	The passive: present and past simple	Art and music; Common verbs in the passive		
8B	Talk about sports and activities	Present perfect with *for* and *since*	Sports and activities	Word stress	
8C	Apologise, make and accept excuses			Tones for continuing or finishing	Apologies and excuses
8D	Write a book review				
Review and extension More practice			WORDPOWER *by*		
Unit 9 Achievements					
Getting started Talk about an unusual student					
9A	Talk about future possibilities	First conditional	Degree subjects; Education collocations	Word groups	
9B	Describe actions and feelings	Verb patterns	Verbs followed by *to* + infinitive / verb + *-ing*		
9C	Make telephone calls			Main stress: contrastive	Telephoning people you don't know; Telephoning people you know
9D	Write a personal profile				
Review and extension More practice			WORDPOWER Multi-word verbs with *put*		
Unit 10 Values					
Getting started Talk about seeing a crime					
10A	Talk about moral dilemmas	Second conditional	Multi-word verbs	Sentence stress: vowel sounds	
10B	Describe problems with goods and services	Quantifiers; *too / not enough*	Noun formation	Word stress Sound and spelling: verbs and nouns	
10C	Return goods and make complaints			Sentence stress	Returning goods and making complaints
10D	Write an apology email				
Review and extension More practice			WORDPOWER Multi-word verbs with *on*		
Unit 11 Discovery and Invention					
Getting started Talk about robots					
11A	Explain what technology does	Defining relative clauses	Compound nouns	Word stress: compound nouns	
11B	Describe discoveries	Articles	Adverbials: luck and chance		
11C	Ask for and give directions			Sound and spelling: /ɔː/ and /ɜː/	Asking for and giving directions in a building
11D	Write a post expressing an opinion				
Review and extension More practice			WORDPOWER preposition + noun		
Unit 12 Characters					
Getting started Talk about taking care of an animal					
12A	Tell a story	Past perfect	Animals	Sound and spelling: /ʌ/, /ɔː/ and /əʊ/	
12B	Talk about family relationships	Reported speech	Personality adjectives	Sentence stress: *that* Word stress	
12C	Agree and disagree in discussions			Main stress: contrastive	Agreeing and disagreeing
12D	Write a short story				
Review and extension More practice			WORDPOWER *age*		
Communication Plus p.127		**Grammar Focus** p.142		**Vocabulary Focus** p.133	

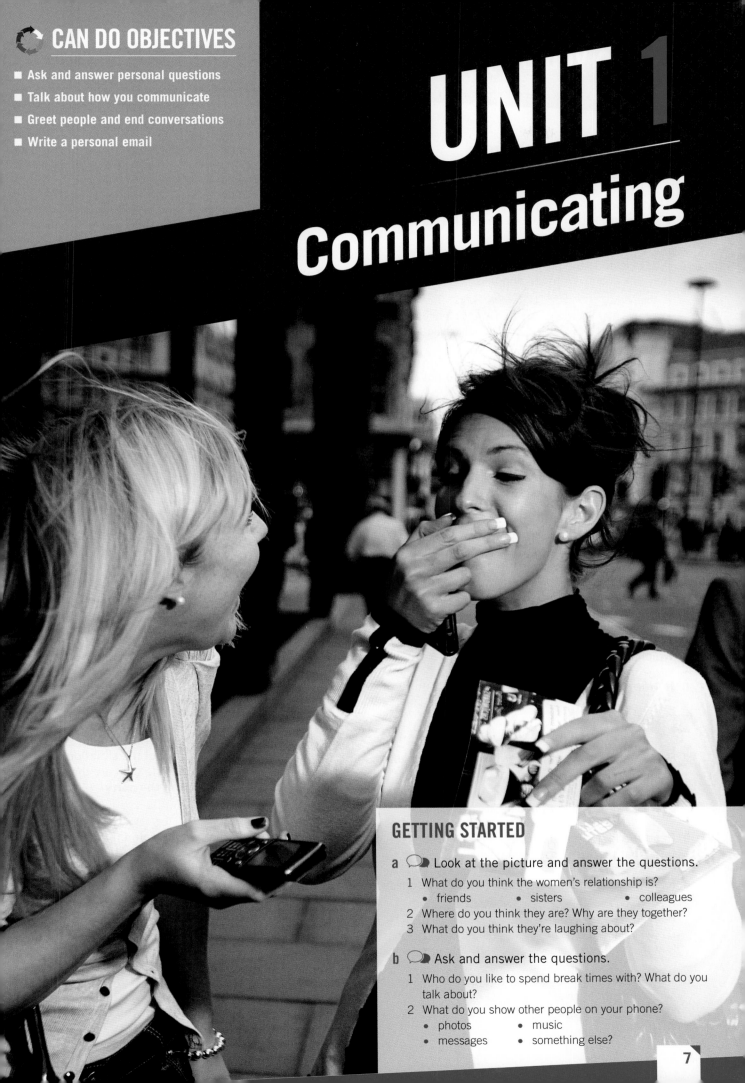

CAN DO OBJECTIVES

- Ask and answer personal questions
- Talk about how you communicate
- Greet people and end conversations
- Write a personal email

UNIT 1
Communicating

GETTING STARTED

a 💬 Look at the picture and answer the questions.

1 What do you think the women's relationship is?
- friends
- sisters
- colleagues

2 Where do you think they are? Why are they together?

3 What do you think they're laughing about?

b 💬 Ask and answer the questions.

1 Who do you like to spend break times with? What do you talk about?

2 What do you show other people on your phone?
- photos
- music
- messages
- something else?

7

1A Do you play any sports?

1 SPEAKING AND LISTENING

a 💬 Look at pictures 1–3 and answer the questions.

1 What event are the people at?
2 Do you think each pair are meeting for the first time? Why/Why not?

b ▶1.2 Listen to the people's conversations 1–3. What do they talk about? Write the numbers.

- the party   <u>1, 2, 3</u>
- people they know _____
- money _____
- where they live _____
- work _____
- their interests _____
- education _____

c ▶1.2 Listen again. Which speakers are not enjoying their conversations? Why?

2 VOCABULARY Common adjectives

a ▶1.3 Complete the sentences with the adjectives the speakers used in the listening. Then listen and check.

| alright awful strange delicious perfect boring |

1 It's a _____ day for a birthday party.
2 The pizza is _____.
3 It's _____, but the music is a bit _____.
4 It's an _____ film.
5 It's a really _____ story.

b Which of the adjectives from 2a are positive? Which adjectives are negative? Which adjective means 'OK'?

c ▶ Now go to Vocabulary Focus 1A on p.133

3 READING

a 💬 Talk to a partner. Answer the questions together.

1 Where do you usually meet new people?
2 Do you usually start conversations or wait for others to speak?
3 What's the first question you usually ask someone?

b Read the first paragraph of *Small Talk*. Who is the article for? What problem does it help with?

c Read the article. Complete gaps 1–8 with the questions.

How do you know Ana?
How much do you earn?
Do you live near here?
How much rent do you pay?
What do you do?
How's the food?
Do you play any sports?
Where did you buy them?

d 💬 Read the article again with a partner. Do you both agree with the advice?

SMALL TALK

Do you have problems when you meet people for the first time?

Is it difficult to think of what to talk about? Don't worry. You don't need to talk about yourself; ask the right questions and you can make the other person talk.

When you start a conversation with a new person, ask about the situation you're in and the people who are there:
What do you think of the party?
1 ....
2 ....

Say something positive and follow it with a question:
This music's brilliant. Do you know what it is?
The match was great last night. Do you watch the football?
I really like your shoes. 3 ....

Then, ask personal questions about interests and hobbies to show you are interested:
Did you see the film? What was it like?
4 .... **Which ones?**
What was the last album you bought?
What kind of music is that?

When you feel more relaxed, ask personal questions about relationships and home life:
Where did you grow up? Are you married? Do you have any children?
5 _____
Holidays are always a good topic if the conversation slows down:
Do you have any holiday plans? Where did you go for your last holiday?
You can ask about work and studies anytime:
6 _____
or **Where do you study?**
But be careful – sometimes people don't want to talk about work at a party!

There are also some topics that are never a good idea.
Money – people usually think talking about money is rude. So unless you know people very well, don't ask:
7 _____
or
8 _____
Politics and religion – you don't want to start an argument!
Age – never guess anyone's age. They won't be happy if you get it wrong!

4 GRAMMAR Question forms

a Complete the tables with the questions in the box.

Where did you meet?   Are you married?
Who do you know at this party?   Why were you late?
Do you like the music?   Is she your sister?

Questions with the verb *be*

Question word	Verb *be*	Subject	Adjective, noun, etc.
Why			late?
	Are		

Questions with other main verbs

Question word	Auxiliary verb	Subject	Main verb	
Where			meet?	
			know	at this party?
	Do		like	the music?

b Look at the two tables in 4a and answer questions 1 and 2.
1 In questions with the verb *be*, which word is first, *be* or the subject?
2 In questions with other main verbs, what kind of word goes before the subject?

c ▶ Now go to Grammar Focus 1A on p.142

d ⏵1.8 **Pronunciation** Listen to the questions in the tables in 4a. Underline the stressed words.

e Put the words in the correct order to make questions.
1 do / like / what kind of music / you ?
2 do / what / your parents / do ?
3 grow up / did / you / in this area ?
4 are / you / how old ?
5 have / you / do / any hobbies ?
6 speak / any other languages / you / do ?

f ⏵1.9 Listen and check. Underline the stressed words.

g 💬 Ask and answer the questions in 4e.

5 SPEAKING

a Write down six questions that you would like to ask other people in the class. You can use questions from this lesson or your own. Think about:

- home
- relationships
- education
- work
- interests
- people you know
- the weekend
- travel
- something else?

b 💬 Work in small groups. Ask the other students the questions you wrote in 5a. Then ask for more information.

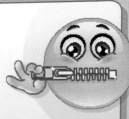

Do you live near here?

No, I live 20 km away.

Oh, how do you get here?

By car.

Learn to talk about how you communicate
- **G** Present simple and present continuous
- **V** Adverbs

1 READING AND LISTENING

a 💬 How do you communicate? Do you do these things with your friends and family? If not, what do you do instead?
- send birthday cards to friends
- write a blog
- send postcards from abroad
- write letters by hand
- make plans with friends by email
- cancel plans by text or instant message
- telephone friends to invite them somewhere

> I always send birthday cards.

> I don't. I write 'happy birthday' on Facebook instead.

b Read the introduction to the article and the line in green under each photo. What do you think the missing words are?

c Read the article and check your answers to 1b. Answer the questions.
1. Why does Julie think her friend will cancel?
2. What does Facebook help Gin to remember?
3. Why is Marc writing a blog?
4. Why does Claudio prefer sending instant messages?

d ▶1.10 Listen to four speakers. Match them with the topics they talk about.

Tara	blogs and emails
Magda	relationships and text messages
Chris	important days and Facebook
Mike	plans and text messages

e ▶1.10 Listen again. Is each speaker happy or unhappy about the use of technology? Why/Why not?

f 💬 Which ideas do you agree with?
- It's rude to cancel by text.
- It's alright to finish a relationship by text.
- Facebook is the perfect place to say 'Congratulations!'
- I love to get postcards and letters.

THE FAST AND THE FURIOUS

Communication is quick and easy with digital technology. But is it making us lazy? Should some things be more personal?

Gin

'Facebook means I don't _____ anything.'

I'm really into Facebook. It's especially useful for birthdays, that kind of thing. When I check my Facebook page, it tells me whose birthday it is. So I never forget and I can just write a message on their wall. And when people have big news – maybe a new baby or something – you can write a comment straight away.

Julie

'I'd prefer a phone call to a _____ .'

I absolutely hate it when friends cancel by text message. It's so rude. My friend Sara and I planned to go to the cinema tonight. But I'm pretty sure she'll cancel – she generally does. I'm waiting for her text message now.

'Writing a blog is a lot easier than sending _____ .'

I'm studying in New York, away from my family. And while I'm here I'm writing a blog so my friends and family at home know my news. I particularly like putting all my photos on there because people leave comments. Most of my friends use Facebook but I prefer writing a blog. It's fairly easy to do and it's quicker than writing 50 separate emails.

Marc

Claudio

'I just send an _____ .'

I normally communicate with people by instant message because they're free. I've even finished relationships with girlfriends by IM. In fact, I mainly do that. I know it's not the best thing to do – but it's better than a lot of shouting and crying. Some of my friends don't even send a message. They just stop all communication and wait for her to realise they're not interested.

2 VOCABULARY Adverbs

a Look at the highlighted adverbs in the text. Answer the questions.

1 Which adverbs make another word stronger?

_____ _____ _____ _____

2 Which adverbs make another word less strong?

_____ _____

b Look at the sentences and complete 1–4 with the frequency adverbs.

I **generally** just send a text.
I **hardly ever** get cards or presents from friends.
I **mainly** finish relationships by IM.
My daughter **rarely** calls me.

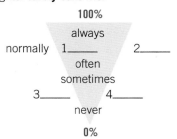

100%
normally always 1_____ 2_____
often
sometimes
3_____ 4_____
never
0%

c ▶1.11 **Pronunciation** Look at the words in the table. Do the letters in **bold** make **long** or **short** vowel sounds? Complete the table headings. Listen and check. Repeat the words.

_____ vowels	_____ vowels
always	pr**e**tty
n**o**rmally	esp**e**cially
h**a**rdly	part**i**cularly
awful	**o**ften
g**o**rgeous	s**o**metimes
alright	n**e**ver
r**u**de	l**o**vely

d ▶1.12 Listen and repeat the sentences.

1 I absolutely hate rude people.
2 I particularly enjoy getting letters.
3 I think Facebook is fairly good.
4 I hardly ever send postcards.
5 I generally text my friends.
6 I'm really into blogs.
7 I'm pretty sure my mum can't use Skype.
8 I mainly see my family at weekends.

e 💬 Change the sentences in 2d so they are true for you. Then compare your sentences with a partner.

3 GRAMMAR
Present simple and present continuous

a Look at these sentences. Which are present simple? Which are present continuous?

present _____
1 I like putting all my photos on my blog.
2 When I plan something, I send a text.

present _____
3 I'm waiting for her text message.
4 She's writing a blog so we know what she's doing.

b Match sentences 1–4 with these uses of present simple and continuous.

We use the present simple to talk about:
• habits and routines ☐
• feelings and permanent situations ☐

We use the present continuous to talk about:
• actions right now ☐
• temporary actions around now ☐

c ▶ Now go to Grammar Focus 1B on p.142

4 SPEAKING

💬 Ask and answer the questions. Give reasons for your answers.

How often do you …?
• send a message to your boss or teacher to say you are sick
• share important news on Facebook
• read English-language websites
• send an e-card instead of a real card
• buy presents for people online
• start conversations with new people
• write emails in English
• call friends and relatives on Skype
• send video by instant message

How often do you read English-language websites?

Not very often. But, I'm planning a holiday in America…

How often do you send 'e-cards'?

Never. I absolutely hate them!

1C Everyday English
It was really nice to meet you

Learn to greet people and end conversations

- **P** Sentence stress
- **S** Showing interest

1 LISTENING

a In your country, what do you normally say and do when you …
- first meet somebody new?
- meet someone you know well?

> We hug and kiss.

> We shake hands and say …

b Look at the photographs. Do you think the people in each photo know each other well? Why?

c ▶ 1.15 Watch or listen to Part 1 and check your answers to 1b.

d ▶ 1.15 Watch or listen again. Are sentences 1–5 true (*T*) or false (*F*)? Correct the false sentences.

1. ☐ The last time Rachel and Annie saw each other was six years ago.
2. ☐ Annie lives a long way from the town centre.
3. ☐ Rachel and Mark got married a year ago.
4. ☐ Annie has a boyfriend.
5. ☐ Rachel, Mark and Annie decide to go to a restaurant together.

2 USEFUL LANGUAGE Greeting people

a ▶ 1.16 Complete the sentences from Part 1 with the words in the box. Listen and check your answers.

meet you	no see	to see you	by the way	are you	these days

1. Long time _____!
2. How _____?
3. Great _____!
4. Where are you living _____?
5. My name's Mark, _____.
6. Nice to _____.

b Look at the phrases in 2a. Which can you use to speak to … ?
1. someone you know
2. someone you are meeting for the first time

c ▶ 1.17 Listen and note down some possible replies to the phrases in 2a. Do you know any different ways to reply to each phrase in 2a?

d Work in pairs. Take turns saying the phrases in 2a and replying.

3 CONVERSATION SKILLS Showing interest

a ▶ 1.18 Listen and complete the conversations from Part 1 with the adjectives in the box.

fantastic	lovely	good	nice

1. Long time no see! How are you?
   I'm great. What a _____ surprise! Great to see you.
2. We live on Compton Road.
   Oh – how _____!
3. Mark's my husband!
   Husband – wow! That's _____ news.
4. Would you both like to come?
   Yeah, that sounds _____.
   Brilliant! Let's go.

b Look at the conversations in 3a. Do the highlighted phrases give information or show interest?

c What kind of word completes each phrase 1–4? Choose the correct form from the box.

adjective + noun	adjective

1. What a + _____!
2. How + _____!
3. That sounds + _____.
4. That's + _____ + news.

d Work in pairs. Take turns to tell your partner about yourself. Reply using the phrases in 3c.

Tell your partner:
- where you live
- something you did at the weekend
- some news
- what job you do / what you are studying these days

4 PRONUNCIATION Sentence stress

a ▶ **1.19** Listen to the sentences. Notice the words with stressed syllables.

I <u>think</u> it was about <u>six</u> <u>years</u> ago!
I <u>live</u> on <u>Hampton</u> Street.
My name's <u>Mark</u>, by the way.
<u>Mark</u>'s my <u>hus</u>band!
I'm <u>going</u> to the <u>café</u> down the <u>street</u> now...
...to <u>meet</u> <u>Leo</u>, my <u>boy</u>friend.

b Look at the sentences in 4a. Which words have stressed syllables – grammar words or words that give information?

5 LISTENING

a 💬 Look at the picture from Part 2. Who is the fourth person at the café? Does he know Rachel and Mark?

b ▶ **1.20** What do you think they will talk about in the café? In pairs, think of three things. Then watch or listen to Part 2. Were you right?

c ▶ **1.20** Watch or listen again. Answer the questions.

1 Do Rachel and Mark have plans for next week?
2 What job does Rachel do?
3 Who helps Rachel at the shop?
4 What does Annie say about her job?
5 What does Mark do?
6 What is Annie doing at the weekend?
7 Why do Rachel and Mark leave?
8 What suggestion does Annie make before they leave?

6 USEFUL LANGUAGE Ending conversations

a ▶ **1.21** Listen and complete the phrases for ending a conversation.

1 We really must _____.
2 It was really nice to _____ you.
3 It was great to _____ you again, Annie.
4 Yeah! We must _____ _____ soon.
5 _____ hello to Dan for me!

b Which phrase in 6a do you use when you say goodbye to somebody you have just met?

c Put the sentences in the correct order to make a conversation.

B ☐ Oh, that's fine. It was great to see you.
A ☐ Not far from here. Look, I'm sorry, but I really must go. I'm late for a meeting.
A ☐ 1 Dan, is that you?
A ☐ Yeah! I think I last saw you at John's wedding. How are you?
A ☐ You, too! I'll give you a call!
B ☐ I'm fine. And you? Where are you living these days?
B ☐ Hi Sarah! Long time no see!

7 SPEAKING

a ▶ **Communication 1C** Student A: go to 7b below. Student B: go to p.129.

Student A

b Read card 1. Think about what you want to say.

c Start the conversation with Student B. Use your own name.

> ① You are walking down the street and you see your friend.
> • say hello
> • give your news:
>   • you've got a new job
>   • *your own idea*
> • listen to your friend's news and respond
> • say goodbye

d Now look at card 2. Listen to Student B and reply. Use your own name.

> ② You meet a colleague for the first time.
> • say who you are
> • give some information:
>   • your office is in building C
>   • *your own idea*
> • listen to what your new colleague says and respond
> • say goodbye

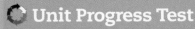

⟳ Unit Progress Test

CHECK YOUR PROGRESS

You can now do the Unit Progress Test.

1 SPEAKING AND LISTENING

a 🗨 Read the messages 1–3 and answer the questions.

1 What do the highlighted phrases mean?
2 Do you ever send or receive these kinds of message? Who to/from? Why?

1 I can't seem to get in touch with you. Call me! SEND

2 Did you get my last text? SEND

3 Are you OK? We haven't heard from you for a long time. SEND

b ▶1.22 Listen to Nina and Chris talking about keeping in touch with friends and family. Who is better at keeping in touch: Nina or Chris?

c ▶1.22 Listen again and answer the questions.

1 Why doesn't Nina send many emails?
2 Why does Chris phone his mother so often?
3 How often does Nina phone her parents?
4 When does Nina prefer to tell her friends her news?
5 When does Chris send photos by email?

d How often do you keep in touch with family and friends? Circle the correct adverb for you.

always   generally   sometimes   rarely

Think about:
1 a family member who lives in a different place
2 a friend who you don't see very often

Which of these do you do with each person?
Write the first letter of their name.
• talk on the phone or Skype
• send emails or messages
• send pictures, video or web links
• hardly ever keep in touch
• meet for a chat

e 🗨 Work in pairs. Talk about your answers to 1d.

I rarely keep in touch with people. I never have time to …

I generally keep in touch with my family. I enjoy sending …

I sometimes send photos to my sister Jane. Usually pictures of…

I send my friend Alex web links to interesting articles.

f 🗨 Which of these opinions do you agree with?

1 'It's nice to see photos of what your friends are doing.'
2 'You don't have to keep in touch with people all the time.'
3 'If your parents worry a lot, you should phone them.'

2 READING

a Simon is a student from England. Look at his pictures from Salamanca in Spain. What do you think he is doing there?

b Read the emails and check your ideas in 2a. Which email is to his … ?

☐ friend Blake   ☐ uncle and aunt
☐ younger sister Mika

c Who does Simon write to about these subjects?

• the weather
• what he does in the evenings
• the family he is staying with
• learning to speak Spanish
• the other students

d 🗨 Answer the questions about Simon's emails.

1 What does he say about speaking Spanish?
2 Why do you think he says different things about this to each person?

Hope you're both well and you're enjoying the summer.
I'm in Salamanca, in Spain. This is a photo I took of the old centre.
It's a beautiful old town, as you can see.
As you know, I'm learning Spanish at the moment. I'm doing a two-month Spanish course here, so my Spanish is slowly improving. The classes are very good and we also watch Spanish films.
It's pretty hot here, but it's nice and cool in the evenings.
Love to all,
Simon

How's it going? Are you having a good time in Berlin?
Here are some photos of my group on the Spanish course. We're all from different countries, so we usually speak English when we're together – not very good for my Spanish! Anyway, I'm having a great time here and the time's going much too quickly. There are lots of good cafés here and we usually all go out in the evening together.
What's Berlin like? Send me some photos! See you back at college next month.
Simon

I'm sending you some photos of the family I'm staying with in Salamanca. They've got a daughter the same age as you (her name's Blanca). She speaks English quite well, but we usually speak Spanish together. She introduced me to some of her friends and I speak Spanish to them, too … some of the time, not always! How's your job in the supermarket? Hope you're not working too hard and you're saving lots of money?!
See you next week.
Love
Simon xx

3 WRITING SKILLS
Correcting mistakes

a Look at the pairs of sentences A–D. Which pair has mistakes in … ?

- [ ] grammar
- [ ] spelling
- [ ] punctuation marks
- [ ] capital letters

A 1 Hope youre both well and youre enjoying the summer.
   2 Are you having a good time in Berlin,

B 1 i'm in salamanca, in spain.
   2 the classes are very good and we also watch spanish Films.

C 1 I having a great time here and the time going much too quickly.
   2 She speak English quite good, but we are usually speaking Spanish together.

D 1 Her are some fotos of my group on the Spanish corse.
   2 We're all from diferent countrys, so we usually speak English.

b Match the rules with mistakes in five of the sentences in 3a (A1–D2).

1 The present continuous is formed *be* + verb + *-ing*.
2 When we leave out a letter, we write an apostrophe '.
3 We use the present simple to talk about habits.
4 If a word ends in *-y*, we change it to *-ies* in the plural.
5 Place names start with a capital letter.

c Correct all of the mistakes in the sentences in 3a. Check your answers in Simon's emails.

4 WRITIN

a Write an email to a friend or family member who you don't see very often. Write about:

- how you are
- what's new for you (the place you're living or the people you're spending time with)
- what you're doing these days

b Work in pairs. Exchange emails and read your partner's email. Circle their mistakes and write these letters at the end of the line.

- grammar **G**
- spelling **Sp**
- punctuation marks **P**
- capital letters **L**

c Work in pairs. Correct the mistakes in your emails together.

d Read other students' emails. Which email is the most interesting? Why?

UNIT 1
Review and extension

1 GRAMMAR

a Put the words in the correct order to make questions.

1 night / did / go / out / you / last ?
2 where / you / last / weekend / go / did ?
3 kind of / like / you / what / do / TV programmes ?
4 do / this school / know / who / at / you ?
5 you / how / play / sport / often / do ?
6 you / do / what / at weekends / do / usually ?
7 tired / you / are / today ?

b 💬 Ask and answer the questions in 1a.

c Complete the conversation with the present simple or present continuous forms of the verbs.

JACKIE Hi Mum.
MUM Oh, hi Jackie. Nice of you to call. You ^{1}_____ (not call) very often!
JACKIE Oh come on, Mum! I ^{2}_____ (work) really hard at university at the moment. I never ^{3}_____ (have) time to call! And I ^{4}_____ (send) you emails all the time.
MUM I ^{5}_____ (like) to speak to you and hear your voice, that's all. Your sister ^{6}_____ (call) me every weekend.
JACKIE Well, we ^{7}_____ (speak) now. But the world ^{8}_____ (change), Mum! Some of my friends never ^{9}_____ (phone) home. They just ^{10}_____ (email) or send a text.
MUM I preferred how things were in the past.

2 VOCABULARY

a Complete the sentences with the correct adjectives.

1 The film was a _ _ _ _ _ t at the beginning, but I didn't like the ending.
2 We ate some really d _ _ _ _ _ _ _ s food at the party.
3 They've got a nice house, but they live in a really u _ _ y part of town.
4 It was a l _ _ _ _ _ y day, so we decided to go to the beach.
5 I bought a g _ _ _ _ _ _ s new dress to wear to my friend's wedding.
6 He listens to really s _ _ _ _ _ e music – I don't know any of the bands.
7 This summer, the weather here was h _ _ _ _ _ _ e – it rained all the time.
8 This is a p _ _ _ _ _ t day for a walk in the park – it's so warm and sunny.

b Choose the correct answers.

1 I *absolutely / fairly* love football.
2 My parents live abroad. I *rarely / mainly* see them.
3 I think American films are *absolutely / really* good, but they're not brilliant.
4 I *normally / particularly* go for a run once or twice a week.
5 I *really / fairly* hate rock music.
6 I love all sports, but tennis is *especially / normally* good.

c 💬 Which sentences in 2b are true for you?

3 WORDPOWER *like*

a Match sentences (1–4) with replies (a–d).

1 ☐ I've got a jacket **like** yours.
2 ☐ **What was** the film **like**?
3 ☐ I enjoy visiting countries with a lot of history, **like** Greece.
4 ☐ We can go for a walk later **if you like**.

a Yes, that would be great.
b And Italy! Me too.
c Yes, this style's popular at the moment.
d I thought it was alright, but my friend hated it.

b Match the expressions in **bold** from 3a with the meanings (a–d).

a what was your opinion of   c if you want
b similar to   d for example

c Complete the sentences with the words in **bold** from 3a.

1 **A** Is your university different from others in your country?
   B No, it's _____ most of the others.
2 **A** We can meet tomorrow _____ .
   B OK – come to my flat for a coffee.
3 **A** Do you want me to bring something to the dinner party?
   B Yes. Bring something sweet, _____ some ice cream.
4 **A** We went to that new restaurant yesterday.
   B _____ it _____ ?

d We often use *like* with the verbs *look* and *sound*. Look at the examples.

- saying people or things are similar
  *John **looks like** his brother – they're both tall with black hair.*
  *I think this new song **sounds like** The Beatles.*

- saying what you think will happen
  *It **looks like** it might rain – it's very cloudy.*

- giving your opinion from what you heard or read
  *I spoke to Sara yesterday. It **sounds like** she had a really good holiday.*

Complete the sentences with the correct forms of *look like* or *sound like*.

1 It _____ their first album. I really like it!
2 Sam invited Tom to the party. So it _____ he'll come.
3 You don't _____ your sister. She's very tall.
4 That was the last bus. It _____ we'll have to walk.

🔄 REVIEW YOUR PROGRESS

How well did you do in this unit? Write 3, 2 or 1 for each objective.
3 = very well   2 = well   1 = not so well

I CAN ...

Ask and answer personal questions	☐
Talk about how you communicate	☐
Greet people and end conversations	☐
Write a personal email	☐

CAN DO OBJECTIVES

- Talk about past holidays
- Describe difficult journeys
- Ask for information in a public place
- Write a travel blog

UNIT 2
Travel and Tourism

GETTING STARTED

a Look at the picture and answer the questions.

1 Where are the people? What are they doing? Why?
2 How is each person feeling?
3 What do you think the woman holding the child is saying?
4 What do you think happens next?

b In pairs, ask and answer questions 1–3.

1 Would you like to do this activity on holiday? Why / Why not?
2 Have you ever ridden a camel, or any other animal? Where? Why? Did you have fun?
3 What kind of activities make you feel like the child in this picture?

1 READING AND LISTENING

a 💬 Ask and answer the questions.

1 Where do you like to go on holiday?
2 Do you like to try new things on holiday? What?
3 Can you think of any kind of holiday you wouldn't enjoy?

b Read *Yes Man changed my life* and answer the questions.

1 What is Danny Wallace's book, *Yes Man* about?
2 What did Richard do after he read *Yes Man*?

c Read *Day One* and *Day Two* and then answer the questions.

Day One
1 Why did Richard go into the travel agent's?
2 What holiday did he book?
3 Did he book the kind of holiday he usually likes?
4 When was his flight?

Day Two
1 Why did Richard go to the beach?
2 How was the weather?
3 What did he buy at the beach?
4 What is he going to do on Day Three? How does he feel about it?

d 💬 Would you like to try water skiing? Do you think Richard will enjoy it?

e ▶1.23 Listen to Richard describing day three. Are sentences 1–5 true (*T*) or false (*F*)? Correct the false sentences.

1 The class began with a lesson before they went out to sea.
2 Richard felt fine when they went out on the boat.
3 He found it difficult to stand up on the water skis.
4 He hated water skiing.
5 When he got back to the hotel, he went to bed.

f 💬 Can you think of a time when you were surprised you enjoyed something?

2 GRAMMAR Past simple: positive

a Underline the past simple form of these verbs in the article.

become	feel	decide	start	ask	do change
have	want	get	see	sleep	go arrive give

b Which verbs in 2a end in *-ed* in the past tense? How do the other verbs change?

You can find a list of irregular verbs on p.176

c Complete the sentences with the past simple form of the verbs in brackets.

1 I _____ as a waiter for a day, for no money. (work)
2 I _____ a day fishing with five Greek fishermen. (spend)
3 I _____ at a beach party until six in the morning. (stay)
4 I _____ a dancing competition. (win)
5 I _____ the same boat trip three times. (take)
6 I _____ swimming at midnight. (go)

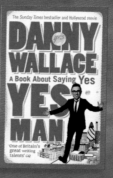

The Sunday Times bestseller and Hollywood movie

DANNY WALLACE
A Book About Saying Yes
YES MAN
'One of Britain's great writing talents' *GQ*

YES MAN CHANGED MY LIFE
by Richard Collins

Yes Man is the best book I've ever read. It's the true story of a year in the life of author, Danny Wallace. Before Danny Wallace became the 'Yes Man', his life was boring and he felt old. So he decided to make things more exciting. He started saying "yes" to every question people asked him. And he did it for a whole year. From the day he started, it completely changed his life and he had all kinds of adventures.
It's a fantastic story. When I finished the book, I wanted to change my life like Danny Wallace. So I took some holiday from work, and became a 'Yes Man' for a week. This is what happened.

3 LISTENING

a ▶1.24 Which of the activities in 2c do you think Richard enjoyed? Tell a partner. Listen and check.

b ▶1.24 Listen again. What is Richard's last question? Do you think he will say *yes* or *no*? Why?

c 💬 Ask and answer the questions.

1 Do you ever say yes when you don't want to? When?
2 Would you like to be a 'Yes Man' for a week? Why / Why not?

Day One

I started on Saturday morning. At 10 am, I got my first question. I saw a poster in the window of a travel agent's. It said, "Tired?" (Yes – I slept badly the night before, so I was tired). Under this, it said, "Do you need a holiday?" (Yes, definitely.) So I went in.
The travel agent asked me where I wanted to go. But before I could answer, she said, "Somewhere hot?"
I don't like hot weather, but I said, "Yes."
"A beach holiday? Maybe in Greece?"
I don't like the beach. I prefer cities. But I said, "Yes."
"What kind of accommodation? A hotel? Or a … "
I hate hotels, but before she could continue, I said, "Yes."
Five minutes later everything was ready. My flight was the next day.

Day Two

I arrived at my hotel on the island of Zante at lunchtime. It was very, very hot. I just wanted to check in and unpack my suitcase, but the receptionist said, "We have a minibus to the beach in ten minutes. Do you want to go?"
You know the answer I gave her.
It was about 40°C at the beach. Luckily, I brought suntan lotion. A man came towards me: "Sunglasses? Do you want sunglasses?"
I had some in my bag, but I said, "Yes."
Five minutes later, another man came: "Beautiful hat, sir?" I tried not to look at him.
Three hours later, I had two pairs of sunglasses, three hats, a watch and a woman's necklace.
It was difficult to carry all my new things back to the minibus. I decided: no trips tomorrow, just rest. When I got back, the receptionist asked, "Did you like the beach?"
I didn't, but I said, "Yes."
"Oh, there's a water skiing course tomorrow. Do you want me to book a place for you?"
I can't swim very well and I don't like the sea. I wanted to cry …

4 GRAMMAR
Past simple: negative and questions

a Complete the sentences with the words in the box.

was	didn't	did	weren't

1 Some of my experiences _____ very good.
2 I _____ like the mosquitoes that bit me.
3 _____ you have a good week?
4 What _____ your favourite thing?

b Look at the sentences in 4a and answer the questions about the past simple.

1 Which sentences include the verb *be*?
2 How do we make negatives and questions …
  • with the verb *be*? • with other verbs?

c ▶ Now go to Grammar Focus 2A on p.144

5 PRONUNCIATION -ed endings

a ▶1.27 Listen and tick (✓) the verbs which have an extra syllable when we add -ed.

change > changed ☐   play > played ☐
need > needed ☐   ask > asked ☐
decide > decided ☐   want > wanted ☐
start > started ☐

b Complete the rule with two sounds.

> -ed endings are pronounced with an extra syllable /ɪd/ after ____ and ____ only.

c ▶1.28 Which of the verbs + -ed in the box have the extra /ɪd/ syllable? Listen and check.

> waited included arrived looked watched
> shouted smiled stopped ended believed

6 VOCABULARY Tourism

a ◯ What useful holiday items can you see on these pages? What else do people normally take?

b ▶ Now go to Vocabulary Focus 2A on p.133

7 SPEAKING

a Think of a holiday you enjoyed. Think about your answers to these questions.

• When did you go?
• Where did you go?
• Was it your first time?
• How long did you go for?
• Who did you go with?
• What kind of accommodation did you stay in?
• Did you do any sightseeing?
• Who did you meet?
• Did you bring back any souvenirs?

b ◯ Tell your partner about your holiday. Listen to your partner and ask questions.

2B Everyone was waiting for me

Learn to describe difficult journeys

Ⓖ Past continuous
Ⓥ Travel collocations

1 VOCABULARY Travel collocations

a 💬 Look at the list of ways to travel. Which do you prefer? Why?

- car
- bus
- train
- plane
- coach
- on foot

b 💬 Look at the travel problems in the pictures. Which situation do you dislike most?

c ▶ Now go to Vocabulary Focus 2B on p.134

2 LISTENING

a 💬 Look at the picture and the headline. What do you think happened?

Woman angry
after flight in toilet

b ⊙ 1.33 Listen to the woman describing her experience. Were your ideas in 2a correct?

c ⊙ 1.33 Listen again. What does the woman say about … ?

- her journey to the airport
- boarding the plane
- what the flight attendant said
- what happened when she was in the toilet
- how she feels about what happened now

d 💬 Do you believe the woman's story? Why? / Why not?

3 GRAMMAR Past continuous

a ▶**1.34** Listen and complete the past continuous verbs in the sentences.

1 It ＿＿＿＿＿＿ when I left the house.
2 When I boarded the plane, all the other passengers ＿＿＿＿＿＿ for me.
3 I ＿＿＿＿＿＿ my book, when one of the flight attendants spoke to me.
4 I ＿＿＿＿＿＿ on the toilet when the turbulence started.

b Underline the past simple verbs in sentences 1–4 in 3a.

c Look at the sentences in 3a again and answer the questions.

1 Which action started first in every sentence? (past simple or past continuous?)
2 Think about when and why the past continuous action stopped in each sentence. Write the sentence numbers (1–4).

The past continuous action
… stopped because of the past simple action. ☐☐
… stopped some time after the past simple action. ☐☐

d ▶ Now go to Grammar Focus 2B on p.144

e ▶**1.36** **Pronunciation** Listen to the sentences. Notice which words are stressed.

1 It was <u>rain</u>ing.
2 It wasn't <u>rain</u>ing.
3 Was it <u>rain</u>ing?
4 We were <u>driv</u>ing <u>fast</u>.
5 We <u>weren't</u> <u>driv</u>ing <u>fast</u>.
6 Were we <u>driv</u>ing <u>fast</u>?

f ▶**1.36** Listen to the sentences in 3e again. Do the vowel sounds in *was* and *were* sound the same in all the sentences?

g ▶**1.37** Listen to five more sentences. Do you hear *was*, *wasn't*, *were* or *weren't* in each?

h Complete the sentences with the past continuous or past simple forms of the verbs in brackets.

1 The train ＿＿＿ (leave) the station, when I ＿＿＿ (realise) I was on the wrong train.
2 When I ＿＿＿ (travel) around Australia, I ＿＿＿ (lose) my passport.
3 I ＿＿＿ (run) for the bus when my bag ＿＿＿ (open) and all my things ＿＿＿ (fall) out.
4 I ＿＿＿ (drive) to a family wedding when my GPS ＿＿＿ (stop) working.
5 Someone ＿＿＿ (steal) my bag when I ＿＿＿ (stand) in the queue for a ticket.

i 💬 Have you had any similar experiences to those in 3h?

> I lost my passport when we were moving house.

> What did you do?

4 READING AND SPEAKING

a 💬 Read the headlines and look at the pictures. What do you think happened to the travellers?

Did you mean Capri? Swedish tourists miss their destination by 600 km

Coach passengers asked to get out and push

b ▶ **Communication 2B.** Student A: go to page p.127. Student B: go to p.128.

c 💬 Tell your partner your story. Use the questions to help you.

- Where were they going?
- How were they travelling?
- What was the problem?
- Who helped solve the problem? How?
- What happened in the end?

> Two Swedish tourists were on holiday in Italy. They …

d 💬 Which journey do you think was worse for the travellers?

e Think of a time you had a difficult journey. Think about your answers to these questions.

- Where were you going?
- How were you travelling?
- What went wrong?
- What happened in the end?

f 💬 Work in small groups. Tell the group about your journey.

> When I was travelling to Florida, we waited for ten hours in the airport. Then they sent us to a hotel.

> Was it free?

g 💬 Who in your group has had the worst experience on … ?
- a plane • a train • a bus or a coach

2C Everyday English
What time's the next train?

Learn to ask for information in a public place
- P Joining words
- S Asking for more information

1 LISTENING

a 💬 What kind of information do people ask for in these places? Think of two kinds of information for each place.
- train stations
- tourist offices
- airports

b 💬 Look at the picture. Where is Annie? What information do you think she is asking for?

c ▶ 1.38 Watch or listen to Part 1 and check your ideas in 1b.

d ▶ 1.38 Watch or listen to Part 1 again. Answer the questions.
1 When does the next train to Birmingham leave? _____
2 How often do the trains leave? _____
3 Which platform does the Birmingham train leave from? _____
4 Which day will Annie come back? _____
5 How much is Annie's ticket? _____
6 What does Annie want to get from the newsagent's? _____

2 USEFUL LANGUAGE Asking for information in a public place

a ▶ 1.39 Match 1–6 with a–f to make questions from Annie's conversation. Then listen and check.

1	☐ What time's	a	is a ticket?
2	☐ How often	b	pay by card?
3	☐ Could you tell me where	c	the ticket office is?
4	☐ How much	d	the next train?
5	☐ Can I	e	do the trains leave?
6	☐ Where can I	f	buy a magazine?

b ▶ 1.40 Listen and complete the questions the assistant asks.
1 Yes, how _____ _____ help you?
2 Is there _____ _____ I can help you with?

c Complete the dialogue with words from the box.

> what time   where can I   can I   how much   could you tell me

A Hi, ¹_____ where the museum is, please?
B Yes, it's not far. It's by the river. Look on the map – here.
A I see. And ²_____ does it open?
B From 8 am till 4 pm.
A ³_____ is a ticket?
B For adults, it's £14.
A ⁴_____ buy a ticket?
B I can sell you a ticket here, or you can buy one at the museum.
A Oh, I'll buy one here. ⁵_____ pay by card?
B Of course – that's no problem.

d ▶ 1.41 Listen and check. Practise the dialogue.

3 PRONUNCIATION Joining words

a ▶ 1.42 Listen to the questions and look at the letters in **bold**.
- Where ca**n I** buy a magazine?
- How mu**ch i**s a ticket?

1 Underline the correct word to complete the rule.

There *is / isn't* a pause between words when a consonant sound comes before a vowel sound.

2 What sound exactly do the letters in **bold** in each question make?

b Underline the letters and spaces where there isn't a pause.
1 Is anyone sitting here?
2 Could I sit next to you?
3 What are you reading?
4 Do you want a drink?
5 Where do you get off?
6 Can I have your email address?

c ▶ 1.43 Listen and check.

d 💬 In pairs, ask the questions in 3b and answer with your own ideas.

4 CONVERSATION SKILLS
Asking for more information

a Look at the <u>underlined</u> phrases. Do the phrases show that the speaker wants to … ?

1 end the conversation
2 ask something else

ANNIE	<u>Sorry, just one more thing.</u>
ASSISTANT	Yes, of course.
ANNIE	Could you tell me where the ticket office is?
ASSISTANT	Is there anything else I can help you with?
ANNIE	<u>Actually, there is one more thing</u>. Where can I buy a magazine?

b ▶1.44 Listen to the phrases and repeat.

c 💬 Work in pairs. Student A: you are a tourist officer. Student B: you are a tourist in town. Use the dialogue below, and ask two more questions.

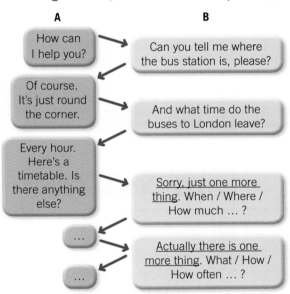

A	B
How can I help you?	Can you tell me where the bus station is, please?
Of course. It's just round the corner.	And what time do the buses to London leave?
Every hour. Here's a timetable. Is there anything else?	<u>Sorry, just one more thing</u>. When / Where / How much … ?
…	<u>Actually there is one more thing</u>. What / How / How often … ?
…	

d 💬 Swap roles. Do the dialogue again.

5 LISTENING

a 💬 Look at the picture from Part 2. Why do you think Annie runs back to the assistant?

b ▶1.45 Watch or listen to Part 2 and check your ideas. What mistake did Annie make? What is her last question?

c 💬 Have you ever made a silly mistake like Annie? What happened?

6 SPEAKING

a ▶ **Communication 2C** Student A: go to 6b below. Student B: go to p.128.

Student A

b Look at Card 1. Think about what you want to ask.

> **1** You need to book a train ticket.
> - 🕐 – first train to Manchester / in the morning?
> - how often / trains to Manchester?
> - £ two adult tickets?
> - pay by card?
> - where / leave luggage?
> - where / the waiting room?

c Listen to Student B and reply. Find out the information you need.

d Now look at card 2. Start the conversation with Student B. Say 'How can I help you?'

> **2** You are a tourist guide in Warwick.
> - castle is in the centre of town
> - opening hours 10 am–6 pm
> - prices: adult £30.60, child £25.80
> - buy tickets at the castle or online
> - tours every hour
> - visitors can bring food, but many places to buy food

🔄 **Unit Progress Test**

CHECK YOUR PROGRESS

You can now do the Unit Progress Test.

1 SPEAKING AND LISTENING

a 💬 Look at the pictures of Indonesia. Ask and answer the questions.

1 What can you see in the photos?
2 What do you know about Indonesia?
3 Have you been there? Would you like to go there? Why / Why not?

b ▶️ 1.46 Listen to Karen talking to her nephew Tim about Indonesia. Answer the questions.

1 Why is Tim phoning Karen?
2 When did she travel to Indonesia?
3 Which of the things in the photographs (a–e) in 1a does Karen describe to Tim?

c ▶️ 1.46 Listen again and answer the questions.

1 How is Tim planning to get to his hostel?
2 What were the problems with Karen's flight to Jakarta?
3 How does Karen describe Indonesian traffic jams?
4 How did Karen feel about the storms in Indonesia?
5 Why didn't Karen write a blog?

d 💬 Ask and answer the questions.

1 Do you write a blog or diary when you travel? Do you know someone who does?
2 Do you like reading other people's blogs? Why / Why not?

2 READING

a Read Tim's travel blog about arriving in Jakarta, Indonesia. Tick (✓) the topic he does not write about.

- his flight to Jakarta
- animals
- the weather
- the traffic
- the people
- food
- tourist places

MY BLOG   ABOUT ME

Indonesian *Adventure*

TUESDAY 22ND APRIL
JAKARTA – EVENING

We've arrived and it's really exciting! It was a long flight, but I slept most of the way, so I'm not tired. When I got off the plane, I noticed the heat first – 32 degrees! It's really humid, because this is the rainy season.

Everything they say about the roads in Jakarta is true! When we left the airport, there was a huge traffic jam. It took a very long time to get to the centre of town.

We got a taxi to the hostel (where we're staying). The taxi driver was very friendly, but he didn't speak much English. I just showed him the address of the hostel on a piece of paper and he brought us here. I think we paid him too much, because he seemed very happy when he drove away!

Sam's telling me to get ready to go and eat, so I have to finish now – more tomorrow.

b Read the blog again and answer the questions.

1 What did Tim do on the flight?
2 Why was the journey to the city centre slow?
3 Why did Tim think the taxi driver was happy?
4 What did he think of the food at the restaurant?
5 What did he see in the Old Town?

3 WRITING SKILLS Linking words

a Read the examples and answer the questions about the linking words in **bold**.

1 I slept most of the way, **so** I'm not tired.
2 **When** I got off the plane, I noticed the heat first.
3 It was really fresh **and** full of flavour.
4 The taxi driver was very friendly, **but** he didn't speak much English.
5 I decided to have *nasi goreng* **because** it's the Indonesian national dish.

Which word do we use to ... ?

a say two things happen at the same time
b add a similar idea
c add a different idea
d give the reason for something
e give the result of something

b Find and <u>underline</u> more examples of the linking words in Tim's blog.

c Put *but, when, so* or *because* where you see ∧ in the sentences.

1 We were very tired, ∧ we went straight to bed.
2 ∧ we got to the hotel, I unpacked.
3 It was the middle of the night, ∧ the streets were completely empty
4 The restaurant looked small and cheap, ∧ the food was amazing.
5 We gave the waiter $5 ∧ the service was excellent.
6 We ran into a shopping centre ∧ the storm began.
7 We went to the National Museum ∧ we wanted to understand more about the country's history.
8 We tried to check in, ∧ we were very early and the desk was closed.

4 WRITING

a You're going to write a blog. Choose one of the topics.

- a holiday experience
- your first day doing something new (for example, starting a new course or job)
- a new place you visited recently

b Make notes. Think about:

- where you were
- how you felt
- what you saw and did
- who you talked to

c Write your blog. Use some linking words from 3a.

d Work in pairs. Read your partner's blog. Do they use linking words? Is it similar to your blog?

WEDNESDAY 23RD APRIL

JAKARTA – THE NEXT DAY!

Sam and I had a delicious meal last night in a small local restaurant – we were the only tourists there, so it seemed to be a place for local people. I decided to have *nasi goreng* because it's the Indonesian national dish. It was really fresh and full of flavour. I felt tired when I got back to the hostel and fell asleep immediately.
Today we visited the Old Town. There are lots of old buildings in different styles. They're very attractive and very different from anything you see in the UK. I took a lot of photos …

UNIT 2
Review and extension

1 GRAMMAR

a Complete the sentences with the past simple forms of the verbs in the box.

ask   not get   learn   meet   need   not spend   wear

1 We _____ a lot of money, because everything was very cheap.
2 She _____ the bus driver for directions.
3 I _____ to change my ticket before I got on the train.
4 I _____ the bus home, because I didn't have any money.
5 He _____ his new shirt to the party.
6 _____ you _____ any interesting people on holiday?
7 I _____ how to surf when I lived in California.

b Choose the correct verb forms.

I had a terrible journey. I ¹*walked / was walking* to the train station and it started raining. And then the train was twenty minutes late. When it ²*came / was coming*, I ³*found / was finding* a seat by the window. Some girls ⁴*played / were playing* music on their mobiles, but it was great music. That was OK, but I ⁵*read / was reading* my book when the train ⁶*arrived / was arriving* at the next station. Two people got on and a man ⁷*sat / was sitting* down next to me and he started talking loudly on his mobile. He ⁸*told / was telling* someone about his new car, his job – everything! He was still talking when the train ⁹*got / was getting* in to the station.

2 VOCABULARY

a Match the clues (1–5) to the words.

suntan lotion   sunglasses   backpack   foreign currency
guidebook   map   passport   suitcase

1 You wear or use these two things when it's sunny.
2 This is money from another country.
3 These two things give you ideas of where to go.
4 You normally need this to travel internationally.
5 You pack clothes in these two things when you go away.

b Complete the sentences with the verbs in the box.

change   check out   do   get
go away   set off   travel around

1 We hope to _____ the world next year.
2 You need to _____ a visa if you want to visit China.
3 You will have time to _____ some sightseeing later.
4 You need to _____ trains at Frankfurt for Berlin.
5 We want to _____ for the weekend later this month.
6 We _____ very early, because our train was at 6.30 am.
7 We need to _____ of our hotel before 10 am.

3 WORDPOWER *off*

a Match the general meanings of *off* (a–c) with the groups of sentences (1–3).

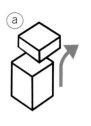 

1 We booked an early ferry, so we **set off** at 5 am.
   OK, **I'm off**. My train leaves in ten minutes.
   The traffic lights turned green and they **drove off**.
   I asked a man for directions, but he just **walked off**.
   The plane **took off** half an hour early.

2 The airline has 20% **off** tickets to New York.
   He **fell off** the chair and hurt his back.
   Can you **cut off** a piece of that cheese for me?
   Why don't you **take off** your coat? It's not cold here.

3 I hate it when people don't **switch off** their phones in the cinema.
   I tried to call him, but his phone **was off**.
   I was tired, so I **turned off** the TV and went to bed.

b Match sentences (1–8) with replies (a–h).

1 There's 10% off if you buy today.
2 Is that your phone? What happened to it?
3 Why is it so cold in here?
4 When are you off?
5 Can I try some of that sausage?
6 Can you turn off the radio, please?
7 We took off an hour late.
8 So, do you know who hit your car?

a It fell off the table.
b Of course. I'll cut off a piece for you.
c Great! I'll take two, please.
d In five minutes.
e What time did you land?
f No, they drove off before I saw them.
g No. I'm listening to it.
h The heating's off.

c 💬 Work in pairs. Cover a–h in 3b and try to remember the replies.

⟳ REVIEW YOUR PROGRESS

How well did you do in this unit? Write 3, 2 or 1 for each objective.
3 = very well   2 = well   1 = not so well

I CAN ...

Talk about past holidays	☐
Describe difficult journeys	☐
Ask for information in a public place	☐
Write a travel blog	☐

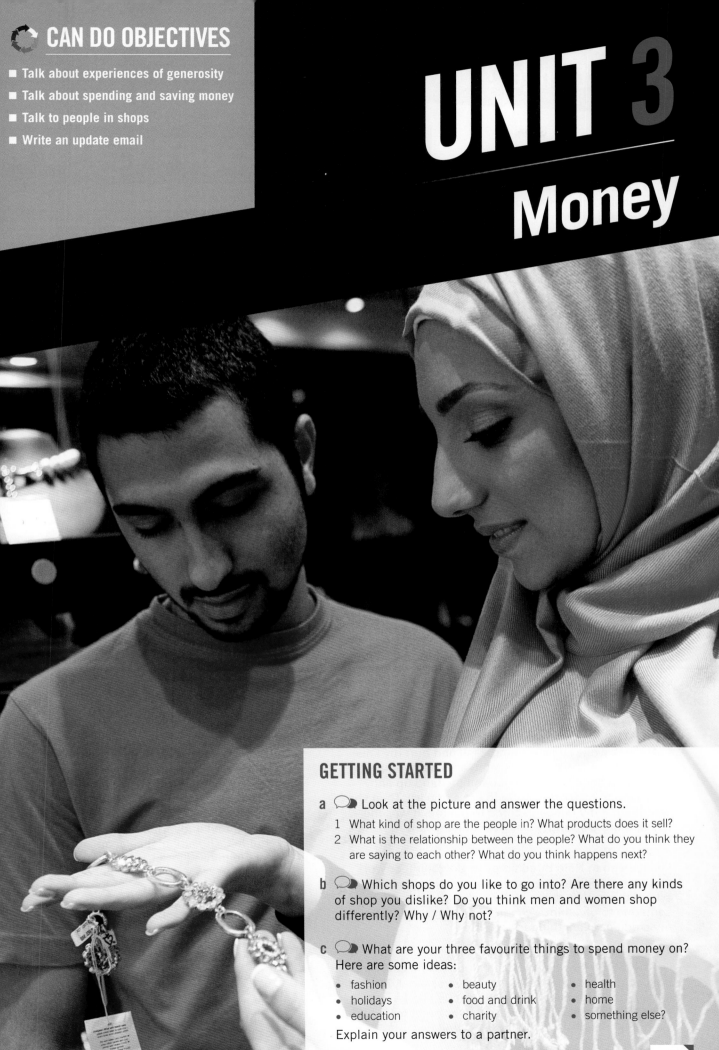

CAN DO OBJECTIVES

- Talk about experiences of generosity
- Talk about spending and saving money
- Talk to people in shops
- Write an update email

UNIT 3
Money

GETTING STARTED

a 💬 Look at the picture and answer the questions.
  1 What kind of shop are the people in? What products does it sell?
  2 What is the relationship between the people? What do you think they are saying to each other? What do you think happens next?

b 💬 Which shops do you like to go into? Are there any kinds of shop you dislike? Do you think men and women shop differently? Why / Why not?

c 💬 What are your three favourite things to spend money on? Here are some ideas:

- fashion
- holidays
- education
- beauty
- food and drink
- charity
- health
- home
- something else?

Explain your answers to a partner.

1 READING

a 💬 Look at the picture. What are the people doing? How do you think they're feeling? Why?

b 💬 Read about Generosity Day. Do you think it's a good idea? Would you like to try it? What would you like to do?

c Read the *Share the LOVE* forum. Which people mention … ?

- helping other people
- receiving help from other people

What kind of help did each person mention?

d Work in pairs. Read the text again. What do the highlighted words and phrases mean?

e 💬 Which writer in the forum do you think is the most generous? Why?

GENEROSITY DAY

Everyone knows that 14 February is Valentine's Day, a day when people spend money on cards, flowers and romantic meals for the people they love. But did you know that 14 February is also Generosity Day? It's a chance to do something nice for someone you don't know. For example, buy a stranger a coffee, smile at ten people you see on the street or give someone who looks sad a hug! So this year, why not do something a bit different?

Share the ♥ LOVE

Home   About   Message board   Search 🔍

Have you ever done something nice for a stranger? What did you do? Has a stranger ever helped you in any way? Write and let us know.

1 SALLY_TM
POSTS 102
Last week while I was running, I fell and hurt my knee quite badly. A few moments later, an older woman stopped in her car. She helped me to stand up and drove me to the corner shop to get some ice. Then she waited until my husband came to get me. It was the nicest thing a stranger has ever done for me.

2 @HELPHAITI
POSTS 1024
I have been to Haiti three times to do volunteer work and I am paying for a young man to finish his high school there. He's doing really well. He just needed someone to give him a chance. I am not rich, but with my credit card anything is possible.

3 NEIL50
POSTS 24
On my fiftieth birthday, I was in a queue in a café and I noticed that everyone looked really stressed. I decided to buy drinks for everyone in the queue and I gave the waitress a big tip, too. It was great to see everyone's faces – I made them all smile!

4 THATGEORGEKID
POSTS 2868
Strangers have helped me lots of times, and I've helped them too. I've given people directions, I've picked up hitchhikers … A few weeks ago, I made a new friend when I called 999. I saw this guy lying on the street and I tried to wake him up, but I couldn't. The ambulance came and he's OK now. He thinks I'm a hero, but I just did what was right.

5 MAYA_FLOWER
POSTS 67
I've never seen a serious accident, so I've never had the chance to save someone's life, like George. But I often help strangers: for example, I buy meals for homeless people and I give away my old clothes to charity. I try to be generous in small ways that don't cost anything, like listening to people when they are lonely, or making a joke when people look bored.

2 GRAMMAR
Present perfect or past simple

a Complete the sentences with the verbs in the box. Check your answers in the forum.

> saw   do   decided   been   done   seen

1 I have _____ to Haiti three times.
2 A few weeks ago, I _____ a man lying in the street …
3 I've never _____ a serious accident.
4 On my fiftieth birthday, I _____ to buy drinks for everyone.
5 Have you ever _____ something nice for a stranger?
6 What did you _____?

b Which sentences in 2a are present perfect? Which are past simple?

☐☐☐ present perfect   ☐☐☐ past simple

c Underline the time expressions in the sentences in 2a. Complete the rules with the time expressions from the sentences.

> We can use the present perfect to talk about past experiences in our whole lives, not at a particular time. We often use adverbs like _____ _____ _____
>
> We use the past simple to talk about a particular time in the past. We often use time phrases like _____ _____

d ▶ Now go to Grammar Focus 3A on p.146

e Complete the questions with present perfect and past simple forms of the verbs in brackets.

1 _____ you ever _____ anything for a charity? (do)
   What _____ you _____? (do)
2 _____ you ever _____ a stranger somewhere? (drive)
   Where _____ you _____ them? (drive)
3 _____ you ever _____ food for a homeless person? (buy)
   What _____ you _____ for them? (buy)

f ⏵1.48 Listen and check. Ask and answer the questions with a partner.

3 VOCABULARY
make / do / give collocations

a Complete the phrases with the verbs *make*, *do* or *give*.

1 _____ a friend   3 _____ volunteer work
   someone smile   something nice
   a joke   well (at school/work)
2 _____ someone directions
   something away
   someone a tip
   someone a hug

b Check your answers to 3a in the Generosity Day text and forum. Try to guess the meaning of new phrases. Check your ideas in a dictionary.

c 💬 Which of the things in 3a have you done this week?

> I haven't given anyone directions.

> I gave my sister a hug this morning.

4 LISTENING

a ⏵1.49 Read the information about Philip Wollen and answer the questions.
1 What was Philip Wollen's job?
2 Why did he leave his job?
3 What do you think Philip Wollen has done with his money?

Listen and check your answer to question 3.

Philip Wollen was once a very successful banker. However, after he became rich, he had a life-changing experience. On his fortieth birthday, he left his job in banking and decided to give away all his money. It is Philip's ambition to spend all his money before he dies.

b ⏵1.49 Listen again and answer the questions.
1 What size are the charities that Philip helps?
2 How many charities has he helped?
3 How did the Morning Star orphanage begin?
4 How did Philip's money help Morning Star?
5 What does the Morning Star's first child do now?
6 What kind of animals do Edgar's Mission help?
7 What do they try to teach people?

c 💬 Would you like to give money to the Morning Star or Edgar's Mission? Why / Why not?

5 SPEAKING

a 💬 You are going to find out about the generosity in your class. Walk around the class and find someone who has done each thing in the grid. Ask more questions.

buy something for a stranger	carry a heavy bag for a stranger
send someone a surprise gift	leave a big tip in a restaurant
smile at a stranger to make them smile	take a lost object back to the owner
do volunteer work	help someone who was hurt
give money to charity	show the way to a lost stranger
pay for all your friends' food or drinks	give away something you like to a friend

> Have you ever bought something for a stranger?

> Why did you buy him a ticket?

> Yes, I have. Once I paid for a man's train ticket.

> He needed to get home to his family.

b 💬 What was the most generous thing you heard?

3B I've already spent my salary this month

Learn to talk about spending and saving mo

G Present perfect with *just*, *already* and *yet*
V Money

1 VOCABULARY Money

a Do you think saving money is easy? Why / Why not?

b Work in pairs. Read the saving tips. What do the highlighted words and phrases mean?

c ▶ Now go to Vocabulary Focus 3B on p.135

2 READING AND SPEAKING

a Read *What kind of spender are you?* and choose the answers (a, b or c) which are true for you.

b In pairs, compare your answers. Are they similar?

c Check your results on p.130. Do you agree with the results?

---

www.moneythings.co.uk

SAVING TIPS

Maureen, Wigan
Always look for special offers on food in the supermarket and go shopping for clothes during the sales.

Paul, Brighton
Don't lend money to people – sometimes they don't pay it back!

Jane, Manchester
Open a second bank account and put some money into it every month.

WHAT KIND OF
SPENDER ARE YOU?

1
What do you think about credit cards?
a They're great. I can buy what I want even when I don't have any money.
b They can be useful if you are careful with them.
c They're a bad idea. It's better not to have them.

2
You want to go on holiday. What's the best idea?
a Forget about the cost. Holidays are only once a year!
b Look around for special offers on the Internet.
c Go just for two or three days and sleep in a tent.

3
You've lost your camera. What do you do next?
a Buy a new one. It was a bit old anyway.
b Look for a good second-hand one.
c Use the camera on your mobile phone.

4
You're at the supermarket check-out. Which statement is true for you?
a Your basket is full of expensive food for dinner tonight!
b You have fifteen packs of coffee. It was on offer!
c You've chosen the basic things and nothing more.

5
Do you know how much money you have in the bank?
a Not really. If my credit card works, then I'm happy.
b Not exactly, but I know I have enough for the month.
c Yes, of course. I checked my balance five minutes ago.

6
Are you a saver?
a What do you mean?
b I save about 10% of my money every month.
c I save all my spare money every month.

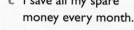

3 LISTENING

a 💬 Look at the pictures of the three people. Who do you think is a ... ?

☐ big spender   ☐ non spender
☐ smart spender

① ② ③

b ▶1.51 Listen to the people being interviewed. Check your ideas in 3a. What has each person bought?

c ▶1.51 Listen again and answer the questions about each speaker.

1 What is he/she saving for?
2 How does he/she feel about borrowing money?

d 💬 Look at the ideas from the listening. Do you agree with the speakers?

1 'I don't want to owe money to a bank.'
2 'Everyone should save for when they're older.'
3 'Life's too short to worry about money!'

4 GRAMMAR
Present perfect with *just*, *already* and *yet*

a Complete the sentences with the past participles of the verbs.

1 I've **just** _____ my food for the week. (buy)
2 I've **already** _____ my salary this month. (spend)
3 I have**n't** _____ it back **yet.** (pay)

b ▶1.52 Listen and check. What tense are all the sentences?

c Look at the sentences in 4a. Then complete the rules with *just*, *already* and *yet*.

Use _____ to say something is complete, often earlier than we expected.
Use _____ to say something happened a short time ago.
Use *not* + _____ to say something is not complete.

d ▶ Now go to Grammar Focus 3B on p.146

e ▶1.54 **Pronunciation** Listen to how the following words spelt with *j* and *y* are pronounced. Then listen again and repeat.

/dʒ/	/j/
just	**y**et
enjoy	**y**ou
join	**y**oung

f ▶1.55 Put the adverbs in brackets in the correct places in the sentences. Then listen and check.

1 I've spent a lot of money on a new pair of glasses. (just)
2 I bought a new mobile last month, but I've lost it. (already)
3 I need some winter clothes, but I haven't had time to go shopping. (yet)
4 I've bought a card for Mother's Day. (already)
5 I bought some amazing shoes last year, but I haven't worn them. (yet)
6 I've seen a special offer on a holiday online, but I haven't decided to buy it. (just, yet)

g Change four sentences in 4f to make them true for you.

h 💬 Compare your sentences with a partner.

> I've just spent a lot of money on my phone bill.

> Really? I've just spent a lot of money on my car. It broke down.

5 SPEAKING

💬 Work in small groups. Ask and answer the questions.

- Are you saving up for anything at the moment? What for? How much money do you need?
- What things do you spend a lot of money on? How do you feel about the amount of money you spend on these things?
- Are there any places you'd like to go, but can't afford to? Where? Why are they expensive?
- Do people often ask for discounts in shops in your country? How about in markets? Are you good at getting discounts?
- Does anyone owe you money at the moment? Who? When do you think they'll pay you back?

3C Everyday English
Do you have anything cheaper?

Learn to talk to people in shops
P Sentence stress
S Changing your mind

1 LISTENING

a 💬 Do you enjoy going shopping? Which of these things do you like shopping for? Why?

- food • gifts • clothes • books

> I like shopping for clothes. It's fun.

> I hate it. I think it's really boring, but I like buying books.

b 💬 Look at the pictures of Mark and Rachel shopping. What do you think they are shopping for?

c ▶ 1.56 Watch or listen to Part 1 and check your ideas.

d 💬 In pairs, look at the products 1–4. Answer the questions.

1 What do you think each product is used for?
2 Would you buy any of the products for someone you know?
3 Would you like to receive any of them as a present?

e ▶ 1.57 Watch or listen to Part 2. Which of the products in the pictures do they buy?

f ▶ 1.57 Watch or listen again. Answer the questions.

1 Why does Mark think 'Football in a tin' is a good present?
2 Why does Rachel disagree about the 'Football in a tin'?
3 Why doesn't Mark like the weather station?
4 Why does Mark decide not to buy the book money bank?

g 💬 Work in pairs. What do you think of the present they chose? Do you think Leo will like it?

2 USEFUL LANGUAGE
Talking to people in shops

a ▶ 1.58 Complete the phrases from Part 2 with the words in the box. Then listen and check.

> anything   sort   cheaper   looking
> take   do   help   show

1 Can I _____ you?
2 We're _____ for a present for a friend.
3 Are you looking for _____ in particular?
4 What _____ of thing does he like?
5 What does it _____?
6 Do you have anything _____?
7 Could you _____ us something else?
8 We'll _____ it.

①
②

③
④

b Answer the questions about the phrases in 2a.

1 Which phrases did the shop assistant say?
2 Which phrase explains why they are in the shop?
3 Which phrases mean they want to see another product?
4 Which phrase asks for information about a product?
5 Which phrase means 'We want to buy this one'?

3 PRONUNCIATION
Sentence stress

a ▶1.59 Listen to the sentences. Notice the stress.
1 This looks perfect.
2 We're only here for Leo.

b ▶1.59 Listen again. Answer the questions.
1 How many syllables does each sentence have?
2 How many stressed syllables does each sentence have?
3 Do we say the unstressed syllables in sentence 2 quickly or slowly?

c ▶1.60 Listen and complete the sentences. The missing words are all unstressed.
1 I'd like ____ look ____ ____ different one.
2 Can you show ____ ____ first one again?
3 I'm looking ____ ____ present ____ ____ brother.
4 Do you have this ____ ____ different size?
5 It'll cost ____ ____ ____ money ____ fix.

4 USEFUL LANGUAGE
Paying at the till

a ▶1.61 Watch or listen to Part 3. What does Mark change his mind about?

b ▶1.61 Watch or listen again. Complete the questions with the words in the box.

| put your   receipt   enter your |
| you like   next, please |

1 Who's ____ ____?
2 How would ____ ____ to pay?
3 Can you ____ ____ card in, please?
4 Can you ____ ____ PIN, please?
5 Here's your ____.

c 💬 Practise the conversation from Part 3. Take turns to be the shop assistant and the customer (Mark).

5 CONVERSATION SKILLS Changing your mind

a Look at the underlined phrases in the sentences. Do the two phrases mean the same or are they different?

On second thoughts, I really think we should get something sporty.
Actually, I think I'll put it on my credit card.

b 💬 Work in pairs. Take turns to change your mind. Start with *I'd like*.
1 a coffee – a cup of tea
2 take the bus – get a taxi
3 a sandwich – a salad
4 go for a drive – go for a walk
5 watch TV – put some music on
6 a first-class ticket – a normal ticket

I'd like a coffee.
OK.
On second thoughts, I'd prefer a cup of tea.
Fine.

6 SPEAKING

▶ **Communication 3C** Work in groups of three. Students A and B: you are buying a present – go to p.130. Student C: you are a shop assistant – go to p.127.

Unit Progress Test

CHECK YOUR PROGRESS

You can now do the Unit Progress Test.

1 LISTENING AND SPEAKING

a 💬 Look at the names of the charities. What do you know about the charities? What do they do?

Match the charities with the sentences.

This charity …
1 protects animals and the environment.
2 protects historic buildings, gardens and the countryside.
3 helps people in poorer countries.

What other large charities do you know? What do they do?

b 💬 Work in pairs. How do people raise money for charity? Add ideas to the list.

- *collect money in the street*
- *sponsor someone to do a sports event, for example, run a marathon*
- *make and sell food, e.g. cakes at work or school*

c ▶1.62 Listen to four people talking about giving money to charity. Do they support a charity? Which one?

1 Shona   2 Jack   3 Jessica   4 William

d ▶1.62 Listen again. Why do/don't the people in 1c support a charity? How do they help? Listen and make notes.

e Work on your own. Make notes on these questions.

1 What charity do you prefer to give money to? Why?
2 Have you ever raised money for charity? What did you do? Who gave you money?

f 💬 Work in small groups. Talk about your answers to 1e.

2 READING

a Anita and her team at work support the National Trust. Read Anita's email. Why is she sending the email? Tick the correct reasons.

1 ☐ to say thank you
2 ☐ to apologise
3 ☐ to tell people how much money they have raised
4 ☐ to tell people about how the team raised money
5 ☐ to tell people about what the National Trust do
6 ☐ to ask people for money

Hello everyone,

(a) We'd like to thank everyone for their help over the past few months raising money for the National Trust. We've successfully raised £500.

(b) Most of you know one of the ways we raised money, because you bought our cakes every Wednesday! But we'd just like to let you know about the different things we did. We also sold our old books, DVDs and clothes online. And, every Friday, we each paid £1 to wear casual clothes to work.

(c) The National Trust will use the money to repair historic buildings and keep them open for the public to visit. It's interesting to see how people lived in the past – some of the rooms and furniture in these buildings are beautiful. Visiting a historic building is a really enjoyable thing for a family to do at weekends, and another way to help the National Trust continue their excellent work.

(d) Thanks again for all your help. Please look out for our next event.

Anita Webb (and team)
Resources Manager

b Read the email again and answer the questions.

1 How did the team raise £500?
2 How will the National Trust spend the money?
3 What is another way Anita's colleagues can help the National Trust?

3 WRITING SKILLS Paragraphing

a Match the descriptions with paragraphs a–d in Anita's email.

1 ☐ closing the email
2 ☐ the introduction
3 ☐ how the team raised money
4 ☐ information about the National Trust

b What information does Anita include in the introduction? What does she mention in the closing paragraph?

c Put the paragraphs below in the correct order to make an email.

☐ Oxfam will use the money on projects around the world to help people have happier and healthier lives. Last year, they helped 13.5 million people. A small amount of money can make a big change. For example, just £15 can give free health care to a mother and her baby.

☐ Many of you have bought tickets to our 'Quiz and Pizza' nights. Others gave their unwanted clothes to the very successful 'Clothes Market' in March. We really hope you enjoyed these events. Your money and time will help Oxfam to continue their important work.

☐ Would you like to help us raise more money for Oxfam? Just email me and I'll tell you what we're planning next. Thanks again for all your help.

☐ This email is to say a big 'Thank you!' to everyone who has helped us to raise money for Oxfam over the last few months. We have now raised £750.

4 WRITING

a Choose one of these emails to write.

1 Write about a real experience of raising money for charity. Write to the people who gave you money to thank them. Tell them about how much money you raised, how you raised the money and about the charity.

2 You and some friends have raised £1,000 for a charity at work/school. Write to everyone who helped you to say thank you. Tell them about how much money you raised, how you raised the money and about the charity.

b Plan the email. Use four paragraphs. What information will you put in each paragraph?

c Write the email.

d Swap emails with a partner. Read your partner's email. Are there four paragraphs in the email? What information is in each paragraph?

UNIT 3
Review and extension

1 GRAMMAR

a Put the words in the correct order to make questions.

1 you / bought / ever / have / something you didn't need ?
2 given / you / a stranger / have / money / to ?
3 ever / to / a very expensive restaurant / have / you / been ?
4 ever / driven / you / an expensive car / have ?
5 lost / ever / you / money / have / on the street ?

b 💬 Ask and answer the questions in 1a.

c Complete the text with the present perfect forms of the verbs in the box.

do   go   have   help   raise   run   spend

My colleague Andrea is really generous. She ¹_____ a lot of work for charity. She ²_____ two marathons and from that she ³_____ lots of money for different charities. She ⁴_____ some time in foreign countries – she ⁵_____ to India to help build a school. At work, she ⁶_____ me a lot when I ⁷_____ problems.

d Put the adverb in brackets in the correct place.

A Have you spoken to John? (yet)
B Yes, he's called me. (just)
A Did you ask him about the party?
B Yes, he's bought the food. (already)
A Great. I haven't been to the shops. (yet)
B Have you decided what music to play? (already)
A Yes, I've made a list. (just)

e 💬 Practise the exchange in 1d.

2 VOCABULARY

a Complete the sentences with the words in the box.

directions   hug   joke   something   volunteer

1 My mum was very upset, so I gave her a _____.
2 I gave the woman _____ to the tourist office.
3 I want to do some _____ work for a charity this summer.
4 He made a _____ and everyone laughed.
5 I always try to do _____ nice at weekends.

b Match questions (1–5) with answers (a–e).

1 ☐ Can you lend me ten euros?
2 ☐ How did you afford your new car?
3 ☐ What are you saving up for?
4 ☐ Did you get a discount on your new bike?
5 ☐ Have you got the money you owe me?

a A new laptop. I want to buy one in the sales.
b Sorry, no. I just spent it on my electricity bill.
c I got a loan!
d No, you won't pay me back!
e Yes, it was on special offer.

3 WORDPOWER *just*

a Look at the different meanings of *just* (in 1–4). Read the example sentences. Match the meanings of *just* in sentences a–d with meanings 1–4.

1 ☐ = *a short time ago*
I've **just** got home from work. I need a rest!
2 ☐ = *only*
He doesn't understand money. He's **just** a child.
3 ☐ = *almost not*
I ran to the station and I **just** caught my train.
4 ☐ = *soon*
Hang on! I'm **just** coming.

a The tickets cost **just** a few dollars.
b I'm **just** finishing this email – I'll be ready in one minute.
c Sorry, he's **just** left – he was here a minute ago.
d You can **just** see the sea from my window, but it's very far away.

b Match sentences (1–5) with replies (a–e).

1 ☐ She looks **just like** her sister.
2 ☐ I think the books cost **just under** £10.
3 ☐ The flight is three hours long.
4 ☐ I've **just about** finished my work.
5 ☐ Look at that rain.

a Yes, they're £9.80. I checked.
b Yes – we got home **just in time**!
c That's good. We need to leave in five minutes.
d Really? It was **just over** two hours when I went.
e Of course – they're twins!

c Complete the sentences with expressions from 3b.

1 Michele leaves home at 8 am and arrives at work at 8.25. It takes him _____ half an hour to get there.
2 Steven looks _____ his brother – they're both tall and they've both got black hair.
3 I normally arrive _____ when I get a train or plane. I never arrive early!
4 My electricity bill is always _____ €50. This time it's €51.20.
5 The new university building is _____ ready – we'll have our lessons there next month.

d 💬 Work in pairs. Make sentences about your life with the expressions in 3b.

CAN DO OBJECTIVES

- Talk about your plans for celebrations
- Plan a day out in a city
- Make social arrangements
- Write and reply to an invitation

UNIT 4
Social Life

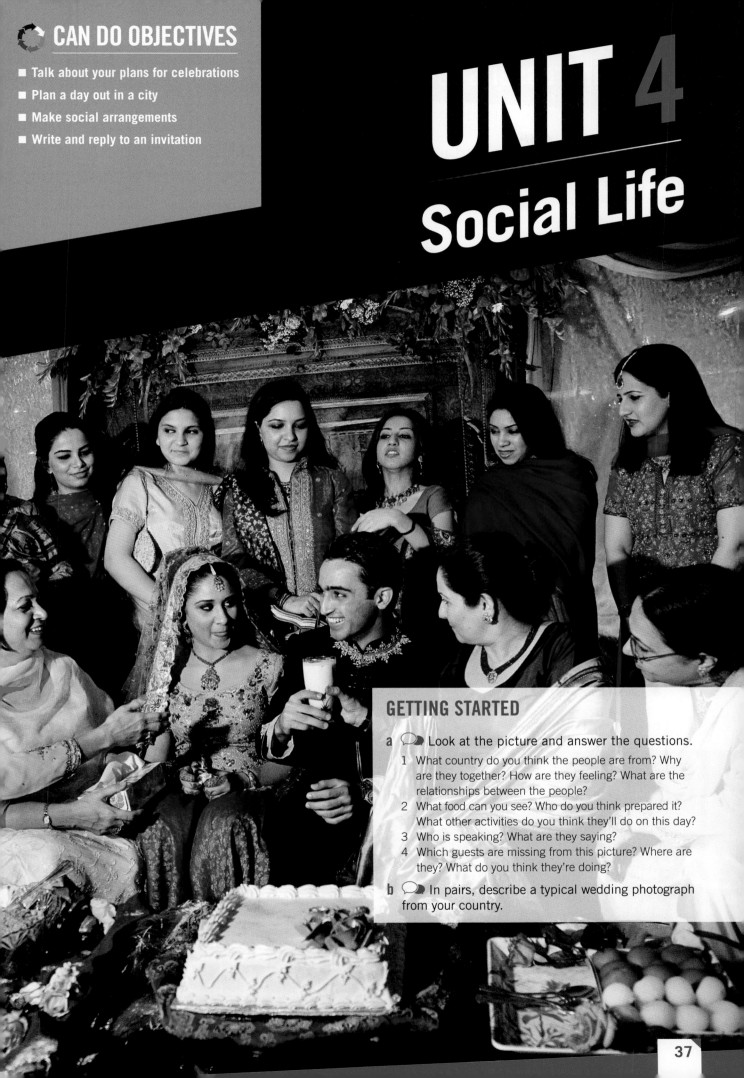

GETTING STARTED

a Look at the picture and answer the questions.

1 What country do you think the people are from? Why are they together? How are they feeling? What are the relationships between the people?

2 What food can you see? Who do you think prepared it? What other activities do you think they'll do on this day?

3 Who is speaking? What are they saying?

4 Which guests are missing from this picture? Where are they? What do you think they're doing?

b In pairs, describe a typical wedding photograph from your country.

4A I'm going to the hairdresser's tomorrow

Learn to talk about your plans for celebrations

- **G** Present continuous and *going to*
- **V** Clothes and appearance

1 VOCABULARY Clothes and appearance

a Look at the pictures on these pages. Answer the questions with a partner.

1 What clothes and accessories can you see?
2 Would you like to wear any of the clothes?
3 Are there any clothes that you would never wear? Why?

b ▶ Now go to Vocabulary Focus 4A on p.135

2 LISTENING

a Look at the pictures of Marta and Craig below. What events are they at? What are they doing in the pictures?

b ▶1.65 Work in pairs. Read sentences 1–6. Do you think Marta or Craig is speaking? Write *M* or *C*. Listen and check.

1 ☐ We're going to stay the whole night – until they serve breakfast!
2 ☐ This year one of my favourite DJs is playing.
3 ☐ They're going to make a special cream from turmeric.
4 ☐ I'm not going to see Monisha until the ceremony begins.
5 ☐ I'm meeting the others at 7 pm so we can start queuing.
6 ☐ My friends are arriving early tomorrow to help me get ready.

c ▶1.65 Listen again and answer the questions.

1 Why does the college organise the May Ball?
2 What is special about Marta's dress?
3 Why is Marta going to stay at home on Saturday?
4 What happens at the end of the May Ball?
5 What are Craig's guests going to do with the special cream?
6 When do the wedding day celebrations start and finish?
7 How does Craig describe the clothes he's going to wear?
8 What happens at the beginning of the wedding day?

d Ask and answer the questions.

1 What's the biggest party you've ever been to?
2 What's the best wedding you've ever been to?

3 GRAMMAR
Present continuous and *going to*

a Read the sentences. Are Craig and Marta talking about the present or the future?

1 My friends **are arriving** early tomorrow.
2 I**'m not going to leave** the house on Saturday.
3 I**'m going to stay** the whole night.
4 A beautician **is doing** our make-up.

b Look at the verb forms in **bold** in the sentences in 3a. Answer the questions with present continuous or *going to*.

1 Which sentences are about future plans with other people?
2 Which future plans are just ideas, not already arranged?

c ▶ Now go to Grammar Focus 4A on p.148

d ▶1.67 **Pronunciation** Listen to five speakers. Which speakers pronounce *going to* /ˈgəʊɪŋ tə/? How do the other speakers say it?

e Answer questions 1 and 2 for each future time in the box.

| today   this week   this weekend |
| this summer   this month   next year |

1 What are your plans? Who are they with?
2 Have you arranged anything yet?

f Tell your partner about your plans.

I'm going to Brazil this summer. *When are you going?*

Marta at the University of Cambridge May Ball

Craig at his Indian wedding

LIFE IN NUMBERS

VIETNAM

Imagine sharing your birthday with the whole country! That's exactly what happens every year in Vietnam. The Vietnamese don't celebrate on the day they were born. Instead everyone gets one year older on the same day – Vietnamese New Year's day or 'Tet'. People don't give birthday presents, but children receive red envelopes with money inside. Children greet older people with the phrase, 'Long life of 100 years!'

Tet is the biggest celebration of the year in Vietnam – and it can last for a week. Everyone takes to the streets to make as much noise as they can and there are fireworks and lion dances.

LATIN AMERICA

Becoming an adult is a very special day for girls in South America and it happens on their fifteenth birthday – the Quinceañera.

In some places, such as parts of Mexico, the father or another relative gives the girl her first pair of high heels as a symbol of becoming a woman. The birthday girl, or quinceañera, often gives out fifteen candles, one to each of the fifteen most important people in her life.

Then there is a meal and dancing. The quinceañera's first dance is always with her father.

JAPAN

In Japan everyone has a day off to celebrate the world's biggest twentieth birthday party.

The second Monday of January every year is 'Coming of Age Day' or 'Seijin no hi' – the day all twenty-year-old Japanese become adults.

Men wear suits and girls dress in beautiful kimonos, which they often have to rent or borrow because they're so expensive. A ceremony is held in the local government office and afterwards the new adults can party with their friends and family.

THE UK

Your 100th birthday is a big day in any country, but it's even more special in the UK – you get a card from the Queen! Don't forget to let her know though – the Queen is a busy woman, so you or your family should apply before the big day.

Each card she sends contains a personal greeting – when twins reach 100 years old together, each one gets a slightly different message. The oldest person who has ever received a birthday card from the Queen was 116 years old.

4 READING

a 🗩 Ask and answer the questions.

1 Do you celebrate your birthday? What do you do?
2 Do people in your country celebrate any specific ages? Which ones?

b Read the article. What do the numbers refer to? (Sometimes there is more than one possible answer.)

1 15 20 100

c Read the article again and answer the questions.

For which celebration do people … ?
1 wear clothes they can't afford to buy
2 need to request something
3 both give and receive something
4 have a party that goes on for several days
5 wear special shoes
6 not go to work so they can celebrate

d 🗩 Work in pairs. Answer the questions.

1 Which celebration in the text did you find most interesting? Why?
2 What other celebrations are important in your country? Which is your favourite?
   - weddings
   - local festivals
   - family celebrations
   - work/school/university events
   - birthdays
   - religious festivals and new year

5 SPEAKING

a Work on your own. Write down three events you are going to in the future. Use the list in 4d for ideas.

1 My best friend's wedding in August
2 21st September – Grandfather's 80th birthday

b 🗩 Now work in a small group. Ask each person questions. Try to guess the three events they are going to. (You can't ask: *What is the event?*)

> When is the event happening?

> In August.

> Who are you going with?

> I'm going with my boyfriend.

> What are you going to wear?

1 LISTENING

a Ask and answer the questions.

1 What do you know about Tokyo? Have you ever been there? Would you like to go? Why / Why not?
2 Look at the places 1–5 in *Tokyo Highlights*. Which would you like to visit?

b ▶1.68 Mike is visiting his friend Harry in Tokyo for one day. Listen and answer the questions.

1 Which places in *Tokyo Highlights* do they decide to visit?
2 Which three other places do they decide to visit?

c ▶1.68 Listen again and answer the questions.

1 Why do they decide not to go to the Imperial Palace?
2 How does Harry describe the noodle restaurant?
3 Why do people do *cosplay*?
4 Why is Akihabara a good place for Mike's shopping?
5 Where will they do karaoke?
6 Why does Harry want to go to the fish market at night?

d Do you think they chose good places to visit? Did they choose any places you would not like to visit?

2 GRAMMAR will / won't / shall

a ▶1.69 Listen to the sentences. Complete the sentences with the words in the box.

'll   won't   shall

1 So we _____ go to Disneyland then!
2 _____ we start with something to eat?
3 **M** I want to look for a new camera.
  H I _____ take you to Akihabara, then.
4 Don't worry – you _____ miss your flight!
5 _____ I come to your hotel in about an hour?

b Are Mike and Harry talking about the present or the future? What are the full forms of *'ll* and *won't*?

TOKYO
HIGHLIGHTS

1 Go to the top of Tokyo Tower for a great view of the city

c Match the sentences in 2a with the uses of *will* and *shall*. Write the numbers.

We use *will* and *won't* to:
☐ make promises
☐ ☐ make decisions while we are speaking

We use *shall* to:
☐ make offers
☐ make suggestions

d ▶ Now go to Grammar Focus 4B on p.148

e ▶1.72 **Pronunciation** Listen to the sentences. Is the vowel in **bold** pronounced /ɒ/ or /əʊ/?

1 I w**a**nt to visit the museum.
2 We w**o**n't have time to see everything.

f ▶1.73 Listen to the sentences. Circle the correct answers.

1 We *want to / won't* come back next year.
2 They *want to / won't* stay in the same hotel again.
3 I *want to / won't* go for a walk in the park.
4 They *want to / won't* see the market.
5 You *want to / won't* find a table at that restaurant.
6 I *want to / won't* take you to see the castle.

g ▶1.73 Listen again and repeat.

h ▶ **Communication 4B** Work in pairs. Student A: go to p.131. Student B: go to p.132.

2 Enjoy a day out at Disneyland Tokyo

3 Walk around the beautiful Yoyogi Park and see people doing cosplay

5 Go shopping in Akihabara

4 Visit Kyokyo – the Imperial Palace

3 VOCABULARY
Adjectives: places

a Look at the sentences. What are the opposites of the highlighted adjectives? Choose the adjectives in the box.

---
tiny   quiet   ugly
---

1 The palace is nice but it's so crowded. _____
2 It's a huge park so it's always really nice. _____
3 Everyone goes to look at the pretty flowers. _____

b Match the opposite adjectives.

1 ☐ modern   a peaceful
2 ☐ high   b wide
3 ☐ indoor   c ancient
4 ☐ magnificent   d outdoor
5 ☐ narrow   e low
6 ☐ noisy   f ordinary

c (▶)**1.74** Listen and check. Underline the stressed syllables.

d (▶)**1.74** Listen again. Repeat the words.

e 💬 Work in a small group. Think about places you all know. Can you think of one place for each adjective in 4b?

> There's an outdoor swimming pool near the river.

> The market in the town centre is really noisy.

4 LISTENING

a (▶)**1.75** Listen to Mike and Harry's conversation. What was Mike's favourite part of the day?

b (▶)**1.76** Listen to the last part of the conversation. What is the problem? What does Harry suggest?

c 💬 Would you stay another day? Why / Why not?

d 💬 Are there any cities in another country that you would like to visit? Is there any city you would like to live in? Which?

5 SPEAKING

a Your partner is going to visit you for one day in a city you know well. Make notes on:

- places to visit
- where to eat
- what to do in the evening

b 💬 Student A: describe the places to your partner. Student B: choose which places you want to visit. Agree on a plan for the day. Then swap roles.

> Shall we go to an art gallery first?

> I don't really like art galleries.

> OK – I'll take you to the National Cinema Museum. It's huge.

> That sounds good.

c 💬 Describe each day out to the class. Vote for the day out you like the most.

4C Everyday English
Are you doing anything on Wednesday?

Learn to make social arrangements
P Sentence stress
S Making time to think

1 LISTENING

a 💬 Do you make arrangements with people by phone? What kind of things do you arrange?

b ▶1.77 Watch or listen to Part 1. Why does Annie call Rachel?

c ▶1.77 Watch or listen again. Answer the questions.
1 Why can't Rachel come on Wednesday?
2 What is she doing on Thursday?
3 Which day do they agree to have the meal?
4 What time do they decide?
5 What does Annie want Rachel to bring?

2 USEFUL LANGUAGE
Making arrangements

a Look at the phrases. Which phrases are for inviting? Which are for responding to invitations? Write *I* (inviting) or *R* (responding).
1 ☐ Would you like to come round for a meal?
2 ☐ Are you doing anything on Wednesday?
3 ☐ We can't do Wednesday.
4 ☐ How about Thursday? Is that OK for you?
5 ☐ This week's really busy for us.
6 ☐ What are you doing on Monday?
7 ☐ What time shall we come round?
8 ☐ Would you like us to bring anything?

b ▶1.78 Listen to how Rachel and Annie replied to each question. Make notes. What different replies could you give?

c ▶1.79 Complete the gaps with words from the box. Listen and check.

---
how about   shall I   are you doing (x 2)
is that OK   would you like   can't do   busy

A ¹_____ anything tomorrow? ²_____ to come round for a coffee?
B I ³_____ tomorrow. ⁴_____ the weekend? ⁵_____ for you?
A No, the weekend's really ⁶_____ for me. What ⁷_____ on Monday next week?
B Nothing – I'm free. What time ⁸_____ come round?
A Any time in the morning.

d 💬 Work in pairs. Practise the conversation in 2c. Change the details.

> Are you doing anything on Friday? Would you like to go to the cinema?

> I can't do Friday.

3 CONVERSATION SKILLS
Making time to think

a Look at the examples from Part 1. <u>Underline</u> the phrases Rachel uses to give herself time to think.
1 Oh, that sounds nice. I'll just check. No, we can't do Wednesday. Sorry.
2 Thursday … hang on a minute … no, sorry.
3 Just a moment … Nothing! We can do Monday.

b ▶1.80 Listen and repeat the phrases in 3a.

c 💬 Work in pairs. Take turns to make an invitation. Check your phone / diary before you reply. Use the phrases in 3a.

> Do you want to come to the cinema on Saturday?

> Saturday … hang on a minute … yes, that would be great!

4 LISTENING

a ▶ 1.81 Look at the pictures. Where are they? Do you think Leo likes his present? Watch or listen to Part 2 and check your ideas.

b ▶ 1.81 Watch or listen again. Answer the questions.

1 Why does Mark want to go for a run tomorrow?
2 What does Rachel find out about Leo?
3 What do Mark and Leo arrange to do and when?

c 💬 Ask and answer the questions.

1 Do people in your country usually open their presents when the giver is there? Why / Why not?
2 Do you ever receive presents you don't like?
3 Do you think you are good at choosing presents for people?

5 PRONUNCIATION Sentence stress

a ▶ 1.82 Listen to two sentences from Part 1. Answer the questions.

We can do Monday.
We can't do Wednesday.

1 Which word is stressed more – *can* or *can't*?
2 Is the vowel in *can't* long or short?

b ▶ 1.83 Listen to the sentences. Complete the rule.

I <u>don't</u> really <u>like</u> <u>sport</u>.
I <u>can't</u> <u>stand</u> <u>football</u>.
You <u>really</u> <u>did</u>n't <u>need</u> to.

> Negative auxiliary forms are *sometimes* / *always* stressed.

c ▶ 1.84 Listen and repeat.

1 I can't do next week.
2 We don't have time.
3 I won't be late.
4 I could see you tomorrow.
5 We didn't go to the party.
6 We can come at six o'clock.

6 SPEAKING

a ▶ **Communication 4C** Work in pairs. Student A: go to 6b below. Student B: go to p.132.

Student A

b You want to invite Student B for dinner one evening. Look at your diary. Complete your diary with plans for three evenings. Decide what you want Student B to bring to the dinner.

Wednesday: _____

Thursday: _____

Friday: _____

Saturday: _____

Sunday: _____

Need guests to bring:

c 💬 Call and invite Student B to dinner. Arrange an evening for dinner. Try to arrange it this week. If you can't, arrange it for next week. Tell Student B what to bring.

🔄 Unit Progress Test

CHECK YOUR PROGRESS

You can now do the Unit Progress Test.

4D Skills for Writing
Are you free on Saturday?

1 SPEAKING AND LISTENING

a 💬 How often do you do the things in this list? Who do you do them with?

- have a party
- go out for a coffee or a meal
- go out and do something (for example, see a film)
- do sport (for example, go swimming or play football)
- invite people for a meal at your home
- go for a walk

b 💬 Which of the activities in 1a do you do to … ?

- celebrate a birthday
- celebrate the end of term
- meet new friends
- spend time with old friends
- spend time with colleagues

c ▶️**1.85** Listen to three people. What is each person going to do this weekend?

1 Susanna
2 Barbara
3 Sven

d ▶️**1.85** Listen again and answer the questions.

Susanna
1 Why doesn't Susanna like parties at home?
2 Where is she going to celebrate her 21st birthday?
3 What is she going to wear?

Barbara
4 Why doesn't Barbara like cooking for people at home?
5 Why does she prefer cooking things together?
6 What's Barbara going to make for the barbecue on Saturday?

Sven
7 What does Sven say people do at parties?
8 What does he prefer to do with friends? Why?
9 What is he going to do at the lake?

e 💬 Which person are you most similar to? Why?

2 READING

a Barbara sent emails inviting people to her barbecue. Read the emails and answer the questions.

1 Has Barbara seen Martina recently?
2 When is the barbecue?
3 What do Martina and Bill need to bring to the barbecue?

b Who do you think Barbara sees more often? How do you know?

Hi Martina,

How are you? We haven't seen you for ages! Hope you're well and you're enjoying your new job. This is just to say that we're having a barbecue at the weekend. Are you free on Saturday and, if so, would you like to come? People are going to arrive around eight o'clock. Everyone's bringing something for the barbecue. Do you think you could bring something?

It would be lovely to see you and have a chance to chat.

Best wishes,

Barbara

Inbox

Hi Bill,

How are things? I hope the cycling trip went well – you had good weather for it!

Are you doing anything on Saturday evening? We're having a barbecue and inviting a few people. Can you come? It'd be great to see you!

Everyone is bringing something. We'll make some salads, but could you bring some meat for the barbecue?

Love,

Barbara

3 WRITING SKILLS Inviting and replying

Look at the emails in 2a again and complete the table.

Type of phrase	Email to Martina	Email to Bill
Asks how the other person is	1 How are you?	5 How _____ ?
Asks if he/she is free	2 Are you _____ on Saturday?	6 Are you _____ on Saturday?
Invites him/her	3 _____ to come?	7 _____ come?
Says she wants to see him/her	4 It _____ to see you.	8 It'd _____ to see you!

Read the replies to Barbara's emails. Which is from Martina and which is from Bill?
How do you know? Who is coming to Barbara's BBQ?

Hi Barbara,

Nice to hear from you. Yes, I'm fine, but I'm very busy. The job's great, but I have to work very long hours. Thanks for inviting me on Saturday. I'm free that evening and I'd love to come. Is it OK if I bring my daughter, Stephanie? We don't eat meat, but we'll bring some vegetables for the barbecue.

I'm looking forward to seeing you and having a good chat.

All the best,

Hi Barbara,

Yes, we had a great time, but my legs still hurt!

I'm really sorry, the BBQ sounds great, but I'm afraid I can't come. Thanks for asking. I'd love to, but I'm staying with my sister at the weekend.

See you soon anyway. Hope you have a nice time!

xx

c Underline the phrases in the replies that each person uses to:

1 say thank you
2 say yes to an invitation
3 say no to an invitation
4 give a reason
5 talk about the next time they'll meet

d Correct the mistakes in each of the sentences. Use the emails in this lesson to help you.

1 You like to come to my birthday party?
2 Thanks that you invited me to your wedding.
3 It's afraid I can't go to the cinema with you.
4 I love to come, but I'm busy that weekend.
5 I'm looking forward to see you tomorrow.

4 WRITING

a Work in pairs. You are organising an activity at the weekend. Write an invitation to another pair of students. Include these points:

- ask them how they are
- invite them to come
- say where and when the event is
- tell them what they need to bring

b Swap invitations with another pair. Write a reply to the invitation. Include these points:

- say thank you
- decide if you can go (If you can't go, give a reason.)
- add a comment or a question

c Give your reply back to the other pair. Look at their invitations and replies. Have they included these points?

- said clearly where and when the event is
- used the correct language for the invitation
- used the correct language to reply to the invitation

UNIT 4
Review and extension

1 GRAMMAR

a Complete the sentences with the correct form of *going to* and the verbs in the box.

buy   go   travel   meet   not take   watch

1 I _____ a film at the cinema soon.
2 They _____ around South America this summer.
3 Sile and Sean _____ on holiday by the sea next summer.
4 I _____ an English exam this year.
5 She _____ something from the shops after work.
6 We _____ some friends for lunch tomorrow.

b Complete the conversation with the present continuous forms of the verbs.

A ¹_____ (you / do) anything this Saturday?
B I ²_____ (go) to my sister's in the evening. She ³_____ (have) a party. I ⁴_____ (not do) anything in the afternoon.
A Great! I ⁵_____ (have) a barbecue. Do you want to come? Tina and Matt ⁶_____ (come).
B Sounds good! Do you want me to bring anything?
A Well, I ⁷_____ (make) vegetarian food. Is that OK?
B Yes, that's great.

c 🗨 Practise the conversation in 1b.

d Complete the text messages with *will, won't* or *shall*.

Hi! I'm almost at the cinema. ¹_____ (I / get) the tickets when I arrive. ²_____ (I / get) you something to eat or drink? Try to be on time ...

Hi. ³_____ (I / have) a lemonade please. ⁴_____ (I / eat) something later. ⁵_____ (we / go) for coffee after the film? I promise ⁶_____ (I / be) late!

📷 _____ Send

2 VOCABULARY

a Where do these clothes and accessories go on the body? Write the correct numbers.

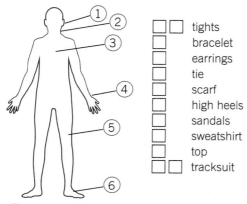

☐☐ tights
☐ bracelet
☐ earrings
☐ tie
☐ scarf
☐ high heels
☐ sandals
☐ sweatshirt
☐ top
☐☐ tracksuit

b 🗨 Talk about the clothes and accessories you are wearing.

3 WORDPOWER *look*

a Match the words in **bold** (1–5) with definitions (a–e).

1 We're really **looking forward to** our holiday in Florida.

2 I'm **looking after** my friend's cat while he's on holiday.

3 I didn't know the address, so I **looked** it **up** online.

4 He doesn't **look** very well – maybe he's got a cold.

5 I was only in the city an hour, so I didn't have time to **look around**.

a ☐ visit a place and see the things in it
b ☐ appear, seem
c ☐ feel happy and excited about a future event
d ☐ try to find information in a book or on a computer
e ☐ give a person or animal what they need

b Choose the correct answers.

1 I really like looking *after / up* young children.
2 I'm really looking *after / forward to* the weekend.
3 I always look *up / out* a film online before I see it.
4 I spend too much time looking *at / to* social media sites.
5 I always look *for / to* special offers when I go shopping.
6 I *look / look like* tired when I don't get much sleep.
7 I love looking *around / up* clothes shops.

c 🗨 Work in pairs. Which of the sentences in 3b are true for you?

🔄 REVIEW YOUR PROGRESS

How well did you do in this unit? Write 3, 2 or 1 for each objective.
3 = very well   2 = well   1 = not so well

I CAN ...

Talk about your plans for celebrations	☐
Plan a day out in a city	☐
Make social arrangements	☐
Write and reply to an invitation	☐

46

CAN DO OBJECTIVES

- Talk about what people do at work
- Talk about your future career
- Make offers and suggestions
- Write a job application

UNIT 5
Work

GETTING STARTED

a ⏵ 2.2 Look at the picture of people at work. What do you think their jobs are? Listen and check your ideas.

b 💬 What are the good things about their jobs? What are the bad things?

c 💬 Why is the man stretching his arms up? What do you think he's saying to his colleague?

d 💬 Work in pairs. Have a conversation using your ideas in **c**. Take turns being the man stretching his arms and his colleague.

47

5A I have to work long hours

Learn to talk about what people do at work
G must / have to / can
V Work

THE HAPPIEST JOBS

We spend most of our time at work. When we're not there, we're probably thinking about it. But what makes us happy at work? And which workers are the happiest? Here are twelve of the happiest and least happy jobs in the UK, according to the City & Guilds 'Career Happiness Index'.

% AGREEING THEY ARE HAPPY AT WORK

Job		%
1 _____	😊😊😊😊😊😊😊😊😊	87%
2 _____	😊😊😊😊😊😊😊😊	79%
plumbers	😊😊😊😊😊😊😊😊	76%
scientists	😊😊😊😊😊😊😊	69%
doctors and dentists	😊😊😊😊😊😊😊	65%
lawyers	😊😊😊😊😊😊	64%
3 _____	😊😊😊😊😊😊	62%
teachers	😊😊😊😊😊😊	59%
4 _____	😊😊😊😊😊	58%
electricians	😊😊😊😊😊	55%
IT workers	😊😊😊😊😊	48%
5 _____	😊😊😊😊	44%

1 VOCABULARY Work

a 💬 Look at the photographs. Which jobs can you see?

b 💬 Work in pairs. Make a list of as many jobs as you can. You have one minute.

c ▶ Now go to Vocabulary Focus 5A on p.136

2 READING

a 💬 Work in pairs. Read the first part of the article: *The Happiest Jobs*. Where do you think these jobs go in the list?

bankers   gardeners   hairdressers   nurses   accountants

b 💬 Check your ideas on p.127. Are you surprised? Why? / Why not?

c 💬 What do you think makes people happy at work? Make a list of ideas with a partner.

d Read the second half of the article. Was your list correct?

e 💬 Work in pairs. Answer the questions.
1 Do you know anyone who does any of the jobs in the article? How do they feel about their job?
2 Which job in the article is the most similar to your (future) job?
3 Did anything in the article surprise you? Was there any information that you already knew?
4 Do you think the results would be the same in your country? Why / Why not?

THE HAPPIEST WORKERS: WHY THEY'RE HAPPY

So what makes us happy at work? What you do in your job and where you do it is very important:
* 89% of gardeners feel their work is important and useful. Only 35% of bankers feel the same.
* 82% of gardeners said they use their skills every day, compared to only 35% of bankers.
* 89% of gardeners said they like their working environment, but only 24% of bankers said the same.

The people we work with matter:
* The most important thing of all is that other people value your work. 67% of all workers put this first.
* Most workers said that good relationships with colleagues are important. Scientists get on best with their colleagues (90%).

More money doesn't make us happier:
* 61% of workers said that it is very important for them to earn a good salary, but ...
* Workers who earn over £60,000 a year are the unhappiest.
* Self-employed people earn less but are much happier at work (85%) than people who work for a company.

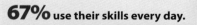

PLUMBERS

74% think their work is important and useful.

67% use their skills every day.

HAIRDRESSERS

Only 7% are unhappy in their jobs.

86% get on well with their colleagues.

GARDENERS

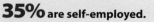

89% think their work is important and useful.

35% are self-employed.

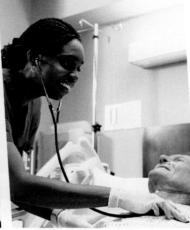

4 GRAMMAR *must / have to / can*

a Look at the sentences. Match the <u>underlined</u> words with the meanings.

1 To become a nurse you <u>have to</u> do well at school.
2 You <u>don't have to</u> wear a suit or go to many meetings.
3 You <u>can't</u> relax because if something goes wrong, you lose money.

a _____ = this is not necessary
b _____ = this is not allowed or not possible
c _____ = this is necessary

b Compare the written rules from John and Alisha's workplaces with the things they said. Complete the rules below.

> Nurses must not lift patients without another nurse present.

> You can't lift a patient on your own.

> You always have to switch off the mains power.

> Electricians must switch off the mains power before they start work.

In written English, we use:
_____ to say that that something is necessary
_____ to say that something is not allowed or is not possible

c ▶ Now go to Grammar Focus 5A on p.150

d What do you have to do if you work in these places? What can't you do?

- office
- restaurant
- bank
- school

> In a school, you can't leave children on their own.

> Yes, and you have to wear a suit.

e Write rules for the people who work in each place in 4d. Use *must* and *must not*.

Teachers must not leave children on their own.
Teachers must wear a suit.

5 SPEAKING

a Choose five of the jobs from the list. Think of three advantages and three disadvantages for each job.

- scientist
- lawyer
- accountant
- electrician
- IT worker
- engineer
- nurse
- pilot
- police officer
- receptionist
- secretary

b Which job do you think is the hardest? Which job is the most interesting?

> Receptionists don't have to have a university degree. And they can find a job quite easily.

> But they have to work long hours. And they don't earn a good salary.

3 LISTENING

a What do you think these people like about their jobs?

1 Alisha, nurse
2 John, electrician
3 Miriam, banker

b ▶ 2.5 Listen to Alisha, John and Miriam and check your ideas in 3a.

c ▶ 2.5 Listen again and answer the questions about each person's job.

1 What qualifications, experience and other abilities are necessary for the job?
2 What is difficult about the job?

d Which of the three jobs would you prefer to do? Why? Would you be good at it?

1 SPEAKING

a 💬 What can you do if you need a job? Where can you go? Who can you speak to?

b Match the worries 1–3 with the situations in the pictures.
1 ☐ I'll say something stupid on my first day.
2 ☐ I won't find a job I'll enjoy.
3 ☐ They'll ask me really difficult questions.

a looking for a job

b having a job interview

c starting a new job

c 💬 Have you ever had any of the worries in 1b? Tell a partner.

2 LISTENING

a ▶ 2.9 Listen to three people talking about finding work. Where are they? Who is the most positive about finding work? Who is the least positive?

Sara

Marco

Kate

b ▶ 2.9 Read the predictions each speaker made. Listen again. What reasons do they give for each prediction?

Sara
1 It won't be easy to find a job I'll enjoy.
2 I don't think I'll get an interview.
Marco
3 I'm sure I'll make some really useful contacts.
4 I might get a job today!
Kate
5 I might not get my perfect job.
6 I'm sure I'll find some kind of work.

c 💬 Have you ever been to a careers fair? What was it like?

3 GRAMMAR
will and might for predictions

a Look at the sentences in 2b again. Then <u>underline</u> the correct word to complete the rule about *will* and *might*.

> We use *will* and *might* to make predictions about the future.
> *will* and *won't* are *more / less* sure than *might* and *might not*.

b ▶ Now go to Grammar Focus 5B on p.150

c Write a positive response to each worry in 1b. Then compare with other students. Whose responses are most positive?

| I won't find a job I'll enjoy. | → | *You might find something really interesting.* |

d ▶ **Communication 5B** If your partner has got a job: go to p.130.
If your partner does not have a job: go to p.128.

4 VOCABULARY Jobs

a 💬 Find the jobs in the photos on the page.

☐ computer programmer   ☐ carer
☐ shop assistant   ☐ postman   ☐ builder

Do you know anyone who does these jobs?

b ▶ Now go to Vocabulary Focus 5B on p.136

c ▶2.13 Pronunciation Listen to the words.
How does the speaker say the consonant sound
/ʃ/ in the part of the words in **bold**?

> musi**ci**an   politi**ci**an   **sh**op assistant

d ▶2.14 Listen to the words. Which words have
the /ʃ/ sound? Underline the letters.

> qualification   question   information
> machine   experience   change

e Practise saying the words in 4c and 4d.

5 READING

a 💬 Look at the jobs in the photos. Answer the
questions with a partner.

1 Which jobs do you think might disappear in the future?
2 Which jobs do you think there will be more of in the future?

b Now read the article and check your ideas in 5a.

c Read the article again. What will happen because
of these things?

- online shopping
- sending emails
- digital photos
- 3D printers
- environmental problems
- living longer
- studying online

6 SPEAKING

a 💬 Work in small groups. Look at the predictions.
Do you think these things will happen in your
lifetime? Why / Why not?

1 3D printers will make parts of buildings or whole buildings.
2 People won't print photos any more.
3 There won't be many shops.
4 There won't be any huge offices. People will generally work at home.
5 Companies will pay the bosses less and other staff more.
6 A normal working week will have four days, not five.

b Work alone. Write three new predictions.

c 💬 Read your predictions to your group.
Do they agree?

Planning a safe future career

**Choose your future career carefully
– experts are predicting big
changes in the jobs we'll do in the
next ten or twenty years. Some
jobs might disappear, but others
will become more important.**

The Internet will have a big effect.
People already choose to do a lot of
their shopping online, so there won't
be as many shops, and there won't
be many jobs for shop assistants.
Some postmen and other post office
staff might lose their jobs, because
people will send everything by email.

Another job that might disappear
because of technology is photo
processors – the people who print
photos. This is because most of us keep
our photos on our computers now and
never print them. Also, there might not be
as many jobs for builders as there are today. 3D printers will
soon make parts of buildings or even whole buildings in
just a few hours.

So which jobs are safe?

- **Computer programmers** – a hundred years ago there were
  none, but now there are lots of them and there will be even
  more in future because almost all jobs will need computers.
- **Environment protection officer** – there will be a lot of new
  'green' jobs as environmental problems get more serious.
- **Carers** – people will live longer and we'll need carers to look
  after us in old age.
- **Online education manager** – many students will take online
  courses. There will be jobs for people to create and organise
  the courses.

And of course, we will still need **actors** and
musicians to entertain us, **lawyers** to argue and
politicians to make the big decisions.

Learn to make offers and suggestions

P Sentence stress: vowel sounds
S Reassurance

1 LISTENING

a 💬 When was the last time someone asked you for help? Who was it? What did he / she ask?

b 💬 Look at the picture of Rachel and read the text message. How is she feeling? Who is the text from? What's the problem?

c ▶ **2.15** Watch or listen to Part 1. Answer the questions.
1 What does Tina think Rachel should do for Annie?
2 What does Tina offer to do?
3 Why is Rachel worried about leaving early?
4 How are they going to deal with the problem?

d 💬 What would you do in Rachel's situation? Would you call Annie or go and see her? Why?

2 CONVERSATION SKILLS Reassurance

a ▶ **2.15** Watch or listen again. Match the sentences with the responses.
1 ☐ But I can't leave you here on your own.
2 ☐ We've still got so much to do.
3 ☐ It means you won't be able to leave early today.
4 ☐ OK, well if you're sure.

a **Never mind**.
b Of course. **It's no problem**.
c I'll be fine! **Don't worry about it**.
d Oh, **it doesn't matter**.

b ▶ **2.16** Why do you think Tina uses the expressions in **bold** in a–d? Listen and repeat the phrases.

c 💬 In pairs, look at situations 1–6. Take turns to apologise for the problems. Respond with expressions a–d in 2a.
1 You can't help your partner this weekend.
2 You lost your partner's book.
3 You have to cancel the dinner party.
4 You don't have the money you owe your partner.
5 You can't come to the cinema tonight.
6 You're going to be late for the party.

> I'm really sorry, but I can't help you this weekend. I have to work.

> Oh, it doesn't matter.

3 LISTENING

▶ **2.17** Watch or listen to Part 2. Which jobs will Tina do before she goes home?
1 ☐ finish off the flowers
2 ☐ start the order for Mrs Thompson
3 ☐ start the order for the birthday party
4 ☐ put the alarm on
5 ☐ take out the rubbish
6 ☐ take the order for the wedding

4 USEFUL LANGUAGE
Offers and suggestions

a ▶ **2.18** Listen and complete the sentences.

1 ☐ _____ finish things here, if you want.
2 ☐ Why _____ you tell me what we still need to do?
3 ☐ _____ I finish off those flowers?
4 ☐ Would you _____ me to prepare some of the orders for tomorrow?
5 ☐ You _____ start with that order for Mrs Thompson.
6 ☐ Maybe you _____ start on the order for that big birthday party.
7 ☐ Do you want _____ to take out the rubbish when I leave?
8 ☐ How _____ taking her some flowers?
9 ☐ Why _____ I deal with this?

b Look at the sentences in 4a again. Mark them *O* (offer) and *S* (suggestion).

c 💬 Work in pairs. What offers and suggestions could you make in situations 1–4? Use the phrases and your own ideas.

> I'll …   Why don't I / you … ?   Shall I … ?
> Would you like me to … ?   Maybe you should …
> How about … ?   Do you want me to … ?

1 It's raining. Your friend has to walk to the station, but doesn't have an umbrella.
2 Your colleague has to write a report for her boss before the end of the day. There's not enough time.
3 Your friend wants to go for a meal. You don't like the restaurant he suggests.
4 You see a tourist. She's lost her bag and doesn't have any money.

> Why don't I drive you to the station?

> How about getting a taxi?

5 PRONUNCIATION
Sentence stress: vowel sounds

a ▶ **2.19** Listen to the phrases from 4a. Are the highlighted modal verbs stressed?

1 Shall I finish off those flowers?
2 Would you like me to prepare some of the orders for tomorrow?
3 You could start with that order for Mrs Thompson.
4 Maybe you should start on the order for that big birthday party.

b ▶ **2.19** Listen again. Which vowel sound do you hear in each of the modal verbs?

c Practise saying the sentences in 5a.

6 SPEAKING

a 💬 Work in groups of four. Choose one of the two events to organise.

A work meeting

- book meeting room
- arrange hotel for guest from advertising company
- book taxis for colleagues from other office
- •
- •
- •

A surprise birthday party for a friend

- buy food and drink
- make and send invitations
- book somewhere for the party
- •
- •
- •

b 💬 Work with a partner in your group. Look at the list of things to do for the event you chose. Add three more things.

c 💬 Work in your group again. Now you have to organise the event. Make offers and suggestions to decide which person in your group will do which job.

> Shall I book a meeting room?

> OK, why don't you call a hotel?

> Would you like me to buy the food?

> Sure. How about going to the supermarket?

◯ Unit Progress Test

CHECK YOUR PROGRESS

You can now do the Unit Progress Test.

53

a CUBA COFFEE

We're looking for keen young people to work in our cafés. No experience necessary – we'll give you the training you need to become a barista!

Contact us at www.cubacoffee.com and send us your CV.

b 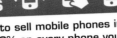 Q.net ✓ Situation Vacant

Students required to work for a market research company. Interview people in the street or on the phone in our offices. Good pay – work when you want to.

Visit our website at www.customer-Q.net

c electrostores

Sales assistants wanted to sell mobile phones in our superstores. Earn 10% on every phone you sell. Find us at www.electrostores.com/mobiles

Free training programme.

d Saveco

Weekend and summer jobs for students

Join our team and earn money. General assistants required for checkout and meat and fish counters. Good pay and conditions.

Contact: reply@saveco.com

1 SPEAKING AND LISTENING

a Have you ever had a summer job or a part-time job? What was it? Did you enjoy it?

b Read the job adverts. Which jobs in the adverts could these sentences describe?

1 ☐ You have to start early in the morning.
2 ☐ You need to be good with money.
3 ☐ You need to like working fast.
4 ☐ It's nice because you can talk to people.
5 ☐ You have to be good at explaining things.
6 ☐ You can earn extra money from tips.

c Work in pairs. Answer the questions about the jobs in the adverts.

1 Which job would you most like to do? Why?
2 Which job would you least like to do? Why?
3 Which job would you do best? Why?

d ▶ 2.20 Listen to two students, Penny and John, and answer the questions.

1 Which jobs in the adverts are they talking about?
2 Do they like the jobs? Why / Why not?

e ▶ 2.20 Listen again and choose the correct answers.

1 John *has / hasn't* worked in the café before.
2 John *likes / doesn't like* working quickly.
3 John *sometimes / always* makes £20 in tips.
4 Penny *has / hasn't* worked in a café before.
5 Penny *is / isn't* going to apply for the job.

2 READING

Read Penny's job application. Are sentences 1–4 true (*T*) or false (*F*)? Correct the false sentences.

1 ☐ She tells them she has worked in cafés before.
2 ☐ She saw the ad in the newspaper.
3 ☐ She can't work this summer, because she's studying.
4 ☐ She wants to know how much she will earn.

① Dear Sir/Madam,

② I am writing to apply for the job of barista at the Cuba Coffee Company, which you advertised on your website.

③ I am a student at the University of Manchester and I am available to work in August and September.

④ A job with you will be an exciting opportunity for me to learn new skills and to work in a new environment. I have a lot of experience of working in a team and helping customers at *Saveco* supermarket. My experience of working in a fast, busy supermarket will be very useful for this job.

⑤ I attach a copy of my CV with details of my past employment.

⑥ Could you please send me information about the salary and working hours, and also more details about your training programme?

⑦ I look forward to hearing from you.

Yours faithfully,

Penny Longwell

3 WRITING SKILLS Organising an email

a Penny's email in 2 has seven parts. What does each part of the letter do?

- [ ] says why she's writing
- [ ] asks for more information about the job
- [ ] describes documents she's sending with the email
- [ ] opens the email
- [ ] closes the email
- [ ] says why she wants the job and describes her experience
- [ ] says what she's doing now and when she can work

b Look at sentences 1–5. Which ones are about … ?

- what you are doing now
- past jobs
- skills

1 I am good at working in a team.
2 I have experience of working in a restaurant.
3 I am currently working as a sales assistant in a bookshop.
4 I am studying engineering in Madrid.
5 I speak fluent English.

c What are the missing prepositions? Complete the sentences.

1 I am writing to apply _____ the job _____ barista.
2 I am a student _____ the University of Manchester.
3 I have a lot _____ experience _____ working _____ a team.
4 I look forward _____ hearing from you.

d Put the parts of the email below in the correct order.

- I attach a copy of my CV. [ ]
- I look forward to hearing from you. Yours faithfully, [ ]
- I am writing to apply for the job of sales assistant. [ ]
- Dear Sir/Madam, [ ]
- I would like to work for your company, because it would be a good opportunity for me to improve my communication skills. I have three years' experience of sales. [ ]
- Could you send me more information about the working hours? [ ]
- I am currently working as a sales assistant in a clothes shop. [ ]

4 WRITING A job application

a Read the adverts on *Jobsearch.com*. Choose one and write an email applying for the job. Include these parts:

- open the email
- say why you are writing
- say what you are doing now
- say why you want the job
- describe documents you are sending
- ask for more information
- close the email

b Work in groups. Read the applications together. Which student would you give each job to? Why?

Jobsearch.com

Home | New Jobs | Advice

Use your English … and your local knowledge!
Get a holiday job as a guide for English-speaking tourists to your town.
You will need:
- *a good level of English*
- *knowledge of your local town or area*

VIEW JOB

Work with children and have a holiday
We're looking for people to work on an international holiday camp for children aged 10–15. You will help organise activities and trips, and speak English with the children. We prefer someone with experience of working with children.

VIEW JOB

Evening jobs with Megapizza
We need people to serve and deliver pizzas in the evenings and at weekends.
Good pay and conditions. Must have driving licence.
Contact: *jobs@megapizza.com.*

VIEW JOB

UNIT 5
Review and extension

1 GRAMMAR

a Choose the correct answers.

1 Employees must not use their computers to send personal emails.
'We _____ use our computers to send personal emails.'
(a) have to   (b) don't have to   (c) can't

2 Employees can leave the building at lunch time.
'We _____ stay in the building at lunch.'
(a) must   (b) don't have to   (c) can't

3 Employees _____ use social media.
'We can't use social media at work.'
(a) must not   (b) must   (c) don't have to

4 Employees _____ make local phone calls on company phones.
'We don't have to use our mobiles to make local calls.'
(a) can   (b) can't   (c) must

5 Employees _____ wear a shirt and tie.
'We have to wear a shirt and tie.'
(a) can   (b) must not   (c) must

b Match sentences (1–5) with meanings (a–c).

1 ☐ It won't be difficult for me to find a job.
2 ☐ I think I'll finish university next year.
3 ☐ I might work for a bank one day.
4 ☐ I'll find a good job in the USA.
5 ☐ I might not find a job I like in my home town.

a completely sure   b fairly sure   c not sure

c 💬 Which of the sentences in 1b are true for you?

2 VOCABULARY

a Choose the best jobs for each person (1–7).

accountant   carer   hairdresser   IT worker
journalist   politician   vet

1 I really like working with animals. _____
2 I enjoy helping older people. _____
3 I want to tell people what's happening in the world. _____
4 I'm good with numbers. _____
5 I like meeting people and helping them look good. _____
6 I want to make my country a better place. _____
7 I enjoy working with computers. _____

b 💬 Which jobs would you like and not like in 2a?

c Match the sentence halves.

1 ☐ In my job, I have to work
2 ☐ My job's interesting, because I have to make
3 ☐ I don't have a boss, because I'm
4 ☐ I enjoy being in my office. We're lucky that we have
5 ☐ I'm tired at the end of the day, because I deal with

a self-employed.
b very long hours.
c a nice working environment.
d important decisions every day.
e lots of serious problems.

3 WORDPOWER job and work

a Look at the sentences. Which word (job or work) is countable? Which is uncountable?

1 I've got a really interesting job.
2 I'm looking for work at the moment.

b Match the uses of work and job (1–4) with the meanings (a–d).

1 ☐ 90% of gardeners feel their work is important and useful
2 ☐ We spend most of our time at work.
3 ☐ I've got a lot of jobs to do at home this weekend.
4 ☐ I enjoy my course, but it's hard work.

a when you use lots of energy to do something
b the activity or activities you do for your job
c activities you have to do, often without getting money
d the place where you work

c Match sentences (1–3) with replies (a–c).

1 ☐ Why isn't my email working on this computer?
2 ☐ Is the medicine from the doctor working?
3 ☐ I can't work this out. Do you know the answer?

a No, it's a very difficult question.
b I don't know. Maybe there's a problem with the Internet.
c Definitely. I feel much better.

d Complete the sentences with work or job.

1 I'm painting my apartment at the moment. It's a lot of hard _____.
2 I'm starting a new _____ soon.
3 My mobile doesn't _____ when I'm inside this building.
4 I've got an important _____ to do at home this weekend.
5 I leave _____ early on Fridays.
6 The education system in my country doesn't _____ well.
7 I know a lot of people who are trying to find _____.
8 I can't _____ out how to download this application form.

e Complete these sentences with your own ideas.

1 I can't work out …
2 I would like to get a job …
3 Two jobs I need to do this week are …
4 … makes me happy at work.
5 I need do some hard work …
6 … doesn't work very well.

f 💬 Compare your sentences in 3e with another student.

🔄 REVIEW YOUR PROGRESS

How well did you do in this unit? Write 3, 2 or 1 for each objective.
3 = very well   2 = well   1 = not so well

I CAN …

Talk about what people do at work	☐
Talk about your future career	☐
Make offers and suggestions	☐
Write a job application	☐

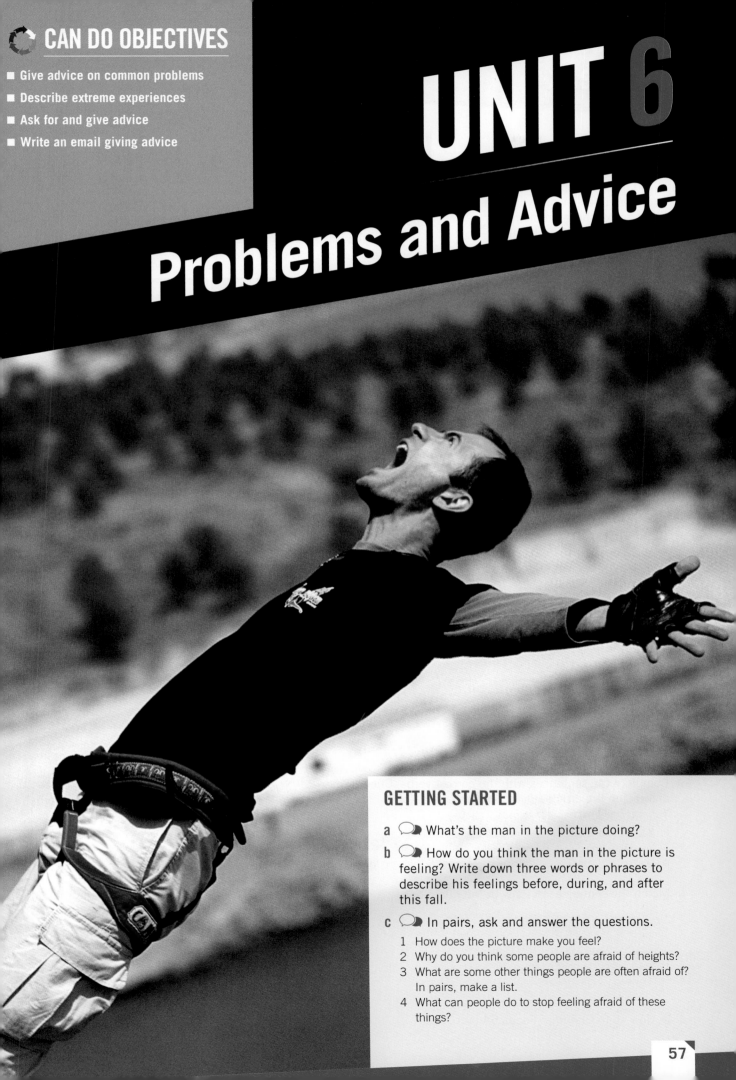

CAN DO OBJECTIVES

- Give advice on common problems
- Describe extreme experiences
- Ask for and give advice
- Write an email giving advice

UNIT 6
Problems and Advice

GETTING STARTED

a What's the man in the picture doing?

b How do you think the man in the picture is feeling? Write down three words or phrases to describe his feelings before, during, and after this fall.

c In pairs, ask and answer the questions.

1 How does the picture make you feel?
2 Why do you think some people are afraid of heights?
3 What are some other things people are often afraid of? In pairs, make a list.
4 What can people do to stop feeling afraid of these things?

1 READING

a 💬 Look at the problems in the pictures. Does anyone you know have any of these problems? How could you solve them? Tell a partner.

b Read the advice. Which four problems in the pictures is it for? Complete the headings 1–4.

c Read the advice again. What is the advice about these things? Make notes.

1
- music
- 15 minutes

2
- rules
- a pile

3
- breaks
- rewards

4
- screens
- milk

d 💬 Cover the article. Use your notes. Try to remember the advice in the article.

e 💬 Do you think the advice in each paragraph is useful? Why / Why not?

How to deal with life's

You don't have any money, you never finish anything you start, your house is dirty, you can't find a good job and your whole life is terrible. Well, maybe it isn't that bad! If you'd like to improve things, we can help. Here are our top ways to deal with some of life's little problems.

I can't concentrate on my work

I'm addicted to my mobile

My home is a mess

I don't sleep well
I have too much work to do

I don't have enough money

I'm always late

I feel tired all the time

2 GRAMMAR Imperative; *should*

a Complete the sentences with the correct verbs. Check your answers in the article.

1 Turn on the TV or _____ to music while you clean.
2 You should _____ to drink less coffee and smoke less, too.
3 You shouldn't _____ for hours without a break.
4 Don't _____ devices with bright screens before you go to sleep.

b Match the sentences in 2a with the rules.

To give advice, we use:
- ☐ infinitive
- ☐ *don't* + infinitive
- ☐ subject + *should* + infinitive
- ☐ subject + *shouldn't* + infinitive

c ▶ Now go to Grammar Focus 6A on p.152

d ▶ **2.23** **Pronunciation** Listen to the sentence. Is the vowel sound long or short in the words *shouldn't* and *use*?

You sh**ou**ldn't **u**se your mobile phone before you go to sleep.

e ▶ **2.24** Listen to the sentences. Do the letters in **bold** have the long vowel /uː/ or the short vowel /ʊ/?

1 You sh**ou**ldn't **u**se your comp**u**ter all day.
2 L**oo**k for n**ew** ways of d**oi**ng exercise.
3 Find a g**oo**d time of day to study.
4 Ch**oo**se the healthiest f**oo**d.
5 Read a b**oo**k before you go to sleep.

f Practise saying the sentences in 2e.

ittle problems

1

Learn to enjoy cleaning and tidying. People who enjoy this usually have clean homes. Turn on the TV or listen to music while you clean. Start by cleaning every day, but only for fifteen minutes. When the 15 minutes are finished, you should stop. Don't worry if things aren't perfectly clean. Do a little bit of cleaning every day and in a week your place will look great.

2

It's important to give yourself rules. When you go out with friends, decide how many times you will look at your phone – maybe only two or three times in an evening. Ask your friends about how they feel. If they have the same problem as you, put all of your phones together, in a pile and out of the way. That way, no one can look at their phone and you can all enjoy each other's company.

3

The machine we use so much for work – our computer – is the same machine we often use to have fun. So control how you use your computer. If your problem is that you check your email every five minutes, you can get programs that stop the Internet from working for a period of time you choose. Use this time to focus on your work. But you shouldn't work for hours without a break. Work for 25 minutes, and then have a five-minute rest. Rewards are really important, too. Have a biscuit or get some fresh air every hour or so.

4

First think about your body. Exercising regularly will help you to fall asleep more easily. You should try to drink less coffee and smoke less, too. These bad habits keep you awake. Don't use devices with bright screens, for example, your mobile phone, before you go to sleep. They make your brain think that it is daytime, instead of night. Read a book and drink a cup of warm milk or herbal tea in the evening. Then you'll feel ready for sleep.

3 VOCABULARY
Verbs with dependent prepositions

a Complete the sentences with the correct prepositions from the box.

| at   about (x2)   with   to   on |

1 What is a problem you have to deal _____ every day?
2 Do you listen _____ music while you clean?
3 How often do you look _____ your phone?
4 What stops you concentrating _____ your work?
5 Do you think _____ your work at weekends?
6 Who can you ask _____ problems at school or work?

b 💬 Work in pairs. Ask and answer the questions in 3a.

c Match the sentence halves to make advice for two problems.

1 ☐ Don't **borrow** money
2 ☐ Only **spend** money
3 ☐ Don't **pay**
4 ☐ You should **wait**
5 ☐ You should **ask**
6 ☐ **Talk**
7 ☐ You should **think**
8 ☐ Eat a good breakfast so you **arrive**

a **for** the sales to buy expensive things.
b **for** friends' meals when you go out.
c **on** things you really need.
d **from** friends because it creates problems.
e **of** ways to save energy.
f **for** a few days off.
g **at** work or school full of energy.
h **to** a doctor about how you feel.

d ▶ **2.25** Listen and check your answers in 3c. Which two problems is the advice for?

e Cover one half of the sentences in 3c. Try to remember the advice.

4 SPEAKING

a ▶ **Communication 6A** Student A: go to p.130. Student B: go to p.132.

b 💬 Work in pairs. Choose one of the problems and write some advice.

- I feel really stressed before exams.
- I'm not creative enough at work.
- I don't laugh very often.
- I never finish anything I start.
- I always lose important things.

c 💬 Work in small groups. Present the problems and your advice. Whose advice is the most useful for you?

1 VOCABULARY -ed / -ing adjectives

a 💬 Look at the pictures on this page. How do you think the people are feeling? Make a list of words.

b Read the sentences and answer the questions.

Johan's day at the beach was very <u>relaxing</u>.
After a day at the beach, Johan was completely <u>relaxed</u>.

a Which adjective describes how he feels?
b Which adjective describes the thing that makes him feel like that?

c ▶ Now go to Vocabulary Focus 6B on p.137

2 READING AND LISTENING

a 💬 Have you tried scuba diving? Would you like to? How do you think you would feel if you saw a shark?

b 💬 Match the words with a–f in the pictures. Use the words to describe the scene.

☐ scuba diver	☐ shark	☐ reef
☐ the surface	☐ breathe (v.)	☐ air

c Read *Sharks saved my life*. Which sentence is true about Caroline's experience in Egypt?

1 She went scuba diving to deal with her fear of sharks.
2 She was afraid, because she went scuba diving in very deep water.
3 She got lost when she was scuba diving.

d Read the article again. Answer the questions with a partner.

1 Why did Caroline go to Egypt?
2 Why did she ask the instructor how deep the water was?
3 How did she feel when they got to the reef? Why?
4 Why didn't Caroline to go back up to the surface o the water fast?

e 💬 What do you think happened next? How d you think sharks saved Caroline's life?

f ▶2.28 Listen to the rest of the story and check your ideas in 2e.

g ▶2.28 Listen again and answer the questions.

1 What happened after Caroline saw the sharks?
2 How did Caroline feel when she was back on the fishing boat?
3 How has the experience changed Caroline?

h 💬 Ask and answer the questions.

1 Were you surprised by anything in the story?
2 Do you think you would feel the same way as Caroline if this happened to you?

SHARKS
SAVED MY LIFE

I started scuba diving because I was interested in sharks. I learnt how to dive in England, but English waters were very disappointing. So I decided to try the Red Sea in Egypt.

The diving there was much more interesting. I saw so many beautiful fish, including sharks. After a few days, my instructor suggested a trip to the Shaab Shagra reef to swim with the sharks there.

We went out in an old fishing boat and I asked him, 'How deep is the water?' 'Not deep. 30 metres,' he said. I thought, 'Good, I can do that but I can't go below 30 metres.' I didn't have any experience of deep diving, and I knew that below 30 metres people often feel strange.

Some people suddenly feel very happy. Other people get confused, and they don't know which way is up or down.

I jumped in and followed my instructor. When we got down to the reef I looked at my diving watch to see how deep we were. I was shocked to see we were at 40 metres! I was scared and I was breathing very quickly. I thought to myself, 'Don't use all your air. Breathe slowly.' But I was really frightened and I couldn't slow my breathing down.

I was really worried about my air. How much did I need? Did I have enough? I remember looking up at the light. I felt terrified, and I just wanted to go back up to the surface fast. But I knew that if you go up too fast you can get 'the bends' and die in terrible pain. I was thinking, 'Don't go up. You'll die.' But my heart was saying, 'Go up! Go up!' I looked for my instructor. But I couldn't get his attention.

3 GRAMMAR Uses of to + infinitive

a Look at the sentences. Complete the gaps with the words in the box.

> to see   to do   to be   to get

1 I didn't really know what _____.
2 I just wanted _____ out of the water.
3 I was happy _____ alive.
4 I looked at my diving watch _____ how deep we were.

b ▶2.29 Listen and check.

c Match the sentences in 3a with the rules.

> We use *to* + infinitive:
> ☐ to give a reason   ☐ after adjectives
> ☐ after certain verbs   ☐ after question words

d ▶2.29 **Pronunciation** Listen to the sentences from 3a again. Which part of the infinitive is stressed – *to* or the verb?

e Look at the article in 2c again. <u>Underline</u> another example for each use of the infinitive in 3c.

f ▶ Now go to Grammar Focus 6B on p.152

g Choose one topic to talk about in each pair of topics 1–4 below. Think about what you will say.

1 • an interesting place you've visited. Why did you go there? (to …)
  • an important course you've done. Why did you do it? (to …)

2 • a time when you decided to do something, but then changed your mind. What was it?
  • a time when you tried to do something difficult. What happened?

3 • a time when you didn't know what to do or where to go. What did you do?
  • a problem that you didn't know how to deal with. What happened?

4 • someone you were surprised to see somewhere. Who was it? Where did you see the person?
  • some information you were shocked to hear. What was it?

h 💬 Work in pairs. Talk about your ideas in 3g.

4 LISTENING

a 💬 You are going to hear about another experience. Look at the words in the box. What do you think happened?

> parachute   6,000 metres   wind (n.)   get stuck
> hang   free (v.)   pull along   lucky

b ▶2.31 Listen to the interview and check your ideas in 4a.

c ▶2.31 Look at the interviewer's questions below. Listen again and make notes on Aaron's answers.

1 What happened to you?
2 How did it happen?
3 What went wrong?
4 How did you feel?
5 Did the others help you?
6 Did that experience stop you from jumping?

d 💬 Tell Aaron's story with partner. Use your notes to help you.

5 SPEAKING

a 💬 Do you know about a person who has had an experience like the situations in this lesson? Try to think of a time when someone:

• had a dangerous or frightening experience
• had a lucky experience
• learned something from a difficult situation
• changed a lot because of an experience
• had an experience that made them very happy.

b Prepare some notes about one experience you talked about in 5a. Use the questions to help you.

• What was the person's situation at the time?
• What exactly was the experience?
• How did the person feel?
• What did other people do?
• How did the experience change the person?

c 💬 Work in new pairs. Tell your partner about the experience. Choose the best story to tell to the whole class.

1 LISTENING

a 💬 When you have a problem, who do you prefer to talk to about it?

b 💬 Look at the picture. Annie is telling Rachel about some bad news. What do you think the news might be?

c ▶2.32 Watch or listen to Part 1 and check your ideas.

2 CONVERSATION SKILLS
Showing sympathy

a ▶2.32 Which of the phrases did Rachel use to show she feels sorry for Annie? Watch or listen again and check.

1 How awful.   4 I'm really sorry to hear that.
2 That's terrible.   5 That's a shame.
3 What a pity.

b Look at the two phrases in 2a that Rachel didn't use. Would you use them in a similar situation or in a less serious situation?

c ▶2.33 Listen and repeat the phrases in 2a.

d 💬 Work in pairs. Take turns to give bad news. Respond with the best phrases from 2a.

• your boyfriend / girlfriend forgot your birthday
• you broke your leg playing football
• you missed your train and waited two hours for the next one
• you spent hours preparing dinner and then burnt the food
• someone stole your phone and money when you were on holiday

3 LISTENING

a ▶2.34 Watch or listen to Part 2. What advice does Rachel give about … ?

1 Annie's boss
2 Annie's colleagues
3 Mark
4 changing jobs

b ▶2.34 Watch or listen again. Which advice in 3a does Annie disagree with? Why?

c 💬 Which of Rachel's advice do you think is most useful? What else could Annie do?

4 PRONUNCIATION Main stress

a ▶2.35 Listen to the sentences. Underline the word in each sentence that Rachel stresses the most.

1 Did you ask when you're going to lose your job?
2 Maybe there'll be other jobs there.
3 You work in marketing, right?
4 Mark works in marketing, too.
5 Changing jobs could be a good thing.

b Why does Rachel stress the words you underlined in 4a? Choose the best answer.

1 to show more sympathy
2 none of the other words are important
3 the underlined words are the most important

c ▶2.35 Listen to 4a 1–5 again and repeat.

d 💬 Practise the dialogues with a partner. Stress the underlined words.

1 A We're meeting at 4 pm.
  B I know. But I don't know where!

2 A I'm really busy at work at the moment.
  B You work in a bank, right?

3 A I used to work for IBM.
  B Really? I used to work for IBM, too!

4 A I don't think it's a good time to change jobs.
  B I'm not sure. I think there are lots of interesting jobs out there.

5 USEFUL LANGUAGE
Asking for and giving advice

a ▶ 2.36 Listen and complete the phrases.

Asking for advice

1 _____ do you think I should do?
2 Do you _____ I should speak to him about it?

Giving advice

3 _____ get all the details first.
4 I think you _____ speak to your boss again.
5 I think it's a _____ _____ to ask.
6 I _____ worry too much.

b Look at Annie's responses to Rachel's advice. Which phrases show that Annie doesn't agree with the advice?

1 I don't think that's a good idea.
2 I suppose so.
3 I don't think I should do that.
4 You're right.

c ▶ 2.37 Listen and repeat the phrases in 5a and 5b.

d Complete the dialogue. Then practise the dialogue with a partner.

A I just heard I didn't get that job. I'm really disappointed. What do you ¹_____ I should do?

B I'm really sorry to ²_____ that. But I wouldn't ³_____ too much – you'll find something soon.

A I ⁴_____ so. But I'm surprised. I thought the interview went very well.

B Well then, I think you ⁵_____ write to the company. ⁶_____ them for some information about your interview.

A I don't think ⁷_____'s a good idea. They won't want to give me information like that.

B I think it's a good ⁸_____ to ask. I've done that before and the information can be really useful.

A You're ⁹_____. I'll send them an email tomorrow.

6 LISTENING

a ▶ 2.38 Annie is worried about Leo. Watch or listen to Part 3 and answer the questions.

1 Why is Annie worried about Leo?
2 What explanation does Rachel give?

b 💬 Ask and answer the questions.

1 What other reasons could there be for Leo's behaviour?
2 Do you think Annie is right to worry?

7 SPEAKING

a You are going to tell your partner about something bad that happened to you. Read the cards 1–4 and choose a problem. Think about what you want to say.

1 Someone stole your bag in a café.
- What was in the bag?
- What were you doing when the person stole it?
- Who do you think stole it?
- How did you feel?
- What problems will you now have without your bag?

2 You failed an important exam.
- What was the exam?
- Why was it important?
- Did you think you would pass?
- Who else will be upset that you failed?

3 You had an argument with your best friend.
- Do you normally argue with your best friend?
- What was the argument about?
- How did it start?
- Do you want to contact your friend again?

4 Your boss said your work wasn't good enough.
- What work was it?
- What did your boss say exactly?
- How did you feel?
- Do you think this will create problems for you in the future?

b 💬 Student A, tell your partner about what happened. Student B, show sympathy and give Student A some advice.

c 💬 Now swap roles.

d 💬 Did your partner show sympathy? Was their advice helpful?

🔄 **Unit Progress Test**

CHECK YOUR PROGRESS

You can now do the Unit Progress Test.

6D Skills for Writing
I often worry about tests and exams

Chloe   Bob

Marisa

1 LISTENING AND SPEAKING

a Are these situations connected to work or study? Write work (*W*), study (*S*) or both (*B*).

1. ☐ doing exams or tests
2. ☐ doing a presentation
3. ☐ managing other people
4. ☐ making business decisions
5. ☐ learning to communicate in a foreign language
6. ☐ reading all the books on a booklist

b 💬 What problems do people sometimes have in the situations in 1a?

c ▶ 2.39 Listen to Chloe, Bob and Marisa talking about problems with work and study. Complete the first row of the table.

	Chloe	Bob	Marisa
What's the main problem?			
What are the details of the problem?			
How does she/he feel?			
What advice has she/he had from friends or family?			

d ▶ 2.39 Listen again and complete the table.

e 💬 What advice would you give to Chloe, Bob and Marisa?

2 READING

a Eliza teaches English. She has a wiki for her class where students can write and ask for advice. Read Sevim's message. What does Sevim want help with?

b Read Eliza's reply. How many suggestions does Eliza make?

c Read the text again. Are sentences 1–5 true (*T*) or false (*F*)? Correct the false sentences.

1. ☐ Eliza always felt relaxed about speaking Turkish.
2. ☐ Eliza thinks language learners should try not to make mistakes.
3. ☐ Eliza says Sevim should use English with the students in her class.
4. ☐ Sevim can pay extra to go to a chat group at the study centre.
5. ☐ Eliza thinks you can practise speaking on the Internet.

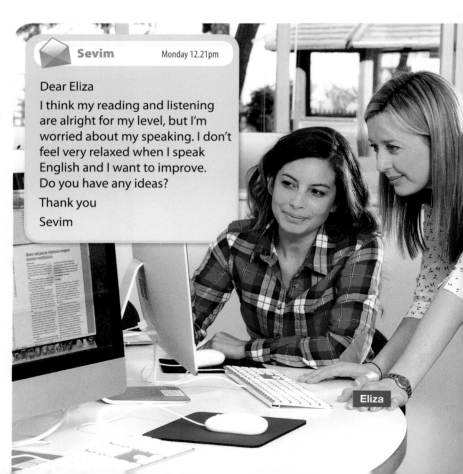

✉ **Sevim**   Monday 12.21pm

Dear Eliza

I think my reading and listening are alright for my level, but I'm worried about my speaking. I don't feel very relaxed when I speak English and I want to improve. Do you have any ideas?

Thank you

Sevim

Eliza

3 WRITING SKILLS Linking: ordering ideas and giving examples

Eliza uses words and phrases to order information in her reply. Notice the <u>underlined</u> example.

<u>First of all</u>, don't worry about making mistakes.

<u>Underline</u> three more words in the message that order Eliza's ideas.

Read the advice on studying vocabulary for an exam. Add words and phrases where you see ∧ to order the information.

> ∧ you can study vocabulary lists at the back of the course book. There are also some practice exercises there to help you. ∧ you should test yourself on the words you have studied. For example, you can try writing down all the words you can remember about a particular topic. ∧ you can work with another student and test each other. If you both speak the same language, you can translate words from your language into English. ∧ it's a good idea to try and think about the words you've learned and use them in a conversation the same day. This is a very active way of studying vocabulary.

c Read the text in 2b again. Notice the highlighted expressions Eliza uses to give examples. Cover the text and complete the sentences.

1 _____, it's a good idea to use only English in class …
2 You can join a conversation group, _____ the chat groups in the study centre.
3 _____, there are lots of websites where you can find speaking partners from all around the world.

d Match the sentence halves.

1 ☐ You can download apps to help you study. For
2 ☐ There are lots of ways to practise listening, such
3 ☐ It's easy to get extra reading practice. For

a as DVDs, podcasts and online videos.
b instance, there are lots of books and magazines in the study centre.
c example, I use the *Cambridge Advanced Learner's Dictionary* on my phone.

Eliza   Monday 14.08pm

Hi Sevim,

Thanks for your message and I'm glad that you wrote to me for ideas.

I remember when I was learning Turkish, I felt embarrassed about speaking. I could remember lots of words and I knew grammar rules, but speaking was difficult. I now feel a lot more relaxed about speaking, so here are some ideas that I've taken from my own experience.

First of all, don't worry about making mistakes. Other people will still understand you and they probably won't notice your mistakes. Secondly, remember that the only way to learn to speak a second language is by speaking. Use every chance you get to speak. For example, it's a good idea to use only English in class and not speak to other students in Turkish. You should also try practising new vocabulary and grammar we learn in class by repeating it at home.

Next, you should think about extra speaking practice outside the classroom. You can join a conversation group, such as the chat groups in the study centre. They are free to join. Finally, you can also practise speaking online. For instance, there are lots of websites where you can find speaking partners from all around the world.

I hope this helps you and please feel free to talk to me after class next week.

Best wishes,

Eliza

---

4 WRITING

a Work in pairs. Read the ideas for Sevim about how to improve her writing. Add three more ideas to the list.

- plan your ideas before you write

- ask another student to check your grammar

-

-

-

b Work in pairs. Write a message giving advice to Sevim. Make sure you order your ideas clearly and give examples.

c Work in groups of four. Read the other pair's message to Sevim. Does it contain similar ideas to your message? Are the ideas ordered clearly? Are there examples?

UNIT 6
Review and extension

1 GRAMMAR

a Complete the exchanges with *should* or *shouldn't*.

1 **A** I can't sleep.
   B You _____ drink coffee in the afternoon.
2 **A** My desk is messy.
   B I think you _____ tidy it at the end of every day.
3 **A** I'm addicted to TV.
   B You _____ watch more than two hours a day.
4 **A** I don't have time to keep fit.
   B You _____ try to walk for ten minutes every day.
5 **A** I don't have much money.
   B I don't think you _____ buy so many clothes.
6 **A** I don't know many people where I live.
   B I think you _____ join a club or a sports team.

b Change the advice in 1a into imperatives.

1 *Don't drink coffee in the afternoon.*

c Complete the sentences with the correct forms of the verbs in the box.

| do   drive   find   go   learn   meet |

1 Do you think people in your country
   should _____ more exercise?
2 Is it difficult _____ parking where you live?
3 Do you need _____ to the shops today?
4 Do you think everyone should _____ a foreign language?
5 Is it easy _____ new people where you live?
6 Do you know how _____?

d 💬 Ask and answer the questions in 1c.

2 VOCABULARY

a Complete the sentences with the correct forms of the verbs in the box.

| arrive   ask   borrow   concentrate   deal   spend |

1 Sometimes I find it hard to _____ on my work.
2 What time did you _____ at the airport?
3 She _____ the waiter for the bill.
4 We _____ a car from a friend for the day.
5 They _____ too much money on food last month.
6 I _____ with a lot of different people in my job.

b Choose the correct answers.

1 I felt so *relaxed / relaxing* during my holiday.
2 The news was really *shocked / shocking*.
3 I needed to rest after my *tired / tiring* day.
4 I had a really *amazing / amazed* time in the city.
5 It's very *annoyed / annoying* when you have to queue.
6 I was *embarrassed / embarrassing* when I fell over.

c 💬 Talk about when the situations in 2b have been true for you.

3 WORDPOWER verb + *to*

a Match sentences (1–2) with the replies (a–b).

1 **My chair at work isn't very comfortable.**

2 **I can't afford to go to the cinema tonight.**

a ☐ I think you should stop **lending** money **to** your friends.
b ☐ I think you should **explain** the problem **to** your boss.

b Which verb + *to* combination in **bold** in 3a is a way of giving? Which is a way of communicating?

c Look at the sentences. Add the verb + *to* combinations to the table.

1 You have to **pay** a lot of money **to** the government when you start a new business.
2 She **wrote to** the newspaper to tell them what happened.
3 I **sold** my car **to** my brother-in-law.
4 I always **read to** my children before they go to sleep.
5 She **described** the building **to** her friend, but he couldn't find it.
6 She **brought** flowers **to** her mother to say sorry.

Communicating	Giving
explain to	lend to

d Where does *to* come in the sentences? Tick the correct answer.

1 ☐ before the object of the verb
2 ☐ after the direct object and before the indirect object

e Put *to* in the correct places in the sentences.

1 They sold their house some friends from another country.
2 When Steve described his holiday his friends, they were amazed.
3 Please bring something to drink the party.
4 I read the joke my friend, because it was funny.
5 Tara lent an umbrella her neighbour, because it was raining.
6 Did you write the letter the bank like I told you?
7 I explained the problem the company, but they didn't help me.
8 I paid the money for my course the school last week.

f Write five sentences about your life using the verbs + *to* from the table in 3c.

🔄 REVIEW YOUR PROGRESS

How well did you do in this unit? Write 3, 2 or 1 for each objective.
3 = very well   2 = well   1 = not so well

I CAN ...

Give advice on common problems	☐
Describe extreme experiences	☐
Ask for and give advice	☐
Write an email giving advice	☐

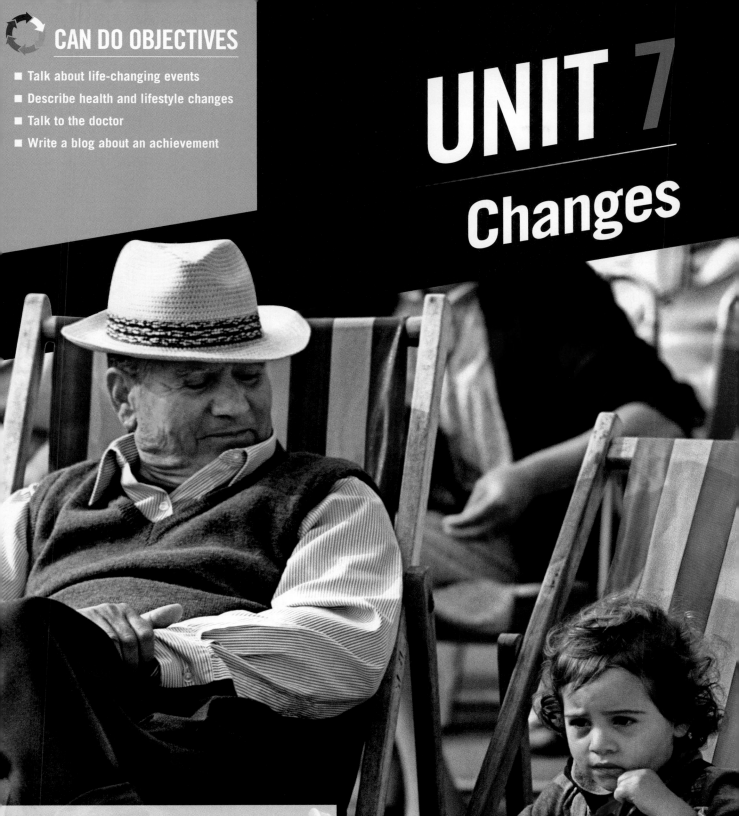

CAN DO OBJECTIVES

- Talk about life-changing events
- Describe health and lifestyle changes
- Talk to the doctor
- Write a blog about an achievement

UNIT 7
Changes

GETTING STARTED

a 💬 Look at the picture and answer the questions.

1 Who are the people in the picture? Where are they? Why have they gone there?
2 What have they done today? What will they do later?
3 How are they feeling? What do they talk about when they are together?

b 💬 In pairs, ask and answer the questions.

1 How does the old man feel about the little girl? What do you think he says about her to his friends?
2 What does he hope for for her future? What does he worry about?

7A I'm the happiest I've ever been

1 READING

a 💬 Look at the pictures. Which of the people are famous in your country? What do you know about them?

b Read the quotes. Which person is talking about these life events?

1 ☐☐ starting a family
2 ☐ the body getting older
3 ☐ becoming a celebrity
4 ☐ making films
5 ☐ reading a life-changing novel

c Read the quotes again. How did the life events in 1b change each person's life?

d 💬 Which quote do you like most? Why?

2 GRAMMAR

Comparatives and superlatives

a Complete the table with the highlighted comparative and superlative forms from the quotes.

	Comparative	Examples	Superlative	Examples
short adjectives	adj + *er*	shorter ¹_____	*the* adj + *est*	the kindest ² the _____
adjectives ending in *y*	adj – *-y* + *ier*	funnier healthier	*the* adj – *-y* + *iest*	the silliest ³ the _____
long adjectives	*more* + adj	more important ⁴_____	*the most* + adj	the most interesting ⁵ the _____
regular adverbs	*more* + adv	more easily ⁶_____	*the most* + adv	the most carefully the most politely

b Read Jane Goodall's quote again. Match sentences 1–2 with the meanings a–b.

1 ☐ I am not as fit as I was.   a I haven't changed. I'm equally fit now.
2 ☐ I am as fit as I was.   b I've changed. I'm less fit now.

c ▶ Now go to Grammar Focus 7A on p.154

d Complete the sentences with the correct forms of the adjectives and adverbs in brackets.

1 My life is _____ than it was five years ago. (good)
2 I'm the _____ I've ever been. (confident)
3 I learn _____ than when I was younger. (slowly)
4 I'm not as _____ as I was a year ago. (busy)
5 This is the _____ town I've ever lived in. (large)
6 My home is _____ these days. (tidy)
7 I work _____ now than I did five years ago. (hard)
8 I speak English _____ than I did a year ago. (good)

e ▶2.41 Listen and check. Practise the sentences.

f 💬 Are the sentences in 2d true for you? Why?

> My life is better than it was five years ago.

> Why?

> Well, I have my own flat, but I still see my friends and family all the time too.

b Brad Pitt
"I always thought that if I wanted to have a family, I wanted it to be big. These days I have very few friends. I have a handful of close friends and I have my family. I am the happiest I've ever been."

a Nelson Mandela
"When I closed that book, I was a different man. It improved my powers of thinking and self-control, and my relationships. I left prison more informed than when I went in."

c Jane Goodall, Primatologist
"I get back twice a year, and sometimes I see the chimps, and sometimes I don't ... I'm not as fit as I was, so if they're way up at the top of the mountain, it's difficult."

d Beyoncé
"Motherhood has changed everything for me, of course. I'm a lot braver and I'm more secure. I feel like you see things a bit differently after you give birth and my biggest job is to protect her."

e Rupert Grint
"You grow up more quickly than other teenagers … but I've become less independent, because people do everything for me."

f PSY
"My parents are really proud. My father is happy, because now he sees that I am more famous than Ban Ki-moon, the secretary-general of the United Nations. He was the most famous Korean before me."

3 LISTENING

a 💬 Read about two famous people. Do you know anything else about them? How do you think their lives were different before they became famous?

Rivaldo
Born: April 19, 1972, Paulista, Brazil
Rivaldo is a Brazilian ex-footballer. He has played for some of the biggest teams in the world and in two World Cups.

Sylvester Stallone
Born: July 6, 1946, New York, USA
Sylvester Stallone is an American actor, writer and director. He is most famous for his roles in the *Rocky* and *Rambo* films.

b ▶ 2.42 Listen to the stories of the two people. Which information did you already know?

c ▶ 2.42 Listen again. Are these sentences true about Rivaldo (*R*), Stallone (*S*) or both men (*B*)? Compare your answers with a partner.

1 ☐ His life was difficult when he was young.
2 ☐ At one time in his life, he couldn't afford to buy food.
3 ☐ He sold something that he loved.
4 ☐ He wanted to forget about his career after a sad event.
5 ☐ He was still poor after he got the job he wanted.
6 ☐ Some people did not believe he could be a big star.
7 ☐ His success happened very suddenly.
8 ☐ He cared about something else more than money.

d 💬 Ask and answer the questions.

1 Which person had the most difficult experience, do you think?
2 Do you know about any other people who started life poor and then became rich?

4 VOCABULARY *get* collocations

a ▶ 2.43 Complete the sentences with the correct form of the phrases in the box. Listen and check.

get a job   get an offer   get paid   get rich

1 Sylvester Stallone couldn't _____ as an actor.
2 *Rocky* won an Oscar and Stallone _____ .
3 Rivaldo _____ from Paulistano football club.
4 He didn't _____ much and he sometimes walked to training.

b ▶ Now go to Vocabulary Focus 7A on p.138

5 SPEAKING

a Think of a person you know and put their most important and interesting life events in order on the timeline. Use expressions with *get* and any other events you like.

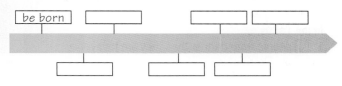

b 💬 Work in pairs. Tell your partner about the person you chose.

> When she was 20, my mother got a place at university in London. She met my father …

c 💬 Ask and answer the questions. Look at the life events in the box.

get a place at university   get engaged   get married
have children   get rich   get a job   get old

1 Which of the life events have you experienced? When do you think you will experience the other events?
2 Which life events do you think change people the most? How do people change?

7B I didn't use to eat healthy food

1 READING

a 💬 Look at the photographs from the 1950s. How do you think daily life was different then? Think about:

- men / women / children
- food and drink / shopping / work / health and exercise

b 💬 Read sentences 1–4 about the 1950s. Do you think they are true (*T*) or false (*F*)? Compare your answers with a partner.

In the 1950s, ...

1 ☐ people were thinner than they are today.
2 ☐ people spent more time at the gym than today.
3 ☐ people lived longer lives than they do today.
4 ☐ people smoked more cigarettes than today.

c Read the article. Check your answers to 1b.

d Read the article again. Answer the questions.

1 In the 1950s, what did the government say people should drink?
2 How is government advice about food different today?
3 How much time do UK women spend on a diet these days?
4 How did women in the 1950s exercise?
5 Why do people put on weight more easily today?
6 In the 1950s, when did people visit the doctor?
7 Which health problems are more common today?
8 Why didn't people stop smoking in the 1950s?
9 Where is it illegal to smoke in the UK?

e 💬 Think about the information you have read. Do you think people are healthier now than in the 1950s? Why / Why not?

1950s and TODAY

People are often shocked by the unhealthy lifestyles shown in TV shows like Mad Men. But are we really any healthier than we were 70 years ago?

Food and drink

People didn't use to worry about how many calories they ate. The government advised people to eat meat, cheese, butter, cereal and bread every day. They also recommended two glasses of milk a day. Today the advice has changed. They say we should eat more vegetables and less meat, cheese and butter. But we don't listen. Not many of us eat a healthy diet. 60% of us are now overweight. In the UK, the average woman will spend 31 years of her life on a diet. For a man, it's 28 years.

AVERAGE WEIGHT IN KG

in the 1950s: ♀55 ♂65   today: ♀70 ♂83

Exercise

Most women used to keep in shape naturally by doing housework – the average housewife did three hours of housework every day. They didn't need to go to the gym to lose weight and get fit. Today, busy working lives make it harder to get enough exercise. Inventions like washing machines, freezers and cars have made our lives easier, so it's now much easier to put on weight.

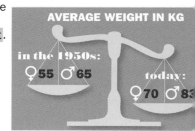

CALORIES BURNT DOING HOUSEWORK

in the 1950s: 1992 per day   today: 556 per day

Health care

People didn't use to live as long as we do today. Hospital operations were much less common and people only used to go to the doctor when they were seriously ill. Today, we live longer, but we have new health problems. In the 1950s, most kids drank milk and ate peanuts without any problems but more people have allergies to various foods today. And the number of people who have diabetes is also increasing, because more people are overweight.

AVERAGE AGE AT DEATH	
in the 1950s:	65
today:	79

Cigarettes

Smoking used to be very popular. The big Hollywood stars like James Dean and Audrey Hepburn all smoked on screen. In the UK, 80% of adults were regular smokers. People just didn't know how dangerous it was and didn't try to give up smoking. Today, we all know the dangers, and it's now illegal to smoke in public places like offices, schools and restaurants.

SMOKERS (% OF POPULATION)

in the 1950s: 80%

today: 20%

2 VOCABULARY Health collocations

a Work in pairs. Look at the highlighted phrases in the article. Which do you think are … ?

1 good for your health   2 bad for your health

b ▶ 2.46 Complete the sentences with phrases from the article. Then listen and check.

1 He _____, because he was doing so much exercise.
2 He decided to _____ smoking, because it was a very expensive habit.
3 After my holiday, I was five kilos _____.
4 It's easy to _____ if you work in an office and don't get any exercise.
5 I'm very healthy – I _____ by running every day.
6 I was a _____ for years, but then I decided to stop.
7 I never do any exercise but I'm thin because I _____.
8 She's _____ again – this time she's only eating bread and carrots for a week.
9 I _____ two _____ – animal hair and bee stings.

c 💬 Which of the ideas in 2b are common in your country? Do you think people are generally healthy in your country? Why / Why not?

d Work in pairs. Find and underline all the words and phrases in the article related to health. Add them to the lists in 2a.

3 GRAMMAR used to

a Look at the sentences about the 1950s. Are these things the same or different today?

Smoking **used to be** very popular. People **didn't use to know** it was dangerous.

Women **used to do** three hours of housework every day. They **didn't use to go** to the gym.

b Look at the sentences in 3a again and complete the rules.

> To talk about something that was different in the past we use _____ + infinitive. The negative is _____ + infinitive.

c ▶ 2.47 **Pronunciation** Listen to the sentences in 3a. Notice the pronunciation of *used to* /juːstə/. Does the pronunciation change in negative sentences?

d ▶ Now go to Grammar Focus 7B on p.154

e Complete the sentences with *used to* and a verb in the box.

> walk   be   think   spend   not suffer   not eat

1 When I was a child I _____ to school every day.
2 When I was a teenager, my parents _____ I was lazy.
3 I _____ from allergies, but now I do.
4 People in my country _____ a lot of fast food, but they do now.
5 I _____ more time outdoors than I do now.
6 The health service in my country _____ better than it is now.

f 💬 Change the sentences in 3e so they are true for you. Compare your answers with a partner.

> I used to go to school on foot.

> Really? My mum used to give me a lift.

4 SPEAKING

▶ Communication 7B Work in pairs. Go to p.129.

7C Everyday English
It hurts all the time

Learn to talk to the doctor
- **P** Tones for asking questions
- **S** Showing concern and relief

1 VOCABULARY At the doctor's

a 💬 Look at the health problems in the box. Which have you had in the last six months?

---
backache   a cold   a temperature   a broken leg
a serious stomachache   the flu   a rash
---

b 💬 What do people in your country do for each of the health problems in 1a? Choose ideas from the list and add more of your own ideas.

- get a prescription from a doctor
- take pills or other medicine
- have some tests
- go to the hospital
- go to the chemist's
- have an operation
- put on cream

2 LISTENING

a ▶️ **2.49** Watch or listen to Part 1. Answer the questions.

1 Why has Leo gone to the doctor?
2 When did the problem start?

b ▶️ **2.49** Watch or listen to Part 1 again. What other information does the doctor get from Leo about his back problem? Compare your notes with a partner.

c 💬 Ask and answer the questions.

1 Do you ever suffer from the same health problem as Leo?
2 What causes it?
3 What treatments would you recommend?

3 USEFUL LANGUAGE
Describing symptoms

a ▶️ **2.50** Complete the phrases with the words in the box. Then listen and check.

---
exhausted   all the time   back   painful   get to sleep
---

1 My _____ hurts.
2 It's very _____.
3 I can't _____.
4 It hurts _____.
5 I feel _____.

b ▶️ **2.50** Listen again and repeat.

c Make eight more phrases with 1–5 in 3a and the words in the box below.

---
when I walk   uncomfortable   concentrate
arm   run   terrible   itchy   sick
---

d 💬 When do people get the symptoms in 3a and 3c? Talk about your ideas with a partner.

> People feel sick when they eat bad food.

> Some people feel sick on car journeys.

4 LISTENING

a ▶️ **2.51** Which treatments do you think the doctor will suggest for Leo? Put a ✓ or a ✗. Then watch or listen to Part 2 and check your ideas.

1 ☐ stay in bed
2 ☐ do the things you normally do
3 ☐ stay in the same position for a long time
4 ☐ do some exercise
5 ☐ take pills for the pain

b ▶️ **2.51** Watch or listen again. Are sentences 1–6 true (*T*) or false (*F*)? Correct the false sentences.

1 ☐ Leo is going to the gym a lot at the moment.
2 ☐ Leo sits down a lot for his job.
3 ☐ Leo isn't taking anything for the pain.
4 ☐ Leo has to take two pills every two hours.
5 ☐ Leo shouldn't take more than 24 pills in a day.
6 ☐ Leo might need to see the doctor again in a week.

5 CONVERSATION SKILLS
Showing concern and relief

a Look at the underlined phrases in the conversations. Which phrases show that Leo is … ?

1 happy with what the doctor says
2 worried about what the doctor says

Doctor	I don't think it's anything to worry about.
Leo	<u>Phew. That's good to hear.</u>
Doctor	But you shouldn't stay in bed – that's not going to help.
Leo	<u>Oh dear. Really?</u>
Doctor	I really don't think it's anything to worry about.
Leo	<u>What a relief!</u>

b ▶2.52 Listen to the phrases in 5a. How do we pronounce *phew*? Repeat the phrases.

c 💬 Work in pairs. Take turns to say the sentences. Respond using the phrases in 5a.

Student A
1 I don't think it's serious.
2 I think you'll need to see another doctor.
3 You should feel better in 48 hours.

Student B
1 I need you to take a few tests.
2 Your foot's definitely not broken.
3 I think it's just a cold, not the flu.

6 USEFUL LANGUAGE
Doctors' questions

a ▶2.53 Match the doctor's questions with Leo's answers. Then listen and check.

1 ☐ So, what's the problem?
2 ☐ When did this problem start?
3 ☐ Where does it hurt?
4 ☐ Can I have a look?
5 ☐ Do you do any exercise?
6 ☐ Are you taking anything for the pain?
7 ☐ Do you have any allergies?

a About three or four days ago.
b Here. This area.
c Yes, I've taken some aspirin.
d No, I don't think so.
e Sure.
f Well, I usually go to the gym, but I haven't been recently.
g Well, my back hurts.

b ▶2.54 Listen to the doctor's questions. Choose the best answer (a or b) for each question.

1	a Yes, I've taken some tablets.	b	My leg hurts.
2	a No, not often.	b	Yes, of course.
3	a I go running.	b	I work in an office.
4	a Not much.	b	I can't eat fish.
5	a I feel tired all the time.	b	No, nothing.
6	a All day.	b	About a week ago.
7	a It hurts a lot.	b	Here – under my arm.

7 PRONUNCIATION
Tones for asking questions

a ▶2.55 Listen to the questions. Does the doctor's voice go up (↗) or down (↘) at the end of each question?

1 So, what's the problem?
2 When did this problem start?
3 Where does it hurt?
4 Can I have a look?

b Which question in 7a does the doctor already know the answer to? Complete the rule.

- In questions where the speaker doesn't know the answer, the voice usually goes **up / down**.
- In questions where the speaker knows the answer, the voice usually goes **up / down**.

c Listen to the questions in 7a again and repeat.

8 SPEAKING

a 💬 Work in pairs. Student A: you are a doctor. Listen to your partner's health problem and give advice.
Student B: choose a health problem from the pictures and explain the problem to your partner. Give details.

What's the problem?

When did this start?

I see …

I've got a stomachache.

Yesterday. After dinner. But it happens quite often.

b 💬 Swap roles. Student A: choose a new health problem.

Unit Progress Test

CHECK YOUR PROGRESS

You can now do the Unit Progress Test.

1 LISTENING AND SPEAKING

a 💬 What kind of things do people sometimes want to change about themselves? Think of one example for each area.

- diet
- exercise
- study
- bad habits
- money
- relationships

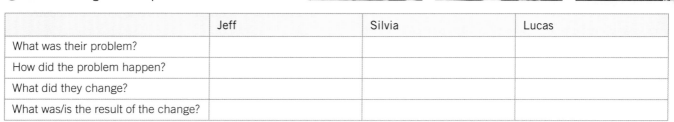
Jeff   Silvia   Lucas

b ▶ 2.56 Listen to Jeff, Silvia and Lucas. What change did each person try to make? Were they successful?

c ▶ 2.56 Listen again. Complete the table.

	Jeff	Silvia	Lucas
What was their problem?			
How did the problem happen?			
What did they change?			
What was/is the result of the change?			

d Think of something you would like to change in your life. Make notes about the questions.

1 What is the change?
2 Why do you want to make the change?
3 How could you make the change?
4 What do you hope the result will be?

e 💬 Work in pairs. Talk about the changes you would like to make.

> I think I should eat less fast food.

> How often do you eat it?

2 READING

a Simon wrote about a change he made for the *Living to Change* blog. Read the blog and answer the questions.

1 What was Simon like before he made a change?
2 What kind of exercise did he start doing?
3 What was the result?

b Are these sentences about Simon true (*T*) or false (*F*)? Correct the false sentences.

1 ☐ Simon had problems with his weight just after he stopped smoking.
2 ☐ He started exercising before he stopped smoking.
3 ☐ He chose running because he liked it when he was younger.
4 ☐ He found it difficult to run when he started.
5 ☐ When he hurt his foot, he was pleased to have a break from running.
6 ☐ He now thinks he might enter a running race.

LIVING TO
CHANGE Talking about how you got even better!

About three years ago, I used to smoke and I was overweight. I was really unfit and I didn't feel very good about myself, so I decided to make a change.

To begin with, I gave up smoking which wasn't too difficult. But then I started eating instead of smoking, and I started putting on a lot of weight. I was getting heavier and heavier and I wasn't doing any exercise. I'm about 1.78 m tall and my weight went up to 98 kg. So, after that I decided I needed to start exercising, too.

Before

When I was at secondary school I used to enjoy running, so I thought that would be an easy way for me to get fit. At first, I could only run for about thirty seconds and then I had to walk. It was terrible. So that's how I got started – I went for walks and every few days I made the walk a bit longer.

3 WRITING SKILLS
Linking: ordering events

Complete the rules with the words in the box. Use the highlighted words in Simon's blog to help you.

to begin with   after that   at first
after a while   soon   then   in the end

To show the order of events we use …
_____ or _____ to talk about the first thing that happened.
_____ or _____ or _____ or _____ to mean *next*.
_____ for the final action, event or result.

b Which word in 3a means … ?
1 after a short time
2 after a longer time period

c Complete the text with words and phrases in 3a.

I stopped drinking coffee.

1 _____, I got headaches and really missed it.
   (This is the first thing that happened.)
2 _____, I started drinking just one cup a day.
   (This is what happened next.)
3 _____, the headaches stopped.
   (This is what happened a short time later.)
4 _____, I started drinking green tea during the day.
   (This is what happened after a longer period of time.)
5 _____, I forgot to make coffee in the morning one day.
   (This is what happened next.)
6 _____, I realised I didn't need coffee at all.
   (This is the last thing that happened.)

Home | News | Articles | Contact us   log in

After a while, I began feeling fitter and that's when I started to run and walk. But then, one day, I fell over and hurt my foot when I was running and I had to stop for about two weeks. I was surprised how much I missed it!

However, when I started again, it was much easier than I thought. Soon, I found I didn't need to walk any more and I found I could run further and further. In the end, I was able to go for a 10 km run without problems. I've lost almost 20 kg and I now weigh just 80 kg. I feel so much better and I'm planning to run a marathon next year. These days, instead of spending all my money on cigarettes, I spend money on going out or buying things.

After

d Complete the text with the time linkers in the box. Use each linker once.

after that   soon   in the end
to begin with   after a while   then

About a year ago, I was walking near a river and I slipped and fell in. I couldn't swim and I was really frightened. I was lucky because a friend was there and she helped me. So I decided that I needed to learn to swim.

1 _____, I hated getting into the water at the swimming pool. My teacher told me to take a shower before getting in, so I was already wet. This was a good idea. 2 _____, I found it easier to get into the water.

3 _____, I started with very easy exercises like putting my head underwater. I felt a little bit stupid. But my teacher made it fun and we laughed a lot. 4 _____, I found it easy to put my head underwater.

Learning how to breathe in and out underwater was difficult and it took a long time. 5 _____, it got easier and I made good progress. 6 _____, I learnt how to swim. I'm not a great swimmer, but I'm not afraid of the water like I used to be. And I'm a lot more careful near the river now!

4 WRITING

a You are going to write an article for the *Living to Change* blog. Think about a difficult change you made or something difficult you tried to do. Choose one of these topics or your own idea.

- health
- education
- work
- money
- bad habits
- relationships

b Make notes on your ideas. Use questions 1–5 to help you.
1 What did you want to do?
2 How did you start? Did your plan change?
3 What was difficult? What was easy?
4 Did anything you didn't expect happen?
5 What happened in the end? How do you feel about it?

c Use your notes to write an article about the change you made. Use time linkers to show the order of events.

d Work in pairs. Read each other's articles. Did you write about similar topics? Did your partner use time linkers?

UNIT 7
Review and extension

1 GRAMMAR

a Complete the sentences using the comparative and superlative forms of the words.

1 Top speed: Kawasa 130km/h, Shumika 140km/h,
TTR 150km/h
The Shumika is _faster than_ the Kawasa, but the TTR is
the fastest (fast)
2 Room price: Grand Hotel 80 euros, Hotel Central 100 euros,
Hotel Europe 130 euros
The Hotel Central is _____ the Grand Hotel, but the Hotel
Europe is _____. (expensive)
3 MP3 players: Soundgood ***, MusicPro ****, iListen *****
The MusicPro is _____ the Soundgood, but the iListen is
_____. (good)
4 Number of fans in the world: Border FC 20 million,
DK Jets 100 million, AK Dynamo 200 million
DK Jets are _____ AK Dynamo, but Border FC is _____.
(popular)

b Complete the text with the correct form of *used to* and the verbs in the box.

| plan   not be   buy   not open   not have   see |

Thirty years ago, we [1]_____ any big supermarkets in my town.
There were some small shops and I [2]_____ everything there. I
liked it because I always [3]_____ people I knew, so it was very
friendly. But it wasn't perfect – there [4]_____ a lot of different
products. And the shops [5]_____ on Sunday or late in the
evening, so I [6]_____ my week carefully.

2 VOCABULARY

a Complete the sentences with the words or phrases in the box.

| a place   in touch   on well   paid   to know |

1 I'm going to get _____ with an old friend this week.
2 I get _____ much more now than in my old job.
3 I'd like to get _____ at a university in a different city.
4 When I was younger I wasn't very close to my parents,
but now we get _____.
5 I got _____ most of my close friends when I was at school.

b Match the sentence halves.

1 ☐ I go running twice a week to keep   a overweight.
2 ☐ I'm healthy now, but I used to be   b on a diet.
3 ☐ I prefer to do exercise than go   c fit.
4 ☐ A lot more people today have   d weight.
5 ☐ When I study a lot, I often put on   e allergies.

3 WORDPOWER *change*

a Is *change* a verb or a noun in sentences 1–8?

1 I just want to **change** into something a bit more comfortable.
2 I have a difficult train journey to work – I have to **change**
twice and take a bus.
3 You've given me the wrong **change** – I gave you $10, not $5.
4 I've **changed my mind** – I'm going to stay in tonight.
5 I took the shirt back to the shop and **changed** it for
another one.
6 I always keep some **change** in the car to pay for parking.
7 We normally go shopping on Saturdays, but we're playing
football **for a change**.
8 Could you **change** my €20 for two €10 notes, please?

b Match the words in **bold** in 3a with meanings a–h.

Verbs
a ☐ get off a train, bus or plane and get on a different one
b ☐ return something and get a new one
c ☐ put different clothes on
d ☐ exchange money for different notes or coins
e ☐ make a different decision

Nouns
f ☐ because you want a new experience
g ☐ coins
h ☐ the money a shop assistant returns to you

c Complete the sentences with the words or phrases in the box.

| change trains   change my mind   change some money
keep some change   the right change   change into
for a change   change |

1 I always _____ in my pocket.
2 I normally _____ comfortable clothes when I get
home in the evening.
3 I have to _____ on my way home.
4 I normally go to the mountains, but this year I'm going on
a beach holiday _____.
5 I think it's better to _____ before you go abroad.
6 I don't often _____ after I've made a decision.
7 It's easy to _____ something after you've bought it in
a shop.
8 When I buy things, I always check the shop assistant
gives me _____.

d 💬 Which of the sentences in 3c are true for you?

⟳ REVIEW YOUR PROGRESS

How well did you do in this unit? Write 3, 2 or 1
for each objective.
3 = very well   2 = well   1 = not so well

I CAN ...

Talk about life-changing events	☐
Describe health and lifestyle changes	☐
Talk to the doctor	☐
Write a blog about an achievement	☐

CAN DO OBJECTIVES

- Talk about music, art and literature
- Talk about sports and leisure activities
- Apologise, make and accept excuses
- Write a book review

UNIT 8
Culture

GETTING STARTED

a 💬 Describe what you can see in this painting.

b 💬 In pairs, ask and answer the questions.

1 Where do you think this was painted?
2 What do you think this painting means?
3 What do you think of the painting?

c ▶ 2.57 Listen to someone talking about the painting. Are their ideas the same as yours?

d 💬 In pairs, ask and answer the questions.

1 Where can you go to see art where you live?
2 Who goes to see it? Why do they go?

8A My favourite book is based on a true story

Learn to talk about music, art and literature

G The passive: present and past simple
V Art and music; Common verbs in the pas.

1 VOCABULARY
Art and music

a 💬 In pairs, match pictures 1–10 with the types of art and music below.

- ☐ TV series
- ☐ novel
- ☐ poem
- ☐ sculpture
- ☐ architecture
- ☐ film
- ☐ photograph
- ☐ painting
- ☐ album
- ☐ classical music

b ▶️ **2.58** Listen and check. Listen again and <u>underline</u> the stressed syllable in each one. Then listen again and repeat.

c 💬 Which kinds of art and music are you interested in?

2 READING

a 💬 Look at the pictures and titles of each thing in the article *Six of the best, biggest and most popular ...* . Which of them have you read, seen or listened to? Do you like them?

b Read the article. Which things ... ?

- took many years to become popular
  _____, _____, _____

- has sold more than any other
  _____, _____

- people have committed a crime to own/see _____, _____

c Read the article again and add the missing sentences a–f.

a But the most popular single novel is much older.

b It's so popular that, in 2012, over 160 baby girls were named *Khaleesi* – the name of a character in the show.

c But now most people recognise the famous *da da da dah* introduction.

d He was wrong – it sold over ten million more than that.

e The author sold the story for only a dollar.

f It was taken by Vincenzo Peruggia, an Italian who wanted to return it to Italy.

d Work with a partner. Look at the highlighted words and phrases in the article. What do they mean?

e 💬 Are you surprised by any of the things on the most popular list?

(1)

Six of the best, biggest and most popula...

We all have our favourite music, our favourite films, our favourite books – but which are the most popular ever?

The most popular album ...
Thriller by Michael Jackson

(2)

At the time Jackson started writing his best-selling album, *Thriller*, he was upset because his previous album, *Off the Wall*, hadn't won a Grammy award. He wrote on the mirror in his room that his next album would sell 50 million copies. ¹_____ Even today around 130,000 copies are sold in the USA every year.

(3) Symphonie № 5.

The most famous classical music ...
Beethoven's Fifth Symphony

When Beethoven was alive, his Fifth Symphony wasn't his most popular piece of music. ²_____ In the twentieth century, the first four notes were used by other musicians to make electro dance, hiphop, surf rock, rock and roll and disco tracks.

The most famous painting ...
La Gioconda

(4)

La Gioconda (which is called the *Mona Lisa* in English-speaking countries) was not always so famous. It only became really well known when it was stolen from the Louvre in Paris in 1911. ³_____ The painting was found two years later and it is now kept behind glass to protect it.

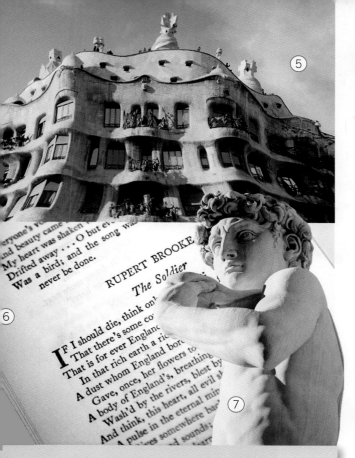

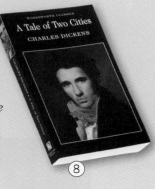

3 GRAMMAR
The passive: present and past simple

a Look at the sentences and answer the questions.

ACTIVE
Charles Dickens **wrote** *A Tale of Two Cities* in 1859.

PASSIVE
A Tale of Two Cities **was written** by Charles Dickens in 1859.

1 Is the information in the active and passive sentences the same or different?
2 Which sentence is about the book? _____
   Which sentence is about the writer? _____
3 How does the verb change in the passive? What are the two parts of the verb form?
   _b_____ + _p____ _p_____

b ▶ Now go to Grammar Focus 8A on p.156

c <u>Underline</u> five more examples of the passive in the article. (There are seven more altogether.)

4 VOCABULARY
Common verbs in the passive

a Complete the sentences using the past participles of the verbs in the box. Not all the sentences are true.

---
set (a story somewhere)   design (a building)
paint (a painting)   base (a film on a book)
perform (a piece of music)   play (a character)
~~write~~ (songs, music)   direct (a film, a TV show)
---

1 All the songs on *Thriller* were <u>written</u> by Michael Jackson.
2 When Beethoven's Fifth Symphony was _____ for the first time, the audience didn't like it very much.
3 The *Mona Lisa* was _____ by Michelangelo.
4 The 2012 Batman film *The Dark Knight Rises* was _____ on the book *A Tale of Two Cities*.
5 The main character in *The Shawshank Redemption* was _____ by Morgan Freeman.
6 *Game of Thrones* is _____ by Peter Jackson, director of *Lord of the Rings*.
7 The Harry Potter stories are _____ in Britain in the 1990s.
8 *Casa Milà* was _____ by Salvador Dalí.

b ▶2.60 Which sentences from 4a do you think are true? Tell a partner. Listen and check.

5 SPEAKING

a Complete the sentences so they are true for you.

My favourite album is …
A painting I like is …
The best book I've ever read was …
A TV show / film I've seen more than once is …
A song I sometimes sing is …
A poem I studied at school was …
A sculpture / building which is famous in my country is …

b 💬 Talk about your answers to 5a in small groups.

The most popular novel …
A Tale of Two Cities

Many people think that the best-selling book of all time is one of the Harry Potter books. It's true that all the Harry Potter books together have sold about 450 million copies. [4]_____ *A Tale of Two Cities* was written by Charles Dickens in 1859 and has sold 250 million copies. It tells the story of a group of ordinary people during the French revolution.

The most popular film …
The Shawshank Redemption

The most popular film ever didn't make much money at the cinema. *The Shawshank Redemption* only became popular later on video, DVD and TV. The film – voted 'Best Film' on the website IMDb – was based on a book by Stephen King. [5]_____

The most popular TV series …
Game of Thrones

The number one TV series on IMDb is currently *Game of Thrones*. The fantasy drama was also the most illegally downloaded series of 2012 and 2013 – people around the world couldn't wait to see it, so they downloaded the programme as soon as it was shown in the USA. [6]_____

8B I've hated rugby since I was at school

Learn to talk about sports and activities
- **G** Present perfect with *for* and *since*
- **V** Sports and activities

1 SPEAKING

a 💬 How do you know when someone is lying? Think of three different ways and tell a partner. Think about:
- what they say
- voice
- eyes
- body

b 💬 Do you know any games where you have to lie?

2 LISTENING

a ▶️ 2.61 Listen to the introduction to a radio show called *I can't believe it!* Answer the questions.

1 What topic are the players going to talk about?
2 How many lies will each player tell?

b Michael, a player on *I can't believe it!*, is going to talk about Usain Bolt. What do you know about him?

c ▶️ 2.62 Listen to what Michael says. Which of the sentences 1–7 do you think are his two lies? Tell a partner.

1 Usain Bolt is the fastest man in the world.
2 His team mates call him 'Giraffe'.
3 Runners as tall as Usain don't usually win.
4 He's held the world record for the 100 metres and 200 metres since 2008.
5 He was the first person to win both races in two Olympics.
6 He forgot to tie his shoes in the 100 metres final in 2012.
7 He slowed down at the end of the 100 metres final in 2012.

d ▶️ 2.63 Listen and check your answers to 2c.

e 💬 Look at the men in the other two pictures. Answer the questions.

1 Where do you think each man is from?
2 What sport/activity is each man doing?
3 What world records do you think they broke?

f ▶️ 2.64 Listen to Alice and Neil talking about the men. Check your answers to 2e.

g ▶️ 2.64 Listen again. Answer questions 1–2 about each man.

1 How did he become famous?
2 What has he done since?

h 💬 Compare your notes with a partner. What do you think the lies about each man are? Tell your partner.

Konishiki Yasokichi	Captain Joseph Kittinger
Lie 1: _____	Lie 1: _____
Lie 2: _____	Lie 2: _____

i ▶️ 2.65 Listen to the next part of the programme and check your ideas in 2h.

j 💬 Which of the three record breakers in the programme do you think is the most interesting? Why?

Usain Bolt

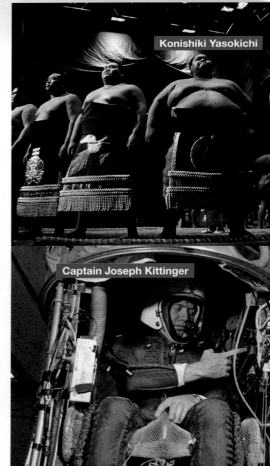

Konishiki Yasokichi

Captain Joseph Kittinger

3 GRAMMAR
Present perfect with *for* and *since*

a Look at the sentence about Konishiki Yasokichi. Does he have a radio show now?

He's had his own radio show for many years.

b Complete the rule with the words *present* and *past*.

> We can use the present perfect to talk about something that started in the _____ and continues in the _____.

c Look at two more sentences from the listening. Choose the correct words. Then complete the rules.

1 Kittinger has held his record *for / since* over 50 years!
2 He's been in the Jamaican Olympic team *for / since* 2004.

> With the present perfect:
> • we use _____ to say the time period,
>   e.g. *ten minutes*, *three years*.
> • we use _____ to say when something started,
>   e.g. *yesterday*, *a year ago*.

d ▶ Now go to Grammar Focus 8B on p.156

e Complete the sentences with the past participles of the verbs in brackets and a time phrase with *for* or *since*. Write four true sentences and two lies.

1 I've _____ (live) in my house/flat …
2 I've _____ (be) a student here …
3 I've _____ (have) my mobile phone …
4 I've _____ (know) _____ …
5 I've _____ (want) _____ …
6 I've _____ (own) my _____ …

f 💬 Read your sentences to a partner. Can your partner guess which two sentences are lies?

4 VOCABULARY Sports and activities

a Look at the pictures on the page. Which sports and activities can you see? Make a list.

b 💬 Have you ever tried any of the sports in the pictures? Would you like to?

c ▶ Now go to Vocabulary Focus 8B on p.138

5 SPEAKING

a You are going to talk about sports and activities. Make notes about (1–4) first.

1 A sport or activity you do
   • when you do it
   • who you do it with
   • why you like it

2 A sport you are a fan of
   • why you like it
   • how long you've been a fan
   • any teams or players you like

3 A sport or activity you've tried, but you didn't like
   • when you tried it
   • why you didn't like it

4 A sport you hate watching
   • why you don't like it
   • when you started hating it

b 💬 Work in small groups. Compare your interests and experiences. Which person in your group are you most similar to?

> Yoga is very dull. I tried it once and I fell asleep.

> I've hated rugby since I played it at school. It's really boring.

> But I love yoga. It's relaxing. Maybe you went to a bad class.

> Me too. I prefer football.

8C Everyday English
I'm really sorry I haven't called

1 LISTENING

a 💬 Do your friends sometimes do any of these things?

- not call you back
- visit unexpectedly
- not reply to text messages or emails

If yes, does it annoy you? Do they do anything else that annoys you?

b ▶ 2.68 Look at the pictures. What do you think is happening? Watch or listen to Part 1 and check your ideas.

c ▶ 2.68 Watch or listen again. Answer the questions.

1 What excuse does Leo give first for not calling?
2 Is Annie happy with Leo's first excuse? What does she ask him?
3 What excuse does Leo give next?
4 What did Annie think the problem was?
5 Why does Leo say he was working so much?
6 Does Annie think this was a good idea?

d 💬 Work in pairs. Answer the questions.

1 When was the last time you apologised to someone? What happened?
2 Do you think it's necessary to apologise if … ?
   - you're ten minutes late when you meet someone
   - you don't reply to someone's text message the same day
   - you forget someone's birthday
   - you have to cancel because you're ill

2 USEFUL LANGUAGE Apologies and excuses

a ▶ 2.69 Listen and complete the sentences from Part 1.

1 I'm _____ _____ I haven't called you.
2 I _____ call or send you a message.
3 I _____ _____ to call you, but I couldn't find my mobile.
4 I _____ _____ to make you worry.
5 I _____ to call you after I went to the doctor.
6 I _____ _____ work that much.
7 No, _____ no excuse.

b In which of the phrases in 2a is Leo … ?

1 apologising
2 giving an excuse

c ▶ 2.69 Listen and repeat the phrases in 2a.

d Complete the excuses with words from 2a.

1 I _____ going to text you, but I didn't have my phone.
2 I _____ to tell you, but I forgot.
3 I _____ work at the weekend, because my boss asked me.
4 I _____ to be so rude.
5 I _____ come to your party, because I was ill.

e ▶ 2.70 Complete the phrases Annie uses to accept Leo's apologies. Then listen and check.

1 It doesn't _____.
2 Well, it's not your _____.
3 Don't _____ about it.
4 No really, it's _____.

f ▶ 2.70 Listen and repeat the phrases in 2e.

g 💬 Work in pairs. Take turns to apologise for the situations and to give an excuse. Respond and accept your partner's apologies. Use ideas from the boxes or your own ideas.

Situations
- being late for a meeting
- not answering an email
- forgetting to pay back some money

Excuses
- lots of traffic
- very busy
- didn't get paid
- missed the bus/train

3 PRONUNCIATION Tones for continuing or finishing

a ▶️ **2.71** Listen to two sentences. Does the voice in the underlined parts (1–4) go down then up (↘↗) or down (↘)?

I was <u>going to call you</u>, but <u>my phone was dead</u>.
       1   2

I <u>meant to call you</u>, but I had to <u>work a lot</u>.
   3   4

b Complete the rule.

> When a speaker wants to show that they have something more to say, their voice often goes **down then up / down**.
> When a speaker wants to show the information they're giving has finished, their voice often goes **down then up / down**.

c ▶️ **2.72** Listen to four sentences. Do you think each speaker has finished or has something more to say?
1 I didn't see John
2 I won't have time tomorrow
3 I was going to tell you what happened
4 I didn't call her

4 LISTENING

a ▶️ **2.73** Watch or listen to Part 2. What does Leo agree to do?

b ▶️ **2.73** Watch or listen again. What are the three other suggestions Annie makes? Why doesn't Leo like them?

Suggestion 1: _____
Leo's response: _____
Suggestion 2: _____
Leo's response: _____
Suggestion 3: _____
Leo's response: _____

c 💬 What do you think of Annie's suggestions? Can you think of anything else to suggest?

5 SPEAKING

a 💬 Work in pairs. Look at the sentences. Who might say each one?

'You still haven't given me the report I asked you to do.'

'You were driving 70 km an hour. The speed limit is 50 km.'

'I'm at the café. Where are you? Is everything OK?'

'You can't sit here unless you order something.'

'Why didn't you get a ticket before you got on?'

'You forgot to buy milk again.'

'Do you know you can't park here?'

'There's a queue here!'

b 💬 What excuses could you give for each situation in 5a?

c 💬 Swap partners. Take turns saying the sentences from 5a to your partner. Apologise and give an excuse. Whose excuses are better?

> You still haven't given me the report I asked you to do.

> I'm sorry. I was at a meeting all morning. I just didn't have time.

> That's OK. It's not your fault. But I need it this week.

🔄 **Unit Progress Test**

CHECK YOUR PROGRESS

You can now do the Unit Progress Test.

1 LISTENING AND SPEAKING

a 💬 Look at the book covers. What do you think the stories are about?

b Read the summaries of the stories and match them with the book covers. Are they similar to your ideas in 1a?

1 In a small village, Megan and Huw fall in love. But Huw has to go abroad and they meet again 50 years later.

2 A man in Florida is out in his fishing boat and a hurricane is coming. His daughter must tell him before it's too late.

3 In Scotland, a woman is murdered. A man has just escaped from prison and the police think he is the murderer … but is he?

c ▶️ 2.74 Listen to three people talking about the books. Answer the questions.

1 Who has finished the book and who is still reading?

2 What do they think about the stories?

d ▶️ 2.74 Listen again and answer the questions.

Two Lives

1 Why does the man leave the village?

2 What has happened while he was away?

Eye of the Storm

3 Did everything in this story happen in real life?

4 What does the girl do to try to save her father's life?

A Puzzle for Logan

5 Why do the police think the prisoner is the murderer?

6 What does Inspector Logan try to do?

e Think of a book you are reading or a book you remember. What happens in the story? Make notes about:

● the characters
● the kind of story it is
● what happens / the main points
● what you think / thought about it

f 💬 Work in small groups. Talk about your book and say if you liked it. Have any other students read it? Would they like to read it now?

2 READING

a Read the online reviews. Match them with the books in the pictures.

b 💬 The first reviewer gave the book three stars (= quite good). How many stars do you think the other reviewers gave?

REVIEWS

HOME   NEWS   REVIEWS   REGISTER

1 EDUARDO ★★★☆☆

This book is quite exciting. Even after the first few pages you want to know who killed the woman, and you don't know until the end. It's well written and the characters are really interesting and realistic. However, the story is quite hard to follow because there are so many different people, so I didn't enjoy it as much as I expected.

2 KATIE

This is the best book I've ever read in English! It's a beautiful story, although it's also very sad and it made me cry. The man and the woman are wonderful characters and they are described very well. You can really understand how they feel. I definitely recommend it!

3 TINA

This book is OK, but it's not brilliant. The story is quite interesting and it's easy to read. However, it's not very exciting, because you know from the start that the girl and her friend will save the girl's father from the storm and they will all live happily ever after. I also thought the characters were a bit dull. In real life, people are not good and kind all of the time!

4 WOO-JIN

I really enjoyed this book. It was interesting to read and it describes Edinburgh very well, so you can really imagine what the city and the people are like. Although the story is quite complicated, you should keep going because the ending is very clever. You can't guess who killed the woman until the very last page. I couldn't put the book down until I got to the end! I can recommend it.

3 WRITING SKILLS
Positive and negative comments; Linking: *although, however*

a Look at the highlighted phrases in the book reviews. Are they positive or negative? Make two lists.

b Look at the examples and answer the questions.

The characters are really interesting and realistic. **However**, the story is quite hard to follow.

The characters are really interesting and realistic, **although** the story is quite hard to follow.

1 Do the words *however* and *although* … ?
   a join similar ideas
   b contrast two different ideas
2 Which word … ?
   a begins a new sentence _____
   b joins two ideas in the same sentence _____

c Underline four examples of *however* and *although* in the texts.

d Where can *although* come in the sentence?
   1 only in the middle
   2 at the beginning or in the middle

e Look at the two sentences in comments 1–4. Join the two sentences in each comment using *however* or *although*. There is more than one possible answer.

   1 I can recommend the book. It's difficult to read.
   2 The story is a bit boring. The characters are interesting.
   3 It's an exciting story. It's not the best story I've ever read.
   4 It's fiction. It's based on a true story.

4 WRITING

a Think of a book you've read. (Use the one you chose in 1e or a different one.) You're going to write a review of the book. Answer the questions.

   1 What are the good and bad points? Think about:
      • the characters   • the story
      • the descriptions
   2 What phrases in 3a can you use to describe the story?
   3 How can you use *however* or *although* to join your ideas?

b Use your ideas in 4a to write a review of the book and give a star rating (1–5).

c Work in pairs. Read your partner's review. Check their work. Does it do all these things? Tick each box.

   ☐ tell you about the characters
   ☐ give a description of the story
   ☐ use *however* and *although* correctly

d Read other students' reviews. Choose a book you would like to read and tell the class why.

UNIT 8
Review and extension

1 GRAMMAR

a Complete the text with present and past simple passive forms of the verbs in the box.

not perform	show	write	love	sell	direct	film

The two most popular DVDs ever are very different. The best-selling DVD is *Finding Nemo* – eight million copies [1]_____ on the first day it was available. Most of the voices for the main characters [2]_____ by famous actors, but they [3]_____ by children all over the world. *Pulp Fiction* – the second best-selling DVD ever – is a much more adult film. It [4]_____ by Quentin Tarantino and it [5]_____ in Los Angeles. It's an unusual film, because the action [6]_____ in a strange order – you see the end of the story at the beginning. Audiences loved the acting; most of the characters [7]_____ for the actors who played them.

b 💬 Work in pairs. Describe a film you like.

c Complete the sentences with the active or passive forms of the verbs.

1 This sculpture _____ in 1870. (create)
2 He _____ some very famous photographs. (take)
3 The film _____ on a true story. (base)
4 Spike Johansen _____ the film while he was still a student. (direct)
5 The author _____ the story in a single day while he was on holiday. (write)
6 The car _____ by a company in Milan. (design)

d Correct the mistakes in these sentences.

1 We live here since 2014.
2 She's studied English since two years.
3 I've had my job from 2010.
4 They're been football fans all their lives.
5 We've been married for 2012.
6 I loved their music since I saw them at a concert.

2 VOCABULARY

a Complete the sentences with the words in the box.

poem	sculpture	series	concert	architecture

1 There's a famous _____ in an art gallery near where I live.
2 I like live music, so I go to at least one _____ a month.
3 I watch a lot of TV _____ like *Game of Thrones*.
4 I can still remember a _____ I wrote when I was a child.
5 I don't really like the _____ in my town.

b 💬 Which of the sentences in 2a are true for you?

c Complete the names of the sports and sports activities.

1 sn __ __b__ __ __ __ __ __ g   5 j __ __ __ __ __ g
2 g__ __ __ __ __ __ __ __ s   6 a __ __ __ __ __ __ __ s
3 wi __ __ __ __ __ __ __ g   7 g __ __ __ __ g
4 s __ __ __ __ __d__ __ __ g   8 y __ __ __

3 WORDPOWER *by*

a Match the sentences with *by* (1–4) with the meanings (a–d).

1 Have you heard the new song **by** Arcade Fire?
2 Can I pay **by** credit card?
3 You need to bring the car back **by** eight o'clock.
4 He was standing **by** the window looking at the rain.

a near or next to
b using
c created or written
d not later than

b Match questions (1–5) with replies (a–e).

1 ☐ Are you going to read your speech from a card?
2 ☐ Can I borrow a pen?
3 ☐ I didn't understand your text message.
4 ☐ Can you recommend a good Italian restaurant here?
5 ☐ Can I put this jacket in the washing machine?

a There are a few, but I think Leonardo's is **by far** the best.
b No, I'm going to learn it **by heart**.
c Yes, of course. Oh, **by the way**, did you speak to Silvia?
d No, you need to wash it **by hand**.
e Sorry, it was for someone else. I sent it to you **by mistake**.

c Which phrase in **bold** in 3b do we use to start talking about something different?

d Match the other phrases in **bold** in 3b with the meanings (1–4).

1 without wanting to _____
2 without using a machine _____
3 much more than anything else _____
4 so you can remember it without reading _____

e Complete the sentences with expressions from 3b.

1 Hello! Are you enjoying the party? My name's Mark, _____.
2 I'm sorry, I turned on the washing machine _____ and now I can't stop it.
3 This form doesn't work on the computer, so I'll have to complete it _____.
4 I think that is _____ the best film in the cinema at the moment.
5 When I was at school, we learnt poems _____ and repeated them to the class.

f 💬 What is something you … ?

• know by heart   • do by hand   • often do by mistake

◑ REVIEW YOUR PROGRESS

How well did you do in this unit? Write 3, 2 or 1 for each objective.
3 = very well   2 = well   1 = not so well

I CAN …

Talk about music, art and literature	☐
Talk about sports and leisure activities	☐
Apologise, make and accept excuses	☐
Write a book review	☐

CAN DO OBJECTIVES

- Talk about future possibilities
- Describe actions and feelings
- Make telephone calls
- Write a personal profile

UNIT 9
Achievements

GETTING STARTED

a 💬 Look at the picture and answer the questions.

1 How old do you think the man in the picture is? How old are the children?
2 How do you think the man feels to be studying at this school? Why do you think he is doing it?

b ▶ 3.2 Listen to some informations about the man. Why do you think they made a film about his life? Would you like to see the film?

c 💬 In pairs, think of three things you will find out about the man in the film.

9A If I don't pass this exam, I won't be very happy

Learn to talk about future possibilities
G First conditional
V Degree subjects; Education collocations

1 VOCABULARY Degree subjects

a 💬 Ask and answer the questions.

1 Do most people in your country go to university? What are three popular degree subjects?
2 Is it important to go to university? Why / Why not?

b ▶ 3.3 Look at the pictures. Match the university degree subjects with the pictures. Listen and check.

☐ law   ☐ drama   ☐ medicine
☐ art   ☐ psychology   ☐ engineering
☐ business management   ☐ education

c 💬 Are the subjects in 1b common degrees in your country? Why do you think people study each subject?

2 READING AND SPEAKING

a 💬 Read the introduction and look at the names of the degree subjects in the article. Which degrees have you heard of before? What exactly do you think students learn in each of the degrees?

b Read the article and check your ideas in 2a. Underline the words which tell you what the students study.

c 💬 Discuss the meaning of any new words you underlined in the article with a partner.

d 💬 Work in pairs. Ask and answer the questions.

1 Which jobs do you think people can do with the degrees in the article? What kind of companies could they work for? Could they be self-employed?
2 Which degree in the article do you think would be the most useful in your country? Which would be the least useful?
3 Which degree would be the most fun or interesting for you? Which would you do well at?

Unusual degrees

Are you thinking about going to university? Do you think mathematics, physics and history sound boring? Well, there are a lot of unusual degrees that you might not know about. Here are some of our favourites.

Football Studies

Students learn about football and business, society and the media. They also study sports injuries and coaching. You don't need to play football to apply – there won't be any footballs in the exam room.

Citrus Studies

Yes, you can do a degree in oranges, lemons and limes! Students learn how to grow citrus fruits, which includes a lot of chemistry and biology. You'll get really healthy from all that fresh fruit!

Toy Design

Not ready to grow up yet? Then maybe you'd like to learn how to design toys for children. But don't think it will be easy just because you see the word 'toy'. Students on this course study child psychology, 3D design and mechanical engineering.

Bakery Science

Eating cake or biscuits is probably something you do for fun. But for students doing this course, it's part of studying. Students learn about chemistry and how to manage production. There is a bakery at the university, so students can practise what they're learning.

3 VOCABULARY
Education collocations

a Look at the words and phrases. Which refer to good students? Which refer to bad students? Write *G* or *B*.

- ☐ pass your exams ☐ fail your exams
- ☐ get low grades ☐ take notes
- ☐ revise ☐ hand an essay in late

b ▶ Now go to Vocabulary Focus 9A on p.139

4 LISTENING

a ▶ 3.5 Listen to five students talking about their studies. Which speakers have good study habits? Which have bad study habits?

good habits _____ bad habits _____

b ▶ 3.5 Listen again. Which speaker … ?

1 ☐ has just finished all their exams
2 ☐ is worried about an exam
3 ☐ has to make an important decision
4 ☐ is finding it difficult to complete a piece of work
5 ☐ knows what subject they want to study at university

c 💬 Which students in 4a are the most similar to you when you study?

Popular Music

You might think that students who do this degree just listen to pop music all day. But that's not true. Pop music involves the science of sound, production and engineering. Students get lectures from some really important people in the music industry.

Ceramics

If you like using your hands, then a course in ceramics might be for you. Students learn how to produce all kinds of ceramics – from fine art to dinner plates. They don't write any essays – all their grades are for exhibitions of their work.

5 GRAMMAR First conditional

a ▶ 3.6 Listen to the sentences and complete the missing words.

1 If I _____, I'm going to have a big party!
2 If I _____ _____ soon, I'll miss the deadline.
3 I might fail the year if she _____ _____ me more time.
4 If the questions _____ too hard, I might be OK.
5 I'm sure I'll get the grades I need if I _____ hard.

b Look at the sentences in 5a. Answer the questions and complete the rules.

1 Are the students talking about the present or the future?
2 Are the events possible or certain to happen?
3 What tense are the verbs in the *if* clause? Complete the rule.

We use *if* + subject + _____ to talk about a possible future situation. We use a future form to talk about the result of this situation.

c ▶ Now go to Grammar Focus 9A on p.158

d ▶ 3.8 **Pronunciation** Listen to the sentences. Notice the pause (//) between the two parts of the sentences.

1 If it rains this weekend, // I'll stay at home.
2 If I don't study hard, // I might not pass the exam.
3 If I see you after class, // I'll give you the book.
4 If I wake up at 10 am tomorrow, // I'll be in trouble at work.
5 If I have enough money next year, // I'm going to buy a new car.

e ▶ 3.8 Listen again and repeat.

f Look at the sentences in 5d again. Change the second half of the sentences so they are true for you.

g 💬 Work in pairs. Student A: read a sentence from 5d. Student B: ask an *if* question. How many exchanges can you make?

> If it rains this weekend, I'm going to watch TV at home.

> What if there aren't any good programmes?

> If there aren't any good programmes, I'll probably …

6 SPEAKING

a Think about your own future. Write down four important plans that you have. Think about:

- jobs
- relationships
- hobbies
- travel

b 💬 Work in small groups. Tell the group your plans. Listen to the other students' plans and ask *if* questions.

> Next week, I'm going to have a job interview in London.

> Will you move to London if you get the job?

9B I managed to stop feeling shy

Learn to describe actions and feelings
- **G** Verb patterns
- **V** Verbs followed by to + infinitive / verb -ing

1 SPEAKING AND LISTENING

a 💬 Which of these situations do you find easy? Which do you feel shy in?

1 speaking to people you don't know at a party

2 speaking to a stranger on a train or bus

3 talking in front of a big group of people

4 asking a stranger for directions

b 💬 Read the sentences about shy people. Do you think they are true (T) or (F) false?
1. ☐ More people are shy now than in the past.
2. ☐ Shy people are not interested in talking to other people.
3. ☐ Technology like the Internet can help shy people.
4. ☐ Shy people often have negative ideas about the future.

c ▶️ 3.9 Listen to an interview about shyness with Dr Lamb on a news programme. Check your answers to 1b.

d ▶️ 3.9 Listen again. What does Dr Lamb say about … ?
1. when shyness becomes a problem
2. why technology may cause shyness
3. the worries shy people have
4. how she helps shy people

e 💬 What do you think of Dr Lamb's advice? What do you do if you feel shy or nervous?

2 READING

a 💬 Are you interested in the lives of celebrities? Why / Why not? Which celebrities are you interested in?

b 💬 Look at the pictures of the celebrities in the article. Which problems from the list do you think each celebrity had?
- family disagreements
- language problems
- shyness
- not finishing school
- bullying

c Read the article. Check your answers to 2b.

THE NOT-SO-EASY LIVES OF
CELEBRITIES

You might think that the rich and famous have easy lives. But many had serious problems before they became successful.

Lady Gaga
Lady Gaga is famous for her unusual clothes and amazing performances. But she says she's actually very shy and she avoids meeting other artists. She says, 'I might not be shy with people that I know, but with people that I don't know I am very shy.'

Michael Phelps
Michael Phelps was bullied at school. Other children laughed at his big ears and long arms – the same long arms with which he won 18 Olympic gold medals. But Phelps says the experience helped him to become a champion. 'I kind of laugh at it now,' he says. 'I think it made me stronger going through that.'

Salma Hayek
When Mexican actress Salma Hayek moved to America, she couldn't speak English. She also has dyslexia, so she found it difficult to read and write. But Salma refused to give up. She learned to speak English quickly and in less than a year she was in her first English-language film. She says, 'Some people read really fast, but you'll ask them questions about the script and they'll forget. I take a long time to read a script, but I read it only once.'

d Cover the article. Can you remember who these sentences are about?

1 He often wears dark glasses and a hat in public.
2 He went to university to do a degree in business.
3 He has managed to win six Oscars.
4 Other children laughed at his big ears and long arms.
5 She learned to speak English quickly.
6 She avoids meeting other artists.

Read the text again and check.

e Answer the questions in pairs.

1 Who does Lady Gaga feel shy around?
2 Does Salma Hayek think it's better to read a script quickly?
3 How did bullying affect Michael Phelps's career?
4 Did Johnny Depp want to be famous?
5 Why did Peter Jackson leave school young?
6 What did Benicio Del Toro's father want him to do?

f Who do you think had the most difficult problem to deal with? Do you admire any of the celebrities? Why / Why not?

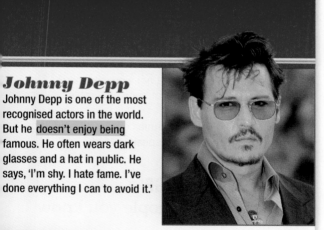

Johnny Depp
Johnny Depp is one of the most recognised actors in the world. But he doesn't enjoy being famous. He often wears dark glasses and a hat in public. He says, 'I'm shy. I hate fame. I've done everything I can to avoid it.'

Peter Jackson
When Peter Jackson – the director of *Lord of The Rings* – was nine years old, he saw the 1933 film *King Kong*, and from that moment he was always thinking about making films. He loved using the family video camera and at only 16 he left school. 'I just wanted to get out of school and into a job, any job, so that I could start saving money for the next piece of film equipment.' Without going to film school he has managed to win six Oscars and he has remade King Kong with a $207 million dollar budget.

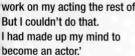

Benicio Del Toro
Oscar winner Benicio Del Toro came from a family of lawyers. His father wanted him to become a lawyer, too. He went to university to do a degree in business, but before he finished he decided to leave to study acting. But Del Toro doesn't regret not finishing university. 'My dad wanted me to go to law school part-time and work on my acting the rest of the time. But I couldn't do that. I had made up my mind to become an actor.'

3 GRAMMAR Verb patterns

a Look at the sentences below. What verb form follows the underlined verbs?

1 He <u>decided</u> to leave to study acting.
2 He <u>loved</u> using the family video camera.

b Look at the table and the highlighted words in the article. Complete the table with the verbs.

Verbs followed by *to* + infinitive	Verbs followed by verb + *-ing*
decide	love

c ▶ Now go to Grammar Focus 9B on p.158

4 VOCABULARY Verbs followed by *to* + infinitive / verb + *-ing*

a Find four more verbs in the article that are followed by *to* + infinitive or verb + *-ing*. Add them to the table in 3b.

b Work in pairs. What do the verbs in 4a mean?

c ▶ Now go to Vocabulary Focus 9B on p.139

5 SPEAKING

a Choose five topics from the list below. Think of an idea for each one. Write key words in each of the boxes, for example:

> visit parents

- A place you've **arranged to go** to soon.
- Something you **regret doing** when you were younger.
- Something you **promised to do** but didn't.
- Something difficult you **managed to do** recently.
- Something you're **avoiding doing** at the moment.
- Something you **forgot to do** that was very important.
- A place you would **recommend visiting** in your town or city.
- Something you **enjoy doing** when you have some free time.
- Something that you **miss doing**.

b Work in pairs. Try to guess your partner's ideas from their key words. Use the words in **bold** in 5a to ask questions.

> Are you avoiding visiting your parents?

> Did you forget to visit your parents?

> No. Of course I'm not avoiding visiting my parents. I love visiting them.

> Yes, I did. We had an arrangement, but I forgot.

91

9C Everyday English
Who's calling, please?

Learn to make telephone calls
- P Main stress: contrastive
- S Dealing with problems on the phone

1 LISTENING

a 🗨 Ask and answer the questions.

1 How often do you use the phone to talk to friends and family? How long are your calls?
2 When do you speak to people you don't know on the phone?
3 Have you ever spoken English on the phone? Who did you speak to? Did you have any problems?
4 Do you ever find speaking on the phone difficult? When?

b ▶3.12 Watch or listen to Part 1. Who is Annie trying to call? Is she going to call again later?

c ▶3.12 Watch or listen again. Answer the questions.

1 Why can't Annie speak to Mark?
2 What does Annie ask Mark's colleague to do?
3 What does Mark's colleague offer to do?
4 What two pieces of information does Mark's colleague ask for?

2 USEFUL LANGUAGE
Telephoning people you don't know

a ▶3.13 Complete the sentences with the words in the box. Then listen and check.

---
available   back   calling   got   there
possible   put   speaking   take
---

1 Is it _____ to speak to Mark Riley?
2 I'll just _____ you through.
3 Is Mark _____?
4 I'm afraid he's not _____.
5 Can I _____ a message?
6 Who's _____, please?
7 This is Annie Morton _____.
8 Shall I ask him to call you _____?
9 Has he _____ your number?

b Which sentences in 2a do you use if ... ?

1 you are calling
2 you have received a call

c Which sentence in 2a do you use ... ?

1 to say that you will connect the call
2 to say that someone else is busy
3 to ask for the caller's name
4 to suggest a future call

d 🗨 Work in groups of three. You are a caller, a receptionist and a colleague. Use the expressions in 2a to have a conversation like the one in Part 1.

3 LISTENING

a ▶3.14 Watch or listen to Part 2. When do Annie and Mark arrange to meet?

b ▶3.14 Watch or listen again. Answer the questions.

1 How is Annie feeling about her work situation?
2 What has Annie done about her work problems since she talked to Rachel?
3 Why does Mark suggest Annie comes to the office?
4 Why does Rachel want to speak to Mark?

4 USEFUL LANGUAGE
Telephoning people you know

a ▶3.15 Listen and complete the sentences.

1 Hi, _____ _____ Annie?
2 Hi, _____ Mark here.
3 Is now a _____ _____?
4 Sorry, can I _____ _____ back?
5 I've _____ _____ go.
6 Speak _____ _____ soon. Bye.

b ▶3.16 Correct five mistakes in the conversation. Listen and check.

A Oh hi, are you Bernice?
B Yes?
A It's Andrea here.
B Oh, hi.
A Is now a free time?
B Well, I'm a bit busy. Can I call you?
A Sure. Call me back when you're free. Is everything OK?
B Yeah, fine. But I've to go. Speak you soon.
A OK, bye.

c 🗨 Practise the conversation in 4b with a partner. Use your own names.

6 PRONUNCIATION Main stress: contrastive

a ▶ 3.18 Listen to the exchange. Which of the <u>underlined</u> words is emphasised most strongly?

Mark Sorry, was that three thirty tomorrow?
Annie No, <u>two thirty</u>.

b Why does Annie say the time differently? Choose the best answer.

1 because she doesn't understand what Mark said
2 because she is correcting what Mark said

c Work in pairs. Complete the questions about your partner. If you don't know, guess.

1 Were you born in _____? (place)
2 Is your birthday in _____? (month)
3 Do you live in _____? (place)
4 Do you come to class by _____? (transport)
5 Do you have a _____ mobile phone? (make of mobile phone, e.g. *Samsung*)
6 Do you prefer to listen to _____? (type of music)

d 🗩 Ask and answer the questions in 6c. Correct any mistakes your partner makes about you.

> Were you born in Madrid?
> No, I was born in Valencia.

7 SPEAKING

a 🗩 Work in pairs. Choose one of the situations and have a telephone conversation.

Caller
1 Call reception and ask for Mr Taylor.
2 Call your friend to arrange a trip to the cinema.
3 Call your friend about the trip next week.
4 Call Mr Colson's office. Ask him to call you back.

Person receiving the call
1 Mr Taylor isn't in. Take a message.
2 You'd prefer to go to a restaurant. There's someone at the door.
3 You're very busy and you can't hear very well.
4 Answer your colleague Mr Colson's phone. Take a message.

> Hello. Is it possible to speak to Mr Taylor?
> I'm afraid he's not in …

b 🗩 Swap roles and have a conversation for a different situation in 7a.

5 CONVERSATION SKILLS
Dealing with problems on the phone

a ▶ 3.17 Listen and complete the exchanges.

Mark Rachel explained you're looking for a new job.
Annie Sorry, Mark, [1]_____ .

Annie How about two thirty tomorrow?
Mark Sorry, [2]_____ three thirty tomorrow?
Annie No, two thirty.

b Look at the completed exchanges in 5a. Which phrase do you use … ?

☐ to say that you didn't hear what someone said
☐ to check that you heard what someone said correctly

C Unit Progress Test

CHECK YOUR PROGRESS

You can now do the Unit Progress Test.

1 LISTENING AND SPEAKING

a 💬 Look at the different ways of learning and answer the questions.

- reading about a topic
- listening to someone explain
- group work
- online or with an app
- in a classroom with a teacher
- one-to-one with a teacher
- studying on your own

1 What different ways have you experienced?
2 Are there any other ways you can think of?
3 Which ways do you prefer?

b ▶️ 3.19 Listen to Janina and Roberta talking about online learning. Who is worried about online learning? Why?

c ▶️ 3.19 Listen again. Are the sentences true (*T*) or false (*F*)? Correct the false sentences.

1 ☐ Janina's going to do an online course next year.
2 ☐ Roberta prefers learning in a classroom.
3 ☐ Roberta likes to choose when she studies.
4 ☐ Roberta couldn't meet her teachers during her online course.
5 ☐ Roberta liked reading the students' online profiles.
6 ☐ Janina needs to have excellent IT skills for the course.
7 ☐ Janina must do the introduction course very soon.

d 💬 Make a list of good and bad points for studying in class with a teacher and studying online.

```
      in class with a teacher              online
        /        \                       /        \
good points   bad points        good points   bad points
```

e 💬 Work in small groups. Talk about your ideas. Decide which kind of study you prefer and tell the group.

2 READING

a Janina decided to do the online learning introduction course. Read her profile and the profile of another student, Gonzalo. What do Janina and Gonzalo have in common?

b Read the profiles again. Make notes and complete the table.

	Janina	Gonzalo
degree subjects		
languages		
reason for doing the online course		
work / free time		

◁▷⌂ ⊕

▦ **WELCOME VISITOR** (Login)

Home   Teach   Learn   **Community**

Janina
Jakubowska

TELL US ABOUT YOU . . .
Hello, everyone. My name's Janina and I'm doing a psychology degree here in Birmingham. [1]It's a great course and I'm really enjoying it, although it's hard work. I've just finished my second year, so I've got [2]one left – the hardest one!

I was born in Poland, but I came to live in England when I was about eight years old. I speak English and Polish, but I'm better at writing in English than in Polish.

HOW DO YOU FEEL ABOUT THIS COURSE?
I'm really looking forward to learning about online courses. [3]They're completely new to me. I think my IT skills are a bit poor so this course might be a good way to improve [4]them.

WHAT DO YOU DO WHEN YOU'RE NOT STUDYING?
I have a part-time job in a restaurant. I work there one night in the week and all day on Saturday. [5]This means I don't have a lot of time for myself, but that's OK. It's not forever.

Gonzalo
Lopez

TELL US ABOUT YOU ...

Hi, everyone. I'm Gonzalo and I come from Mexico. Next year, I really want to do a business degree. I've already got one in sports science. I did it here in Mexico City, but ⁶it was in English and not in Spanish. I'm sure you've already guessed that I can speak Spanish as well as English – ⁷it's my first language after all.

HOW DO YOU FEEL ABOUT THIS COURSE?

If I pass this online introduction course and an English test, then I'll get a place on a business degree programme. I'm excited about being in Mexico, but studying with people in the UK! ⁸It's really cool.

WHAT DO YOU DO WHEN YOU'RE NOT STUDYING?

I work as the manager of a gym, and that's why I want to do the Business Administration degree. Some day I'd like to own it, or ⁹one that is similar. In my free time, I watch sport. I'll watch any sport and I'll try anything, but my favourite sport is football. I also have a girlfriend, Claudia. Luckily, she likes football too, so I can watch matches with ¹⁰her!

3 WRITING SKILLS Avoiding repetition

a Look at the sentences. How is the second sentence different from the sentence in Janina's profile? Underline the different words.

> My name's Janina and I'm doing a psychology degree here in Birmingham. My psychology degree is a great course and I'm really enjoying the course, although the course is hard work.

Why didn't Janina use the sentence above?

b We use different pronouns to avoid repeating information. Notice the highlighted words in the profiles. Find and underline the information the pronouns replace.

c Look at these sentences from Gonzalo's profile. What is the difference between the pronouns *it* and *one*?

> I work as the manager of a gym and that's why I want to do the Business Administration degree. Some day I'd like to own it, or one that is similar.

d Read Muneera's profile and change the highlighted words to pronouns.

Muneera
Farzath

TELL US ABOUT YOU ...

Hello, everyone. My name's Muneera. ¹Muneera's an Arabic name and ²Muneera means 'brilliant'. I have a degree in International Studies, which I did in English. Arabic is my first language, but I can speak and write English well. I live in Kuwait with my family – my father, my mother and my two brothers. ³My family all work in my father's electronics shop.

HOW DO YOU FEEL ABOUT THIS COURSE?

I'm looking forward to this course and I hope ⁴this course will help me to study online more easily. ⁵Studying online is something I find quite difficult.

WHAT DO YOU DO WHEN YOU'RE NOT STUDYING?

In my free time I like seeing my friends. I often go to the cinema with ⁶my friends. One of ⁷my friends, Aaminah, is also taking this course, so you'll meet ⁸Aaminah here too!

4 WRITING

a Write a student profile about yourself for an online English language course. Use the same headings as the students on this page. Make notes.
- Tell us about you ...
- How do you feel about this course?
- What do you do when you're not studying?

b Write your student profile. Make sure you use pronouns to avoid repeating information.

c Work in pairs. Exchange profiles. Check your partner has used pronouns to avoid repetition.

UNIT 9
Review and extension

1 GRAMMAR

a Choose the correct answers.

1 If I *study / will study* hard, I think I'll pass my exams.
2 I *go / 'm going to go* on holiday later in the year if my boss lets me.
3 If I *don't / won't* go to the lesson, I might miss something.
4 I might get a pay rise if I *work / 'll work* hard this year.
5 I *might buy / buy* tickets for the concert next week if I have enough money.
6 If I *won't / can't* find a job in my country, I'll move abroad.

b Complete the conversation between a careers adviser and a student with the best answers.

A So, have you thought about what to do after your course?
B I've decided ¹*to leave / leaving* education and find a job.
A OK, and what kind of job do you want ²*to do / doing*?
B I'm not sure, but I need to start ³*to think / thinking* about it!
A OK, well let's think about the work environment. Imagine ⁴*to work / working* in an office – does that sound good?
B Not really. I really love ⁵*to be / being* outside. And I don't like ⁶*to use / using* computers.
A Right. I'd like you to go away and make a list of outdoor jobs you could do. Then we can arrange ⁷*to talk / talking* again.
B All right, I'll come back next week then.
A Great. And don't forget ⁸*to bring / bringing* the list!

c 💬 Practise the conversation in 1b.

2 VOCABULARY

a Write the names of the degree subjects.

1 I'm learning to become an actor. d _ _ _ a
2 When I finish I'm going to work as a teacher. e _ _ _ _ _ _ _ n
3 I've always wanted to be a doctor, so it's the right course for me. m _ _ _ _ _ _ _ e
4 I want to be a manager at a big company one day. b _ _ _ _ _ _ _ s m _ _ _ _ _ _ _ _ _ t
5 I'm learning to design roads and bridges. e _ _ _ _ _ _ _ _ _ g
6 I study how the brain works. p _ _ _ _ _ _ _ _ y

b Complete the sentences with the verbs in the box.

fail get (x2) hand in revise take

1 If you _____ into a good university, you'll find a good job.
2 It's important to _____ notes when you're in a lesson.
3 It's embarrassing to _____ an exam.
4 It's difficult to _____ good marks without studying.
5 It's a bad idea to _____ the evening before you have an exam.
6 If you _____ work late, the teacher should give you zero.

c 💬 Do you disagree with any of the sentences in 2b?

3 WORDPOWER Multi-word verbs with *put*

a Match sentences (1–7) with the replies (a–g).

1 ☐ It's too dark to read in here.
2 ☐ Have you seen my glasses?
3 ☐ Don't you have a meeting with your teacher today?
4 ☐ You don't look very happy.
5 ☐ Come on – the exam starts in 20 minutes.
6 ☐ Can I borrow your dictionary?
7 ☐ Are you still on the phone?

a I think you **put** them **down** there, next to your books.
b No, the university has **put up** its prices. I don't think I can pay for my course.
c OK – but **put it back** in my bag once you've finished.
d I'll **put on** the light.
e Yes. I'm waiting for them to **put me through** to the right person.
f I just want to **put on** my coat. It's always cold in that big room.
g No, she **put it off** until next week – she's too busy at the moment.

b Match the multi-word verbs with *put* in 3a with the meanings.

1 ☐ decide to do something later than you planned
2 ☐ start to wear
3 ☐ turn on (something electrical)
4 ☐ put an object on the floor or on top of something
5 ☐ connect someone on the telephone to the person they want to speak to
6 ☐ make a price higher
7 ☐ return something to the right place

c Complete the sentences with expressions with *put*.

1 My mum _puts_ her things _down_ and then can't find them!
2 The government _____ _____ the prices of train and bus tickets every year.
3 I _____ my work _____ until I really need to do it.
4 I _____ _____ the TV as soon as I get home.
5 Most receptionists _____ you _____ to the right person when you phone.
6 I _____ _____ my favourite clothes at weekends.
7 I _____ things _____ when I've finished using them.

d 💬 Work in pairs. Which of the sentences in 3c are true for you?

CAN DO OBJECTIVES

- Talk about moral dilemmas
- Describe problems with goods and services
- Return goods and make complaints
- Write an apology email

UNIT 10
Values

GETTING STARTED

a Describe what is happening in the picture.

b What do you think happens next? Think of three ideas.

c In pairs, ask and answer the questions. Say why.

1 If you were looking from a window and you saw this happening, would you call the police?

2 Would your answer be the same if … ?
- you were abroad
- it was your car
- you knew the man
- you were in the street (not looking out the window)

1 SPEAKING

a Match the activities to pictures 1–5.

a ☐ driving too fast on the motorway
b ☐ parking your car illegally
c ☐ taking printer paper from work to use at home
d ☐ taking a towel from a hotel
e ☐ illegally downloading a film from the Internet

b 💬 Work in pairs. Which of the things in the pictures do you think is the worst thing to do? Put the activities in order from 1 (worst) to 5 (least bad).

c 💬 Do people in your country often do these things? Which ones?

2 LISTENING

a 💬 Read the text about illegal downloading. Do you agree with Philip Pullman?

b ▶3.20 Listen to a radio programme about illegal downloading. Would each speaker download anything illegally? What would they download?

Speaker 1 _____
Speaker 2 _____
Speaker 3 _____
Speaker 4 _____
Speaker 5 _____

c ▶3.20 Listen again. What reason does each speaker give for their answers in 2b?

d 💬 Which speakers 1–5 do you disagree with? Which speakers do you feel similar to?

Illegal downloading is wrong, says author Philip Pullman

" Philip Pullman, the author of the famous *His Dark Materials* book series, says in an article that downloading illegally from the Internet is like stealing money from someone's pocket. In the article, he writes that it's wrong to steal an artist's work. He says that people who want to enjoy an artist's work should have to buy it first. "

3 GRAMMAR
Second conditional

a ▶ **3.21** Complete the sentences from the listening with a verb. Listen and check.

1 If you _____ to watch a TV programme, would you download it illegally?
2 If the programme _____ available, I'd download it.
3 If I _____ the album, I'd buy it afterwards.
4 I wouldn't download an album if it _____ for charity.
5 I'd ask my granddaughter to download it for me if I really _____ to see it!

b Look at the sentences in 3a. Choose the correct option, a or b, to complete the sentences.

1 We use the second conditional to talk about:
   a a real future situation
   b an imagined present or future situation
2 The verb form that follows *if* is:
   a a present tense
   b a past tense
3 The highlighted verb in the examples is:
   a *would* + infinitive
   b *had* + infinitive

c ▶ Now go to Grammar Focus 10A on p.160

d ▶ **3.23** **Pronunciation** Listen to the sentences. Notice how the vowel sounds in **bold** are pronounced.

1 **Wou**ld you download the album?
2 Yes, I **wou**ld.
3 No, I **wou**ldn't.
4 I **wou**ldn't download a charity album.
5 What **wou**ld you download?

e ▶ **3.23** Listen again and answer the questions about the sentences in 3d.

1 Do you hear the /l/ or is it silent?
2 When is *would* (or *wouldn't*) unstressed? Tick ✓ one.
   ☐ questions   ☐ negatives   ☐ short answers
3 When *would* is unstressed is it pronounced … ?
   ☐ /wʊd/   ☐ /wəd/

f Think of two different ideas to complete each sentence.

1 If it wasn't against the rules, … *I'd listen to music at work.*
2 If it wasn't so expensive, …
3 … if I practised.

g ◯ Compare your sentences with a partner's.

> If it wasn't against the rules, I'd play my music at work.   It helps me concentrate!   Why?

4 VOCABULARY Multi-word verbs

a ◯ What's happening in each picture below? Choose the best thing to do next from the two phrases.

- **carry on** driving
- stop and look at the damage

- **look after** a lost cat
- not do anything

- **hand in** lost money to the police station
- look for the person who dropped it

Can you finish this tonight?

Dinner – Georgie 7.00pm

- **put off** your arrangements
- say no

b Look at the multi-word verbs in **bold**. Match them with the dictionary definitions.

1 _____ take care of something or someone
2 _____ decide or arrange to do something at a later time
3 _____ continue doing something
4 _____ give something to someone in a position of authority

c ▶ Now go to Vocabulary Focus 10A on p.140

5 SPEAKING

a ◯ Ask and answer the questions.

1 Do you always tell the truth? Why / Why not?
2 Who is the most honest person you know? Why did you choose that person?

b ▶ **Communication 10A** How honest is your partner? Do the quiz to find out. Student A: go to p.129. Student B: go to p.131.

Learn to describe problems with goods and service

G Quantifiers; *too / not enough*
V Noun formation

1 READING AND SPEAKING

a 💬 In your country, is it OK to complain in a shop? What do people complain about?

b What are these people complaining about? Match the complaints (1–4) with the words in the box.

> service   quality   price   delivery

1 This pizza is much cheaper in the other shop.
2 I bought this watch last week and it's already broken.
3 I ordered the rug two weeks ago, but it hasn't arrived yet.
4 I've been in this queue for 20 minutes now – they're so slow.

c 💬 Have you had any similar problems to b1–4 recently?

d 💬 Read the title of the text below. Does the information surprise you?

e Read the text quickly and underline:

1 the top four nations of complainers in Europe
2 the survey questions
3 what the British complain about most
4 the maximum time British people are happy to queue
5 the most common reason not to complain

f 💬 Read the text again. Are there any things that people in your country wouldn't complain about, but the British do? Why / Why not?

2 GRAMMAR Quantifiers; *too / not enough*

a Look at the complaints and answer the questions.

The service is <u>not</u> good <u>enough</u>.
31% are <u>too</u> embarrassed to complain.
There are<u>n't enough</u> shop assistants.
The queue is<u>n't</u> moving quickly <u>enough</u>.
There are <u>too many</u> people in the pool.
There's <u>too much</u> salt on my food.

1 Which of the <u>underlined</u> words say something is … ?
   a more than the right amount
   b less than the right amount

2 Do we put *enough* before or after … ?
   a adjectives   b adverbs   c nouns

3 Which word do we use after *too* with … ?
   a countable nouns
   b uncountable nouns

b ▶ Now go to Grammar Focus 10B on p.160

c Choose the correct options to complete the complaints.

1 The water was *too much / too cold*.
2 There were *too much / too many* children running around.
3 The room wasn't *warm enough / enough warm*.
4 There was *too / too much* noise, so we couldn't hear everything.
5 There weren't *enough seats / seats enough* for everyone.
6 We didn't stop for *long enough / enough long* in each place.

d 💬 What do you think the situation was for each complaint in 2c?

UK shoppers are some of the biggest complainers in Europe

CUSTOMER SERVICE

A recent survey has found that British people complain more than any other European nation. 96% of British people said that they would complain if they received poor service in a shop. The top four complaining nations also included the Germans, the Italians and the Swedish.

In the survey, shoppers across Europe were asked how often, why and when they complain. Shoppers who don't complain were asked why not?

What do the British complain about?

The most common reason British shoppers give for a complaint is that the service is not good enough. If there aren't enough shop assistants or the queue isn't moving quickly enough, the British get angry. The British love a well-organised queue. When asked how long they queue before they get annoyed, they said more than five minutes was too long. Poor-quality products, rude staff and delivery problems are also common reasons. 76% of British shoppers feel 'If customers don't complain, companies can't improve.'

Why do some choose not to complain?

For the few British people who don't complain, 42% don't have time, 37% feel it doesn't help and 31% feel too embarrassed.

COMPLAINTS AROUND THE WORLD

A recent survey has revealed the countries where people like to complain the most. 30,000 people in 30 different countries were asked the question, 'Have you made a complaint in the last 12 months?'

Top of the list was the UK, with Sweden second and Australia third. At the bottom of the list were Saudi Arabia, China and Poland.

TOP TEN	BOTTOM TEN
1 UK	30 Saudi Arabia
2 Sweden	29 China
3 Australia	28 Poland
4 Canada	27 Russia
5 USA	26 Turkey
6 Brazil	25 Spain
7 Argentina	24 Egypt
8 South Africa	23 Thailand
9 France	22 Indonesia
10 Venezuela	21 Japan

3 LISTENING

a Look at the results of an international survey above. Where is your country on the list? If it's not there, where on the list do you think it would be?

b ▶3.26 Listen to a radio programme about the survey. Answer the questions.
1 What two countries are the guests from?
2 Are the guests surprised by the survey results?

c ▶3.26 Listen again. Answer the questions.
1 What two reasons does the first guest give for why people in her country complain more these days?
2 What does the second guest say are two advantages of buying things online in his country?

d Is your country similar to the guests' countries?

e Work in pairs. Complete the sentences to make seven good pieces of advice.
1 Don't wait to complain. Do it _____ the problem happens.
2 Be polite: choose your words carefully and don't _____ .
3 Be clear: give a good _____ of the problem.
4 Give the company a time limit. Say you want a _____ within ten days.
5 Don't be afraid to go to the top: speak to the _____ or write to the _____ of the company.
6 Letters are usually the best way to complain: you can _____ the problem in detail and avoid getting too _____ .
7 Tell them how you _____ . Say how the problem spoiled your _____ .

f ▶3.27 Now listen to an interview with an expert on complaining. Is his advice the same as yours?

g Ask and answer the questions.
1 Which advice from the listening would work in your country? Which advice wouldn't? Why?
2 Is there any different advice you would give to a visitor to your country if they wanted to complain about something?

4 VOCABULARY Noun formation

a Complete the table with words from this lesson.

Verb	Noun
_____	choice
complain	_____
deliver	_____
_____	explanation
decide	_____
describe	_____
enjoy	_____
_____	queue

b ▶3.28 **Pronunciation** Listen to the words in 4a. Underline the stressed syllable in each word.

c ▶3.28 Listen again. Notice when the vowel sound changes, for example *choose* /uː/ *choice* /ɔɪ/. Then listen again and repeat.

d Complete the sentences with words from 4a.
1 Do you have a good c_____ of shops where you live?
2 When was the last time you made a c_____ in a shop?
3 Does it annoy you when you have to q_____ in a shop?
4 Have you ever bought something online that was different from the d_____ when it arrived?
5 Have you ever had a problem with the d_____ of something you bought?
6 What's the worst d_____ you've ever made when buying something?

e Ask and answer the questions in 4d.

5 SPEAKING

Ask and answer the questions. Who is the biggest complainer?
1 Would you complain if … ?
   • your bill at a restaurant was a bit too high
   • you booked a hotel room with one large bed but you got a room with two single beds
   • you ordered a pizza but they delivered the wrong one
   • you ordered something online and it arrived a week late
   • you couldn't hear a film in the cinema because other people were too noisy
2 How would you complain in each situation? What would you say?

10C Everyday English
Can I exchange it for something else?

Learn to return goods and make complaints

P Sentence stress
S Sounding polite

1 LISTENING

a 💬 What reasons can you think of for returning each of these things to a shop?

- a pair of jeans
- a DVD
- a sandwich
- a present you've received

b Look at the notice in a shop. Match the highlighted words with the definitions.

> **For customers who wish to return goods to this shop**
>
> We will give a refund or exchange your goods for products of equal value if:
> i) you bought the goods less than 14 days ago
> ii) you have a receipt.
>
> Thank you for shopping with us.

1 _____ a piece of paper that shows how much you paid for something
2 _____ to change a product you bought for a different one
3 _____ money given to you when you return something to a shop
4 _____ _____ something which is sold in a shop

c 💬 Are the rules in 1b the same as shops in your country? Do all shops in your country have the same rules? Explain any differences.

d ▶3.29 Watch or listen to Part 1. What does Leo want to return? Why? Why isn't it possible?

2 USEFUL LANGUAGE
Returning goods and making complaints

a ▶3.29 Look at the phrases. Which of the phrases did you hear in Part 1? Watch or listen again and check. Tick ✓ the phrases.

Returning something to a shop
- ☐ Could you help me, please?
- ☐ I'd like to return this clock, please.
- ☐ It doesn't fit.
- ☐ I've changed my mind.
- ☐ It was a present, but [I've already got one].
- ☐ I'd like a refund.
- ☐ Can I exchange it for something else?

Complaining
- ☐ Could I speak to the manager, please?
- ☐ I'd like to make a complaint.
- ☐ I've been here for [a very long time].
- ☐ Your sales assistant hasn't been very helpful.
- ☐ This isn't what I ordered.
- ☐ It doesn't work.

b 💬 Look at the phrases you didn't tick in 2a. What shopping situations could you use them in?

c ▶3.30 Now look at the phrases that shop assistants use. Complete them with the missing words. Listen and check.

refund	receipt	replace	sorry	right away	exchange

1 Would you like to _____ it for something?
2 Do you have a _____?
3 I'm terribly _____ …
4 I'll ask someone to look at that for you _____.
5 I'll _____ it immediately.
6 I'll give you a full _____.

d Complete the conversations with words from 2a and 2c. Where are the people in each conversation?

1 A I'd like to make [1]_____ _____.
B What's the problem?
A This phone doesn't [2]_____. It's completely dead.
B I'm [3]_____ sorry. I'll ask someone to [4]_____ _____ that for you right away.

2 A I'd like to exchange these jeans please. They don't [5]_____ – they're too small.
B OK. Do you have a [6]_____?
A Yes, here you are.

3 A Excuse me?
B Yes, sir?
A We've been [7]_____ for an hour, but we haven't ordered yet.
B I'm terribly sorry, sir, but we're extremely busy. We'll be with you as soon as we can.
A Right. Could I speak to the [8]_____, please?

e 💬 Work in pairs. Practise the conversations in 2d.

3 LISTENING

a ▶️**3.31** Leo is going to speak to the manager about his clock. Do you think he will get a refund? Why / Why not? Watch or listen to Part 2 and check.

b ▶️**3.31** Watch or listen again. Answer the questions.

1 What three questions does the manager ask Leo?
- What _____?
- Is there anything _____?
- Why do you _____?
2 What reasons does Leo give for returning the clock?
3 Why does the manager agree to let Leo return the clock?
4 What does Leo decide to do in the end?
5 What reason does he give for his decision?

c 💬 What was the last thing you returned to a shop? Why did you return it?

4 PRONUNCIATION Sentence stress

a ▶️**3.32** Listen to the questions. Which of the highlighted words are stressed?

1 Do you have a receipt?
2 Could you help me, please?
3 Could I speak to the manager, please?
4 Why do you want a refund?
5 What would you like to exchange it for?
6 How can I help?

b Look at your answers in 4a. Which kinds of word are not normally stressed in questions?

- [ ] question words (e.g. *why*, *what*)
- [ ] auxiliary verbs (e.g. *do*, *be*, *can*, *could*)
- [ ] pronouns (e.g. *I*, *you*)
- [ ] main verbs (e.g. *help*, *speak*)

c ▶️**3.32** Listen again and repeat the questions in 4a.

5 CONVERSATION SKILLS
Sounding polite

a Look at the pairs of sentences. Which sentence in each pair is more polite? Which did Leo use?

1 a It's a bit ugly. 2 a It's not very adult.
  b It's ugly.   b It's childish.

b Choose the correct words to complete the rules.

> To describe a problem more politely, we use:
> - *not very* / *a bit* + negative adjective
> - *not very* / *a bit* + opposite positive adjective

c Write two ways to say each adjective more politely.

1 *dirty*: a bit _____, not very _____
2 *slow*: not very _____, a bit _____
3 *rude*: not very _____, a bit _____
4 *cold*: a bit _____, not very _____

d 💬 Work in pairs. Think of things you could complain about using the phrases in 5c. Make sentences.

> This seat isn't very clean.

> The waiter was a bit rude.

6 SPEAKING

a 💬 Work in pairs.

Student A: you are a customer. Choose something to complain about. Use ideas from this lesson or your own ideas. Think about:

- where you are
- what the problem is
- what you want

Student B: deal with Student A's complaint.

b 💬 Swap roles. Choose a different thing to complain about and deal with the complaint.

> Could you help me, please?

> Of course. What seems to be the problem?

> This food isn't very hot …

♻ Unit Progress Test

CHECK YOUR PROGRESS

You can now do the Unit Progress Test.

10D Skills for Writing
We're really sorry we missed it

Learn to write an apology email

W Formal and informal language

Tim

Vicki

Rebecca

1 LISTENING AND SPEAKING

a What would you do in these situations? Read and make notes.

1 You invite a lot of people to a party and ask them to reply to your invitation. However, some people don't reply.
2 You go into a shop and the two shop assistants continue having a private conversation and do not offer you any help.

b 💬 Compare your ideas in 1a with a partner.

c ▶ 3.33 Listen to Tim, Vicki and Rebecca. Match each person with a situation in 1a. Who talks about a different situation? What is it?

d ▶ 3.33 Listen again and answer the questions.

1 What did Tim want to ask the shop assistants?
2 What did he do when the shop assistants didn't help him?
3 What would Vicki do if she was the manager of a company?
4 What does she say she won't do in the future?
5 Why did Rebecca want people to reply to her invitation?
6 Why did she feel embarrassed at her party?

e Think of an experience you had where you felt someone's behaviour was rude. Make notes. Use the questions to help.

- When? • Who? • Where? • What happened?
- What was the result?

f 💬 Tell a partner about your experience.

2 READING

a Read the three apology emails. Which email is about … ?

1 ☐ customer service
2 ☐ work
3 ☐ a social situation

b Read the emails and answer the questions.

1 What is each person apologising for?
2 What offer or suggestion does each person make?

c What are the relationships between the writer of each email and the person they are writing to? Which relationship is the most formal?

(a)

Hi Jack and Brenda,

A quick message to say we're really sorry we had to leave early last Saturday. The dinner was terrific and we had a great time. It's a shame the woman looking after the kids felt unwell and we had to go home. You must come round to our house for dinner.

We'll be in touch soon.

All the best,

Don

3 WRITING SKILLS Formal and informal language

a Look at the sentences from the texts in 2a. Match 1–4 with a–d.

	Informal language	Semi-formal	More formal
1	Hi Jack and Brenda,	Dear Celia,	Dear Mrs Palmer,
2	A quick message to say …	I'm writing to let you know …	We are writing to …
3	We're really sorry …	I'm very sorry to …	We are writing to apologise …
4	All the best, Don	Best wishes, Katie	Yours sincerely, Keith Hughes

a ☐ reason for writing   b ☐ sign off   c ☐ greeting   d ☐ apology

b Look at the examples in the table. Which type of email does not use contractions? Why?

c Make this email between two close friends more informal. Use the examples in 3a to help you.

> Dear Mark,
>
> I hope you are well. I am writing you a quick message to say we got the invitation to your party. We apologise, but we cannot come. We are going to a wedding that day. We will be in touch soon.
>
> Yours sincerely,
>
> Paul

d Look at the first paragraph of each apology email in 2a. How do the writers organise their ideas?

1 apologise then explain
2 explain then apologise

Do they apologise and explain in the same sentence? Or in two separate sentences?

4 WRITING

a You are going to write an informal email of apology. Write to Rebecca in 1a, or use your own idea. Make notes using these ideas.

- think about how you can say sorry
- think of an explanation for what you did
- make an offer or a suggestion to make things better

b Write the email. Use informal language.

c Read other students' emails. Is the correct kind of language used? Would you feel better if you received this apology?

(b)

> Dear Mrs Palmer,
>
> Thank you for your email of 22 May about the delivery problem you had. We are writing to apologise about the long delivery time you experienced. Recently, we have had a few problems and we are working hard to reduce these times for our customers.
>
> We hope you will shop with us again, so we are offering you a 10% discount on the next book you buy from us. This is our way of saying sorry about the problems you have had.
>
> Yours sincerely,
>
> Keith Hughes
>
> Customer Services Manager

(c)

> Dear Celia,
>
> I'm writing to let you know that we need to rearrange tomorrow's meeting. I'm very sorry about that.
>
> Unfortunately, Garry has just asked me to prepare a report on the staff we have here in our London office – he says it's urgent. Could we meet next Monday afternoon instead? I'm very sorry to put our meeting off, but I have to finish this report by end of the day tomorrow. Let me know if next Monday afternoon is possible for you.
>
> Best wishes,
>
> Katie

UNIT 10
Review and extension

1 GRAMMAR

a Complete the conversation with the correct form of the verbs.

A There was an interesting story in the newspaper yesterday. A man found €10,000 in a bag on the train and he gave it to the police.

B He sounds very honest. What ¹_____ you _____ (do) if you ²_____ (be) in the same situation?

A Well, I think if it ³_____ (be) a lot of money, I ⁴_____ (keep) it!

B But if someone ⁵_____ (see) you take it, you ⁶_____ (get) into trouble. And if you ⁷_____ (hand) it in, I think the owner ⁸_____ (give) you some money to say thank you.

A Maybe, but the newspaper said the owner of the bag wanted to take the man out for dinner.

B Only dinner? I ⁹_____ (expect) more than that if I ¹⁰_____ (give back) a bag full of money!

b 💬 Practise the conversation in 1a.

c Choose the correct answers.

1 I can't work here. There's too *much / many* noise.
2 It's not *warm enough / enough warm* to sit outside.
3 We had *a few / a bit of* time before our flight to look round the duty free.
4 It was a great concert – there were *too many / a lot of* fans in the crowd.
5 We don't have *money enough / enough money* to buy it.
6 They don't have *many / much* kinds of bread in this shop.

2 VOCABULARY

a Choose the correct answers.

1 There isn't much *choice / choose* in shops in my town/city.
2 I never *complain / complaint* in shops.
3 I'm not very good at making a quick *decide / decision*.
4 I don't believe the *descriptions / describes* of products.
5 I really *enjoy / enjoyment* going shopping.

b 💬 Which of the sentences in 2a are true for you?

c Complete the sentences with the correct form of the verbs in the box.

break	carry	come	feel	look	pass	join	turn

1 Can you _____ after my bag while I go and get a ticket?
2 I was sorry to hear that Sara and Michael have _____ up.
3 We don't really _____ like going out this evening.
4 He got offered a great job, but he _____ it down.
5 Mrs Robson isn't here at the moment, but I can _____ on a message.
6 This is fun. Why don't you _____ in?
7 I asked him to be quiet, but he _____ on talking.
8 _____ round for a coffee tomorrow if you've got time.

3 WORDPOWER Multi-word verbs with *on*

a Read the sentences. Which of the expressions in **bold** are about … ?

• continuing to do something
• wearing something

1 He was really tired, but he **carried on** jogging.
2 Louise really needs to **get on with** her essay tonight.
3 It was sunny, so he **put on** his sunglasses.
4 I don't know if I can **go on** living in this flat.
5 I **tried on** the trousers, but they weren't very comfortable.
6 I asked him to be quiet, but he **kept on** talking.
7 It was cold inside, so he **kept** his coat **on**.

b Read the definitions of the 'continuing' expressions. Complete the sentences with the best verbs.

go on, carry on – continue to do
keep on – continue to do, often something annoying
get on with – continue work or activities you need to do

1 My phone _____ on switching off. It's really annoying.
2 I'm going home now. I have to _____ on with my revision.
3 My father _____ / _____ / _____ on working until he was 80

c Match the 'wearing' expressions (1–3) with the meanings (a–c).

1 ☐ try on clothes
2 ☐ put on clothes
3 ☐ keep clothes on

a you do this in the morning or when you feel cold
b this is when you continue to wear clothes longer than norma
c you normally do this in a clothes shop

d Match the sentence halves.

1 ☐ I always try on
2 ☐ I want to carry on
3 ☐ I have to get on with
4 ☐ I normally keep my shoes on
5 ☐ In winter, I usually put on

a studying English next year.
b when I go to someone's house.
c clothes before I buy them.
d a hat and scarf when I go out.
e some really important work tomorrow.

e 💬 Which of the sentences in 3d are true for you?

⟳ REVIEW YOUR PROGRESS

How well did you do in this unit? Write 3, 2 or 1 for each objective.
3 = very well   2 = well   1 = not so well

I CAN …

Talk about moral dilemmas	☐
Describe problems with goods and services	☐
Return goods and make complaints	☐
Write an apology email	☐

CAN DO OBJECTIVES

- Explain what technology does
- Describe how discoveries were made
- Ask for and give directions in a building
- Write a post expressing an opinion

UNIT 11

Discovery and Invention

GETTING STARTED

a 💬 Look at the picture and answer the questions.

1 What is the robot dog doing?
2 Why do you think the boy's parents bought him a robot dog?
3 Do you think he would prefer a real dog? Why?
4 What can the robot dog do that a real dog can't do? What can't it do?
5 In pairs, make a list of the good and bad things about having a robot dog (not a real dog).

b 💬 In pairs, ask and answer the questions.

Would you like to own any kind of robot?
- If yes, what would it do?
- If no, why not?

107

Learn to explain what technology does

- **G** Defining relative clauses
- **V** Compound nouns

1 READING AND LISTENING

a 💬 Look at titles of the films and books in the article. What kind of stories are they? Have you seen or read any of them? What are they about?

b Read the introduction to the article. What do e-book readers and cash machines have in common?

c Read the article. What ideas come from each sci-fi book/film?

Back to the Future II <u>flying cars</u>
AI _____
Iron Man _____
Minority Report _____ and
_____

d ⏵**3.34** Do you think people have invented the technology in 1c in real life yet? Tell a partner. Then listen and check.

e ⏵**3.34** Listen again. How is the real technology different from the book/film?

f ⏵**3.34** Listen again. Are the sentences 1–8 true (*T*) or false (*F*)? Correct the false sentences.

1 ☐ The *Terrafugia* flying car can go on normal roads.
2 ☐ Anyone who has a driving licence can fly a *Terrafugia* car.
3 ☐ The *Kirobo* robot was designed to fall in love with the astronauts.
4 ☐ The *Kirobo* robot knows what the astronauts look like.
5 ☐ Robotic suits are used to help people with health problems.
6 ☐ *Cyberdyne* hope their robotic suit is used to save lives.
7 ☐ *Blue CRUSH* has not reduced crime in Memphis.
8 ☐ The *NEC* billboards know if you are interested in their adverts or not.

g 💬 Answer the questions.

1 Which of the new technologies from the listening do you think are the most useful? Why?
2 Think of three more kinds of technology you have seen in sci-fi books/films. Is it real yet? Do you think it will be real one day?

SCIENCE FICTION:
THEY THOUGHT OF IT FIRST!

Did you know that a lot of the technology we use today appeared in science fiction *before* scientists invented it?

 E-book readers didn't appear until 1999, but as long ago as 1961, author Stanislaw Lem wrote about them in his book, *Return from the Stars*.

Cash machines were invented in the 1980s. But Ray Bradbury thought of them first, in his 1953 novel, *Fahrenheit 451*.

Scientists are working on all these ideas from science fiction. How far have they got?

Back to the Future Part II, Steven Spielberg (1989)

When the heroes of the film travel to the future, one of the most amazing machines they find is flying cars. The cars fly along 'roads' in the sky which have signs and streetlights.

AI, Steven Spielberg (2001) based on Super-Toys Last All Summer Long, Brian Aldiss (1969)

When a young child dies, his mother is given an android which looks and behaves exactly like a real boy. The robot loves her like a son.

Iron Man Marvel Comics (1963) Marvel films (2008 onward)

A rich scientist and engineer is badly hurt. To save his own life, he builds himself a robotic heart and a powerful metal suit which makes him stronger and faster than any other man. He becomes a cyborg – part man, part machine.

Minority Report short story by Philip K. Dick (1956) and a film by Steven Spielberg (2002)

Tom Cruise plays a detective who can stop crimes before they happen. His team use information from psychics, who can see the future. They know who will break the law and when it will happen, but they don't know where.

Another idea that appeared in *Minority Report* is personalised advertising. All around the future city there are advertising billboards which use cameras to recognise the people walking by. The billboards speak to people by name and suggest things to buy.

2 GRAMMAR Defining relative clauses

a Look at the words from the reading and listening. Can you remember what they mean? Complete the definitions with the words in the box.

| androids billboards cyborgs psychics space |

1 _____ are people <u>that</u> can predict the future.
2 _____ are robots <u>that</u> look like humans.
3 _____ are people <u>who</u> have some robot body parts.
4 _____ are large signs <u>which</u> show adverts.
5 _____ is the place <u>where</u> astronauts go.

b Look at the <u>underlined</u> words in 2a. Complete the rules.

In defining relative clauses use:
- _____ or _____ to describe people
- _____ or _____ to describe things
- _____ to describe places

c Complete the sentences with *who*, *which* or *where*.

1 Robots are machines _____ do human jobs.
2 Detectives are police officers _____ solve difficult crimes.
3 Earth is the planet _____ we all live.

d ▶ Now go to Grammar Focus 11A on p.162

e Look at the sentences. What are A and B describing?

> **A** It's a person who gives you medicine when you're not feeling well.

> **B** It's a thing that is very comfortable. You sleep on it.

_____   _____

f ▶ **Communication 11A** Work in pairs. Student A: go to p.129. Student B: go to p.131.

3 VOCABULARY Compound nouns

a Match one noun from each column to make compound nouns. Use the article on p.108 to help you.

science ——————— programme
cash ——————————fiction
street   machines
television   sign
road   lights

b Look at the first word in each compound noun. Is it singular or plural?

c ▶ Now go to Vocabulary Focus 11A on p.140

4 SPEAKING

a 💬 Have you started using any new technology recently? What is it? Why did you get it?

b 💬 Look at the inventions in the pictures. What do you think they are for? Compare your ideas with a partner.

c Check with your teacher. How many did you get correct?

11 B I think they discovered it by chance

Learn to talk about discoveries
G Articles
V Adverbials: luck and chance

1 READING

a 💬 Look at the pictures and match the headlines 1–3 to the stories. Which story are you most interested in reading? Why?

① **5,000-year-old body found in the Alps**

② **Farmers uncover ancient army in the fields**

③ **Scientist discovers how to cook food in seconds**

b Now read the stories and answer the questions for each story.
1 Who made the discovery?
2 What were they doing when they made the discovery?
3 What exactly was the invention/discovery?

c Read the stories again and answer the questions.
1 How did Percy LeBaron Spencer test his machine?
2 Why weren't the police careful with Ötzi's body? What damage did they do?
3 Why don't archaeologists know exactly how many terracotta soldiers there are?

d 💬 Ask and answer the questions.
1 Which discovery do you think was the luckiest?
2 How important do you think each of the discoveries was? Put them in order (1–3).
3 What important discoveries can you think of from your lifetime?

Lucky discoveries

Some of our most important discoveries happen when we aren't expecting them at all ...

Percy LeBaron Spencer, an engineer, was working on radar for the army. One day, he was walking past a machine when the chocolate bar in his pocket melted. He was curious, so he did a test. He put a small bowl of popcorn in front of the machine. As expected, a minute later it started popping and jumping out of the bowl.

Spencer realised the microwaves from the radar were heating the food. Next, he made a metal box and sent microwaves into it through a hole. When he put some food in the box, it cooked. This was the first microwave oven – invented totally by chance.

In 1991, two German tourists, Helmut and Erika Simon, were hiking in the mountains in Italy, near the border with Austria. They were coming back down the mountain when one of them saw something in the ice. As they got closer, they realised that they were looking at a man's body. They reported the body and carried on hiking.

When the police arrived the next day, they tried to get the body out of the ice. Everyone thought that it was the body of an unlucky mountain climber and they weren't very careful. They accidentally tore the clothes and also broke one arm. But when scientists studied the body they were shocked. Amazingly, the body was 5,000 years old. He was quickly given the name 'Ötzi the Iceman'. Ötzi is one of the oldest, most complete human bodies ever found.

In 1974, local farmers were digging in Xi'an, a city in China. They were looking for water, but instead they found a life-size soldier made out of terracotta. Fortunately, the farmers stopped digging before they damaged anything and soon archaeologists arrived to look at the area. Surprisingly, there was not just one, but thousands of clay soldiers. They were made around 2,200 years ago and they were buried on purpose – together with the body of the First Emperor of China.

Archaeologists now believe that there are around 6,000 soldiers and their horses in the Terracotta Army, but most of them are still buried underground. All of the soldiers look different. Some are tall, some are short and they all have different clothes and faces. Archaeologists think 700,000 people helped to make them.

2 GRAMMAR Articles

a Read the sentences and the rules for articles.
Match the rules with examples 1–7.

He put ¹**a small bowl** of popcorn in front of the machine. A minute later, it started popping and jumping out of ²**the bowl**.

In 1974, some local farmers were digging in ³**Xi'an**, a city in ⁴**China** ... Fortunately, ⁵**the farmers** stopped digging ...

⁶**Archaeologists** think 700,000 people helped to make ⁷**the Terracotta Army**.

a ☐ Use no article before plural nouns to talk generally.
b ☐☐ Use no article before most countries and place names.
c ☐ Use *a/an* the first time you talk about something.
d ☐☐ Use *the* if you have already mentioned something.
e ☐ Use *the* when there is only one of something in the world.

b ▶ Now go to Grammar Focus 11B on p.162

c Complete the text with *the*, *a/an* or no article.

New species of lizard discovered on menu

In 2010, Ngo Van Tri, of ¹_____ Vietnam Academy of Science and Technology, was at ²_____ small village restaurant. While he was eating, he saw ³_____ box of lizards on ⁴_____ cooking bench. He thought they looked unusual, so he sent some pictures to ⁵_____ biologist in America, L. Lee Grismer.

When Grismer saw ⁶_____ pictures he was sure ⁷_____ lizards were special. He wanted to be ⁸_____ scientist to make ⁹_____ discovery, so he got on ¹⁰_____ plane to ¹¹_____ Vietnam. Then he rode on ¹²_____ motorbike for eight hours to get from ¹³_____ airport to ¹⁴_____ restaurant. But, unfortunately, while he was travelling ¹⁵_____ restaurant owner cooked ¹⁶_____ lizards and served them to his customers. When Grismer arrived, they were all gone. Luckily, ¹⁷_____ nearby restaurant also had the same kind of lizards on their menu. The species of lizard was new to scientists – but not to the Vietnamese villagers!

d ▶3.38 Listen and check.

e Work in pairs. Answer the questions about the story in 2c.

1 Who discovered the lizards?
2 Why did he take pictures of the lizards?
3 How did Grismer travel to Vietnam?
4 What happened while Grismer was travelling?
5 Where did Grismer find the lizards in the end?

f 💬 Cover the story and try to tell it with a partner. Use the prompts to help you.

- small village restaurant
- box of lizards
- biologist
- plane
- motorbike
- restaurant owner
- luckily
- new species

3 VOCABULARY
Adverbials: luck and chance

a Work in pairs. Look at the highlighted words and phrases in the four stories on these pages. What do they mean?

b Add the opposite words and phrases from the stories to the table.

1 _____ 2 _____	unfortunately
3 _____ 4 _____	on purpose
5 _____ 6 _____	as expected

c ▶3.39 Listen to the words and phrases. Underline the stressed syllables.

luckily   fortunately   accidentally   by chance
unfortunately   surprisingly   amazingly
on purpose   as expected

d Write about three occasions when something unexpected happened to you. Use three of the new words and phrases.

I lost my house keys last week. Luckily, my neighbour had an extra key.

e 💬 Compare your sentences with other students in the class. Whose are the most interesting?

4 SPEAKING
▶ **Communication 11B** Student A: go to p.128. Student B: go to p.132.

1 LISTENING

a 💬 Ask and answer the questions.

1 Have you ever got lost? When was the last time it happened?
2 Do you like to ask for directions or do you prefer to use maps?
3 Have you ever got lost in a building?

b ▶️ 3.40 Annie goes to visit Mark at his office. Why does she get lost? Watch or listen to Part 1 and find out.

c ▶️ 3.40 Watch or listen to Part 1 again. Complete the directions the receptionist gives to Annie.
It's on the ¹_____ floor. Go ²_____ the stairs and turn ³_____. Go through the ⁴_____ and turn ⁵_____. Then go ⁶_____ the corridor and it's the ⁷_____ door on the ⁸_____.

2 USEFUL LANGUAGE Asking for and giving directions in a building

a ▶️ 3.41 What phrase does Annie use to ask for directions? Complete the question with the words in the box. Then listen and check.

| is | tell | you | can | me |

Excuse me, _____ _____ _____ _____ where the reception _____?

b ▶️ 3.42 Match the phrases with the pictures. Listen and check. Repeat the phrases.

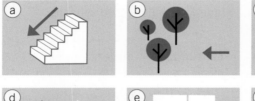
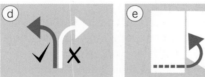
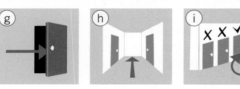

1 ☐ It's over there, by the trees.
2 ☐ It's on the second floor.
3 ☐ It's straight ahead.
4 ☐ Go through the door.
5 ☐ Go down the corridor.
6 ☐ Turn left.
7 ☐ Go down the stairs.
8 ☐ It's the third door on the left.
9 ☐ Take the lift to the third floor.
10 ☐ Go round the corner.

c Cover the phrases and try to remember the directions for each picture.

3 CONVERSATION SKILLS
Checking information

a ▶️ 3.43 What do you think Annie does next after she gets lost? Watch or listen to Part 2 and check your ideas.

b ▶️ 3.44 Read and listen to the three exchanges. Look at the underlined phrases 1–4. Which phrases do we use … ?

- to check information by repeating it
- to show we understand

R First, go up the stairs to the first floor and turn left.
A ¹So go up the stairs to the first floor and turn left.

A ²Sorry, the fourth office?
R No, the first.
A ³Right, I think I've got that.

A ⁴So can I just check? Go up the stairs and turn right …
R No, turn left.

c 💬 Work in pairs. Student A: write three directions for the building you are in and read each one to your partner.
Student B: listen and repeat the information to check it's correct. Use the phrases in 3b. Then swap roles.

> Go through that door. Then go up the stairs to the second floor.

> So I go through that door, then I go up the stairs to the second floor?

> That's right.

d ▶️ 3.45 Watch or listen to Part 3. What does Mark think about Annie getting a job at his company?

e 💬 Would you give Annie a job at your company? Why / Why not?

4 PRONUNCIATION
Sound and spelling: /ɜːː/ and /ɔː/

a ▶3.46 Listen to the vowel sounds in **bold**.
Then listen and repeat.

/ɜːː/ the f**ir**st office
/ɔː/ the f**our**th office

b Look at sentences 1–5. Which of the words in
italics have the /ɜːː/ sound?

1 The *third* / *fourth* floor.
2 On *Tuesday* / *Thursday* evening.
3 It's office number *thirty* / *forty*.
4 It's hard to *walk* / *work* there.
5 There's a *board* / *bird* in the meeting room.

c ▶3.47 Listen to the sentences in 4b. Circle the
words you hear. Listen again and repeat.

5 SPEAKING

Look at the building. Take turns to ask for directions to different places. Give your
directions from the entrance. Follow your partner's directions. Are they correct?

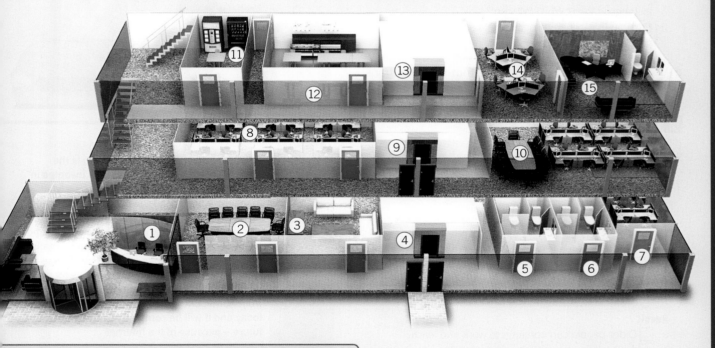

1 Reception
2 Meeting room 1
3 Staff lounge
4 Lift – Ground Floor
5 Gents toilets
6 Ladies toilets
7 HR / Finance
8 IT
9 Lift – First Floor
10 Meeting room 2 / Sales and Marketing
11 Snacks and drinks machine
12 Buildings and maintenance
13 Lift – Second Floor
14 Administration
15 Director's suite

◯ **Unit Progress Test**

CHECK YOUR PROGRESS

You can now do the Unit Progress Test.

Learn to write a web post giving an opinion

Ⓦ Giving opinions; Expressing results and reasons

1 LISTENING AND SPEAKING

a 💬 Look at the pictures of ideas for inventions. What do you think the inventions are?

b ▶ 3.48 Listen to people talking about the inventions. Complete the first row of the table.

c ▶ 3.48 Listen again and complete the table.

	Amir	Uta	Pierre
What's the invention?			
Why is it important / useful?			
Do they think it will happen?			

d Think about each invention and answer the questions. Make notes.

1 Is it a good idea? Why / Why not?
2 Can you think of any other ways to solve the same problems?

e 💬 Work in small groups. Talk about the inventions and compare your answers.

2 READING

a People were asked the question *What is the most important invention of the last 2,000 years?* Read the web posts and write the names of the inventions.

Invention

1 _____
2 _____
3 _____
4 _____

b Match the inventions 1–4 with their results a–d.

Result

a ☐ Older people can continue to work and learn.
b ☐ All the different sciences could develop.
c ☐ Everyday life will change completely.
d ☐ People could record and send information.

c Read the web posts again and answer the questions.

1 Which of the four inventions was the earliest? Which was the latest?
2 In what way might schools, offices etc. change as a result of the Internet?
3 How did the invention of paper change communication?
4 How would the world be different without numbers?
5 How do reading glasses make a difference to the writer of the web post?

¡Hola! ¿Cómo estás?

Hello! How are you?

Mark Turner

I think the most important invention is the Internet. The 'world wide web' was invented in 1989 by Tim Berners-Lee and now nearly all of us use it in our daily lives. We haven't even started to see how much the Internet will change our lives in the future. We still have schools, post offices, newspapers, cinemas, shopping malls, but not for long. All these things will change as a result of the Internet. For example, we may stop using shops or offices as we will do everything from home. Choose any part of the way we live today and it will be completely different in the future – because of the Internet.

Comment added at 12.35   Like Reply Send Mark a message

Eva Sorensen

Around 100 AD, the Chinese invented paper, and by 600 AD paper was used all over Asia. As a result of this, people were able to write down information, keep it and send it over long distances. Paper completely changed the way people communicated, as previously people wrote on clay or stone, which was heavy and broke easily. Later there were printed books and then, in our time, the Internet, but it all started with the invention of paper. So it seems to me that paper is a really important invention, perhaps one of the most important ever.

Comment added at 11.16   Like Reply Send Eva a message

3 WRITING SKILLS
Giving opinions; Expressing results and reasons

a Look at the example and <u>underline</u> the phrase which shows the writer is giving an opinion. Then <u>underline</u> four more phrases for giving opinions in web posts 2–4.

I think the most important invention is the Internet.

b Look at the sentences. Correct the phrases for giving opinions.

1 From my view, the most important invention is the wheel.
2 According to my opinion, the steam engine changed the world the most.
3 I belief the car is a very important invention.
4 It seems like me that the jet engine has made the biggest difference.

c Each example 1–4 below describes a change. What is the cause or reason for each change? What is the result?

1 **Because of** the invention of numbers, science could develop.
2 Around 100 AD, the Chinese invented paper. **As a result of** this, people could send messages long-distance.
3 We may stop using shops and offices, **as** we can now do everything online at home.
4 **Because** they had reading glasses, people could stay active in old age.

d Look at the words and phrases in **bold** in 3c. Which … ?
  • are followed by a noun / noun phrase / pronoun and a comma
  • join two clauses in the same sentence

Home • Forum • Useful links • Contact us

Tomas Valnek

I believe the most important invention is the Hindu-Arabic number system, which was invented around the sixth century in India. It spread throughout the Middle East and was finally brought to Europe in the 13th century. People could add numbers together easily for the first time, so because of this system, science could develop. Numbers are essential to almost all aspects of life, and without this invention there might be no science, engineering or computers.

Comment added at 10.55   Like   Reply   Send Tomas a message

Hiroko Okuzawa

In my opinion, the most important invention has been reading glasses. Reading glasses were invented in Italy around 1280 and they changed the world. Because they had reading glasses, people could read, stay active and work even in old age. In my view, that's really important, especially as I'm over 60 myself. I can still do lots of things because of my reading glasses. I don't know where I would be without them.

Comment added at 10.47   Like   Reply   Send Hiroko a message

---

e Which two words or phrases from examples 1–4 in 3c can go in each gap?

1 _____ they can use email, most people have stopped sending letters by post.
2 _____ cheap air travel, people are able to visit countries anywhere in the world.
3 Most people now have mobile phones. _____ this, they can now keep in touch wherever they are.

f Look at these notes about the invention of the telephone. Make sentences using:
  • a phrase for giving your opinion
  • two words / phrases from 3c to connect a cause with a result.

The telephone:
most important invention /
  19th century
  talk to people in other places
  we can communicate more quickly

g Write one more sentence about the telephone using your own ideas.

4 WRITING

a 💬 Choose one of these inventions to write about or use your own idea.
  • cars   • the aeroplane   • glass
  • photography • boats   • TV

Think about the questions below and make notes. Walk around the class and collect ideas from other students.
  • Why is the invention important?
  • What good or bad results has it had?
  • How was life different before?
  • What other things have changed because of it?

b Write a web post for the website. Remember to explain results and reasons using *as*, *because*, *because of* and *as a result of*.

c Read another student's web post and respond to it. You can:
  • agree or disagree and say why
  • add another idea

d Look at the response you received. Have they … ?
  • agreed or disagreed with your comment
  • used phrases to give opinions
  • used the correct language to connect reasons and results

UNIT 11
Review and extension

1 GRAMMAR

a Write sentences with relative clauses. Add *be* and a relative pronoun.

1 He / the man / invented the colour TV.
2 These / the mobile phones / work under water.
3 That / the machine / makes the screens for the computers.
4 This / the place / they found the statue.
5 These / the people / discovered the ancient city.
6 This / the shop / they sell that delicious bread.

b Complete the conversation with *a/an* or *the*.

A I saw ¹_____ brilliant film last week.
B Oh yeah, why was ²_____ film so good?
A It was ³_____ great story. I think it's probably ⁴_____ best crime film I've ever seen. It's about ⁵_____ group of criminals in ⁶_____ USA. They want to steal ⁷_____ painting from ⁸_____ gallery.
B It sounds good. I saw ⁹_____ good film last week, too. ¹⁰_____ story's simple, but ¹¹_____ actors are great. And it's got ¹²_____ amazing ending.

c 💬 Practise the conversation in 1b.

2 VOCABULARY

a Choose two words in the box to make a compound noun for definitions (1–8).

bag bottle cash kitchen knife lights
machine office road rock shopping
signs star street ticket top

1 You get money from this when the banks are closed.
2 This is a famous musician.
3 People go here to pay for a journey on a train, or a concert.
4 These tell you what to do when you're driving your car.
5 These help you see when you're driving in the dark.
6 You put the things you buy in a supermarket into this.
7 You use this to cut things when you're making food.
8 You put this back on when you've finished drinking.

b Choose the correct answers.

1 I *accidentally / luckily* broke your mug – I'm really sorry.
2 We thought our product was probably too expensive, and *as expected / on purpose* it wasn't successful.
3 The money was found *by chance / unfortunately* by an old man while he was looking for a book.
4 They wanted to build a house there, but *amazingly / luckily* someone told them about the plan to build an airport.
5 A: You did that *on purpose / as expected*!
   B: No, it was just an accident!
6 They thought it was a modern painting. *Surprisingly / By chance*, after some tests, they found that it was much older.

3 WORDPOWER preposition + noun

a Match the phrases (1–7) with their meanings (a–g).

1 ☐ People who go abroad **on business** are lucky.
2 ☐ Buses and trains where I live normally arrive **on time**.
3 ☐ There are lots of houses **for sale** on my street.
4 ☐ I once met an old friend **by chance** when I was abroad.
5 ☐ You should book a hotel **in advance** if you visit my city.
6 ☐ I sometimes broke things **on purpose** when I was a child.
7 ☐ You can always tell if two people are **in love**.

a available to buy
b having strong romantic feelings
c not by chance, because it was planned
d at the expected time
e without planning it
f working, but in a different place
g before something happens

b 💬 Which of the sentences in 3a are true for you?

c We sometimes use a preposition without an article before a place name. This means 'in a particular place for the usual reason'.

He's at home. NOT *He's at the home.*

Match the sentences (1–4) with the pictures (a–d).

1 ☐ Mara's in hospital. She's got a broken leg.
2 ☐ My brother's at university. He studies Physics.
3 ☐ My daughter's not in school today. She's on a class trip.
4 ☐ The police found the stolen painting in his house. Now he's in prison.

d Underline the preposition + noun combinations in sentences 1–4 in 3c. Write a sentence about somebody you know (of) who is in each place.

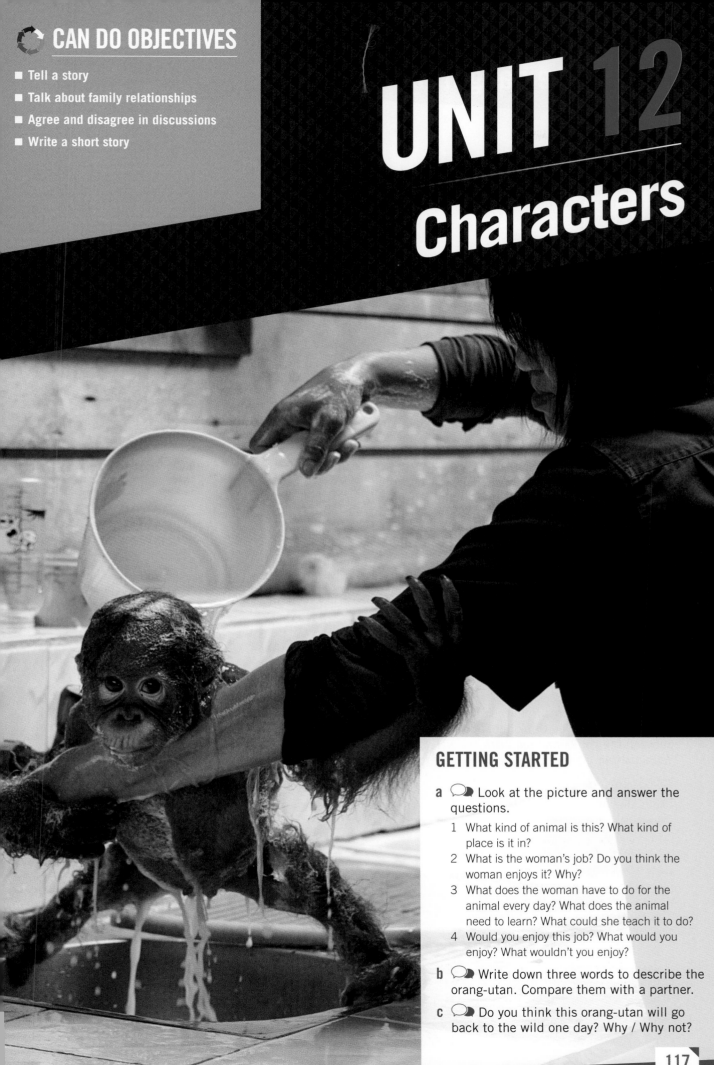

Characters

CAN DO OBJECTIVES

- Tell a story
- Talk about family relationships
- Agree and disagree in discussions
- Write a short story

GETTING STARTED

a 💬 Look at the picture and answer the questions.

1 What kind of animal is this? What kind of place is it in?
2 What is the woman's job? Do you think the woman enjoys it? Why?
3 What does the woman have to do for the animal every day? What does the animal need to learn? What could she teach it to do?
4 Would you enjoy this job? What would you enjoy? What wouldn't you enjoy?

b 💬 Write down three words to describe the orang-utan. Compare them with a partner.

c 💬 Do you think this orang-utan will go back to the wild one day? Why / Why not?

117

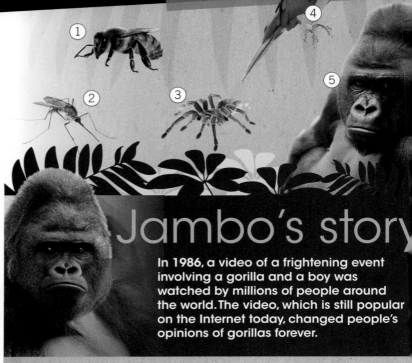

1 VOCABULARY Animals

a 🗨 In pairs, match pictures 1–8 with the names of the animals below.

- ☐ whale
- ☐ mosquito
- ☐ spider
- ☐ gorilla
- ☐ tiger
- ☐ parrot
- ☐ camel
- ☐ bee

b ▶3.49 Listen and check your answers. Practise saying the words in 1a.

c 🗨 Which of the animals in the pictures … ?

1 have you seen
2 have you touched
3 would you like to see and why
4 would you be scared to be close to and why

> I touched a whale when I went diving in Tonga.

> I'm not frightened of most spiders, but this one probably bites.

2 READING

a 🗨 What do you know about gorillas? Do you think they are dangerous?

b Read the introduction to *Jambo's story*. Answer the questions.

1 What was the video about?
2 Why was it important?

c 🗨 Look at the words from the story in the box. What do you think happened between the gorilla and the boy? Tell a partner.

> five-year-old boy   rescue   enclosure
> wall   disappear   scream   seriously hurt
> stroke (v.)   zookeeper   alive   hero

d Work in pairs. Start at square 1. Read each section and answer the questions together. Follow the instructions.

e 🗨 Ask and answer the questions.

1 Why do you think Jambo protected the boy?
2 Have you changed your opinion of gorillas after reading the story?
3 Would you like to watch the video of what happened?

Jambo's story

In 1986, a video of a frightening event involving a gorilla and a boy was watched by millions of people around the world. The video, which is still popular on the Internet today, changed people's opinions of gorillas forever.

1 On 31 August 1986 a couple took their two young sons to Jersey Zoo. When the family arrived, they went to see the gorillas straight away. The father noticed that the children were too small to see the animals, so he picked up his five-year-old son, Levan, and put him on top of the enclosure wall. Then he turned round to pick up his other son.

🗨 *What do you think happened next?*

Go to 3 to find out.

2 Jambo! People had always thought that gorillas were dangerous animals, but the video changed their minds. Journalists named Jambo 'the Gentle Giant', and soon letters, cards and even boxes of bananas arrived for him at the zoo. Jambo died in 1992, but a statue at the zoo reminds the world of this wonderful animal.

🗨 *Go to 2e and answer the questions.*

3 When the father turned back, Levan had disappeared. The boy had fallen off the wall, into the gorilla area. The shocked parents looked down and saw that their son was lying on the ground, about four metres below them. He wasn't moving.

🗨 *What do you think the father did next?*

Go to 5 to find out.

4 Jambo moved carefully around Levan. He softly stroked his back. Then he sat down between Levan and the other gorillas. When he saw that a young gorilla had come too close, Jambo stood up and did not let him pass. His message to the other gorillas was clear: "Don't touch him!" Jambo pulled gently at Levan's clothes and after a while Levan opened his eyes and started to cry.

🗨 *What do you think Jambo did when Levan started to cry?*

Go to 6 to find out.

5 Levan's father tried to climb down into the enclosure to rescue the boy, but he was stopped by the other zoo visitors. Slowly, the gorillas came closer to Levan. A large crowd of people had come to see what was happening. Everyone was screaming and shouting. They were scared that the gorillas might seriously hurt the boy.

Jambo, a 200kg male gorilla, got to Levan first.

🗨 *What do you think Jambo did?*

Go to 4 to find out.

6 Jambo ran away and his gorilla family followed him. Some time later, zookeepers rescued Levan from the enclosure. He had broken several bones in the fall, and had seriously hurt his head, but he was alive. A man had filmed everything and millions of people around the world watched the video on the news. The zookeepers became heroes and so did …

🗨 *Who else do you think became a hero?*

Go to 2 to find out.

⑥ ⑦ ⑧

3 GRAMMAR Past perfect

a Look at the verbs in **bold** in the sentences. Which action happened first? Write *1* (first) or *2* (second) after each of the verbs.

1 When the father **turned back** (__), Levan **had disappeared** (__).
2 Zookeepers **rescued** (__) Levan from the enclosure. He **had broken** (__) several bones.

b Look at the sentences in 3a again. Complete the rule with the words in the box.

> simple   perfect   participle

> We use the past _____ to make it clear that something happened **before** a past _____ action.
> We form the past perfect with *had* + past _____ .

c Read Jambo's story again and <u>underline</u> more examples of the past perfect.

d ▶ Now go to Grammar Focus 12A on p.164

e ▶3.51 **Pronunciation** Look at the vowels in **bold** in the past participles in the box. Put the words in the correct column in the table. Then listen and check.

> ~~br**ou**ght~~   ~~ch**o**sen~~   ~~dr**u**nk~~   bec**o**me   b**ou**ght   c**au**ght
> fl**ow**n   th**ou**ght   sw**u**m   st**o**len   thr**ow**n   w**o**n

/ʌ/	/ɔː/	/əʊ/
drunk	brought	chosen

f ▶3.52 Practise saying the sentences with the correct vowel sounds. Then listen and check.

1 He'd never **thought** of getting a pet.
2 Had you ever **swum** with whales before?
3 The camel had **thrown** him off before it started to run.
4 A mosquito had **flown** into the room in the night!
5 I went to the zoo because I'd **won** a free ticket.
6 After three hours I still hadn't **caught** a fish.

g 💬 What kind of animal do you think caused problems 1–5?

1 When I woke up my skin was red and itchy …
2 This morning I found a dead mouse on the kitchen floor …
3 I suddenly felt a pain in my arm …
4 There was hair all over my new coat …
5 Suddenly, she screamed …

h Complete sentences 1–5 in 3g using the past perfect.

i 💬 Have you ever had any bad experiences with animals? What happened?

4 SPEAKING AND LISTENING

a 💬 Work in pairs. Look at the pictures. Put them in order to make a story.

b ▶3.53 Listen to the story. Check your answers to 4a.

c 💬 Tell the story of Willie the Parrot. Use the pictures to help you.

d 💬 Do you know any stories about … ?

- animals helping or saving humans
- humans helping or saving animals

119

12B He said I was selfish!

1 LISTENING

a 💬 When you were a child, did you get on well with other children? How about with your brothers and sisters?

b 💬 Look at the pictures below. What do you think is happening in each picture?

c ▶ 3.54 Listen and match stories 1–3 to the pictures. Were you right about what was happening?

d ▶ 3.54 Listen again. Are the sentences true (*T*) or false (*F*)? Correct the false sentences.

Claire
1 ☐ Claire told her sister that the cows were horses.
2 ☐ Claire found it funny when her sister jumped on the cow.
3 ☐ Claire's sister went back home on her own.
4 ☐ Claire told her mum the truth about what had happened.

Jeremy
1 ☐ Jeremy wanted to do something nice for his brother.
2 ☐ Jeremy's brother thought the soup looked good.
3 ☐ Jeremy drank some of the soup first.
4 ☐ Jeremy's brother was ill after eating the soup.

Tanya
1 ☐ Tanya couldn't read as well as her sister.
2 ☐ Tanya hated her father saying nice things about her sister.
3 ☐ Tanya's father asked her to read aloud to the visitors.
4 ☐ Tanya knew the stories in the books.

e 💬 Answer the questions in small groups.
1 Which story did you like best? Why?
2 Did you do anything like this when you were a child?

2 GRAMMAR Reported speech

a Look at these examples of reported speech from the stories. What did the people actually say? Match 1–7 with a–g.
1 I said that she could ride one of the horses.
2 I told my mum that my sister had tried to ride a cow and I had saved her.
3 My brother said that he wasn't feeling very well.
4 I told my brother that I was going to make 'grass soup'.
5 I told him that I had drunk some.
6 My dad told them that he was very proud of my sister.
7 I said that I had just finished reading the books.

a ☐ 'I'm not feeling very well.'
b ☐ 'I'm very proud of Lisa.'
c ☐ 'I'm going to make grass soup.'
d ☐ 'You can ride one of the horses.'
e ☐ 'She tried to ride a cow and I saved her.'
f ☐ 'I've just finished reading these books.'
g ☐ 'I've drunk some.'

b How do verb forms change when we report what someone said in the past? Look at the sentences in 2a and complete the rules.

present simple	➤ *past simple*
present continuous	➤ _____
present perfect	➤ _____
past simple	➤ _____
am / is / are going to	➤ _____
can	➤ _____

c Look at the reported speech in 2a again. Complete the sentences with *said* or *told*.
1 I _____ him that I had drunk some.
2 I _____ that I had drunk some.

d ▶ Now go to Grammar Focus 12B on p.164

e ▶ 3.56 **Pronunciation** Listen to how *that* is pronounced in the following two exchanges. What difference do you notice? Do you think they both have the same meaning?

A Hi, Chris. Jane wants to know where her diary is.
B I haven't got it. I told her [1]*that* yesterday.

A Hi, Chris. Jane wants to know where her diary is.
B Yeah, I've just seen her. I told her [2]*that* I hadn't got it.

f (▶)**3.57** Report the sentences 1–6. Then listen and check your answers.

1 You can't read my diary. *I told her …*
2 I'm going to tell Dad. *She said …*
3 I'm not talking to you. *I told him …*
4 I don't want to play with you. *She said …*
5 It's not fair! *He told me …*
6 You broke my toy! *I said that he …*

g Practise saying the reported sentences in 2f.

h (💬) Do you remember anyone saying any of the things in 2f to you?

> My sister always said it wasn't fair when I won games.

i Can you remember any other things people have said to you? Make notes on:
- something a teacher said to you
- something someone told you to frighten you
- something that made you feel good
- something that wasn't true

j (💬) Tell a partner about your answers in 2i.

3 VOCABULARY Personality adjectives

a (💬) Write down the names of four family members. What kind of people are they? Tell your partner one thing about each person.

b ▶ Now go to Vocabulary Focus 12B on p.141

4 READING AND SPEAKING

a (💬) Ask and answer the questions.
1 Which people in your family are you closest to? Why?
2 Does anyone in your family have a strong personality? What are they like?

> I'm very close to my younger sister. We tell each other everything.

> My father is very easygoing and he has a very loud laugh.

b (💬) Work in pairs. Complete *Brothers and Sisters: The Facts* with words in the box. There are different possible answers.

are more sociable   play together   live to over 100 years old!
get on with women   fight   do activities   ~~possessions~~
earns a higher salary   do better at school   talk

c ▶ Communication 12B Go to p.131

BROTHERS AND SISTERS
THE FACTS

1 **80%** of fights between brothers and sisters are about <u>possessions</u>.

2 Children who are of a similar age _____ less.

3 Children who are more than three years apart in age _____ less.

4 When sisters are together, they prefer to _____ than do anything else.

5 When brothers, or brothers and sisters, are together, they prefer to _____.

6 Children with no brothers and sisters _____ and get better jobs.

7 The oldest child in a family is normally more intelligent and usually _____ than younger brothers and sisters.

8 Younger brothers and sisters _____ when they become adults.

9 Boys with older sisters find it easier to _____ when they are adults.

10 Older brothers and sisters have more allergies, but more of them _____.

1 LISTENING

a 💬 Ask and answer the questions.
1 What kind of things do you normally talk about with your friends?
2 Do you ever argue? What do you argue about?
3 Do you think male friends and female friends argue about the same things? What are the differences?

b 💬 Look at the logos. What do you know about the companies?

c ▶3.59 Watch or listen to Part 1. What is wrong with Leo's car? What kind of car does he have? Why do they start arguing?

d ▶3.59 Watch or listen again. Who agrees with the statements below, only Mark (M) or both Leo and Mark (B)?
1 ☐ Japanese cars are reliable.
2 ☐ Nissan cars are made in South Korea.
3 ☐ Toyota is the biggest car company in Japan.
4 ☐ Mazda is a larger company than Suzuki.

e ▶3.60 Watch or listen to Part 2. What does Mark do to end the argument? Do you know who is right?

2 USEFUL LANGUAGE
Agreeing and disagreeing

a ▶3.59 Look at these phrases. Which of the phrases do Mark and Leo use? Watch or listen again to Part 1 and tick ✓ phrases you hear.
☐ That's true.
☐ I'm afraid …
☐ Exactly.
☐ I don't think so.
☐ I'm sorry, but …
☐ You're absolutely right.
☐ Definitely.
☐ That's right.
☐ Oh, please.
☐ I'm not sure about that.

b Look at all the phrases in 2a and answer the questions.
1 Which phrases show we agree?
2 Which phrases show we disagree?
3 Which phrases show we very strongly agree?
4 Which phrase shows we very strongly disagree?

c ▶3.61 Listen and repeat the phrases from 2a. There are sometimes some extra words.

d ▶3.62 Complete these conversations with the expressions from 2a. Then listen and check.
1
A Rock music is the best kind of music.
B I'm not _____ _____ that. Classical music is more relaxing.
2
A Basketball is the most interesting sport.
B _____ true. It's so fast and exciting.
3
A Beach holidays are boring.
B You're _____ right. I prefer to stay in big cities.
4
A English food is boring.
B Oh, _____. It's much more interesting than it used to be!
5
A It's a bad idea to listen to music when you study.
B I'm _____, but I think it helps you concentrate.

e Complete the sentences with your own ideas.
1 _____ is the best artist ever.
2 _____ is really boring.
3 _____ is an amazing singer.
4 _____ is a great film.
5 _____ is a really relaxing place.
6 _____ is a very funny person.

f 💬 Compare your sentences with your partner. Use phrases from 2a to agree or disagree.

3 PRONUNCIATION
Main stress: contrastive

a ▶ **3.63** Listen to Leo and Mark talking about Nissan. Notice how the <u>underlined</u> words have extra stress.

Leo   Nissan's a Japanese company.
Mark   Err, it's actually a <u>Korean</u> company.
Leo   No, it's <u>Japanese</u>.

b Complete the rule.

> To show that we disagree with someone, we put **extra** / **less** stress on the information we think is different.

c 💬 Practise the exchange in 3a using these ideas.

1 Coffee's really bad for you. (good for you)
2 Business management is an easy subject. (difficult)
3 The best way to travel is by plane. (by train)
4 Tennis is a really boring sport. (exciting)
5 The shops in this area are excellent. (terrible)

> Coffee's really bad for you.

> Err, it's actually <u>good</u> for you.

> No, it's <u>bad</u> for you.

d 💬 What's your real opinion about each idea in 3c? Tell your partner. Do you agree?

4 SPEAKING

a Think about these opinions. Which do you agree with? Think of reasons why you agree or disagree. Make notes.

- Money makes people happy.
- Celebrity magazines are fun to read.
- Italian food is the best in the world.
- There should be no speed limits on motorways.
- Children should stay at school until 5 pm.
- Video calls are better than normal phone calls.

b 💬 Work in pairs. Compare your ideas. How many opinions do you agree about?

> I think celebrity magazines are fun to read.

> Oh please. They're silly. I don't care about celebrities.

> I'm sorry, but I think they're fun. It's interesting to read about other people's lives.

○ Unit Progress Test

CHECK YOUR PROGRESS

You can now do the Unit Progress Test.

1 LISTENING AND SPEAKING

a 💬 Ask and answer the questions.
- Where do you normally read or hear stories?
- Who do you know who is good at telling stories?

b ▶3.64 Listen to Olga telling a story about when she was a child.
1 Who did she play with?
2 Where did they play?
3 Who did she see?

c ▶3.64 Put the events from the story in the correct order. Then listen and check.
- ☐ Olga saw an old lady.
- ☐ Olga's mother spoke to the neighbour.
- ☐ Olga was playing with her sister.
- ☐ Olga told her mother.
- ☐ Olga found out the old lady was dead.
- ☐ Olga's family went to live in the country.

d 💬 Do you think the story is true? Which of these opinions is closest to your own? Why?
- 'Yes, it's quite possible. Things like this often happen.'
- 'It could be true, but I don't really believe it.'
- 'Things like this only happen in stories. She probably imagined it.'

e ▶3.64 Work in pairs. Practise telling the story. Then listen again and check. Did you remember all the details?

2 READING

a 💬 Cover the story and look at the picture at the bottom of the page. Answer the questions.
1 Why do you think the people are walking in the rain?
2 Do you think they know the man?
3 What do you think happens in the story?

b Read the story. How similar is it to your ideas in 2a?

c Read the story again and answer the questions.
1 Why didn't they take a map on their walk?
2 How did they find the cottage?
3 Why did the man invite them in?
4 How long had the man lived in the house?
5 How did they find their way to the hotel?
6 What was different about the path when they went back?
7 Why didn't they give the old man the present?

d 💬 Answer the questions.
1 Can you explain why they didn't find the cottage again?
2 Do you think the story is true? Why / Why not?

We were cold, wet and tired. We'd walked for hours by the sea, following a path that had become smaller and smaller and then stopped. We had been very careless and we hadn't brought a map. Mary, who is more confident than she is reliable, had told me she knew the way and I had believed her. But, of course, she didn't know the way and we were lost. We knew we could be several kilometres from the nearest house. We sat down under a tree, feeling very sorry for ourselves.

Suddenly we heard a sound. It was a dog barking, not far away. We got up and walked on quickly. A minute later we came to the top of a small hill, and saw a very old stone cottage. An old man with a black dog was looking out from the front door. 'Oh dear! You look wet!' the man called to us. 'Yes, we're completely lost,' Mary replied. 'Well,' the man said, 'why don't you come in and get dry?'

We went inside and I started to feel better. We sat next to the fire and the man went into the kitchen.

3 WRITING SKILLS Linkers: past time

a Complete the sentences from the story with time linkers. Check your answers in the story.

> a minute later   suddenly   after a while   later that week
> the following day   about an hour later

1 We sat down under a tree, feeling very sorry for ourselves. _____ we heard a sound.
2 We got up and walked on quickly. _____ we came to the top of a small hill.
3 _____, the rain stopped and we got up to leave.
4 _____, we didn't think much about what had happened.
5 _____, we decided to visit the old man and take him a present.
6 _____, we got to the place where the cottage had been.

b Which of these expressions from 3a … ?

> after a while   suddenly

1 tells you that an event was not expected _____
2 tells you that an event happened after another event, but doesn't say how long _____

c We can use time expressions in two ways:

1 to show the period when something happened:
   • the following day   • later that week
2 to show the time between two events:
   • a minute later   • after a while

Which phrases in the list below could you use instead of the highlighted words? Write *1* or *2*.

☐ five minutes   ☐ year   ☐ a few days
☐ evening   ☐ about a month   ☐ morning
☐ a short time   ☐ many years   ☐ night

d Correct the mistakes with time linkers.

1 She left university. About two years after, she got a job.
2 He started reading his book. Sudden, the plane dropped 500 metres.
3 Jose and Amal met on an English course. Week later he asked her to marry him.
4 He bought a new car. Later morning he crashed it.
5 We went straight to bed. Following the morning we went to the Old Town.

4 WRITING

a Work in small groups. Take a sheet of paper. Choose one of these sentences to begin your story and write it at the top.

> After the party, Amanda felt very pleased with herself.

> Riccardo found his seat on the plane and sat down.

> Anton felt lucky to be alive.

b Follow these steps:

1 Write the next few sentences of the story. Write about what *had happened* earlier. Then give your paper to the next group.
2 Continue the story. Begin *Suddenly …* and write a few more sentences. Give your paper to the next group.
3 Continue the story. Begin *A few minutes later, …* or *About an hour later, …* and write a few more sentences. Give your paper to the next group.
4 Continue the story. Begin *After a while, …* and write a few more sentences. Give your paper to the next group.
5 Write the end of the story. Begin *The following week, …* and write a few more sentences to finish the story. Give the paper back to the group who started the story.

c Read your story. Did the other groups use time linkers correctly?

d 💬 Read your story to the class. Which story did you enjoy the most?

He came out with coffee and biscuits and we chatted for a while. He told us he had always lived in that house. 'Ever since I was a child … but that was many years ago,' he said.

About an hour later, the rain stopped and we got up to leave. 'Just walk down that path and you'll come to a village,' the man told us. He said goodbye and we started walking. And he was right – soon we were back in the village and back at the hotel where we were staying.

The following day, we didn't think much about what had happened, but later that week, we decided to visit the old man and take him a present. We wanted to say thank you. So we went back up the path the old man had shown us. But everything was a bit different this time. Plants were growing across the path, making it difficult to walk. After a while, we got to the place where the cottage had been and we stopped and looked around. There was no cottage by the sea – just grass and some very old stones.

UNIT 12
Review and extension

1 GRAMMAR

a Which action in the sentences happened first? Write *1* or *2*.

1 ☐ I arrived late for my flight, because ☐ I'd written the wrong time in my diary.
2 ☐ The man had run away by the time ☐ the police got there.
3 ☐ When I saw the questions in the exam, I realised ☐ I'd revised the wrong things.
4 ☐ It had snowed in the night and ☐ some of the roads were closed.
5 ☐ I was tired, because ☐ I'd worked so hard the day before.

b Choose the correct answers.

A ¹*Did you read / Had you read* the story about the man who was almost attacked by a shark yesterday?
B No, what ²*happened / had happened*?
A He was swimming and he ³*saw / had seen* a dolphin next to him. Then suddenly, the dolphin ⁴*hit / had hit* a shark. The swimmer ⁵*didn't see / hadn't seen* the shark before the dolphin hit it!
B That's incredible. Well, I ⁶*read / had read* another nice animal story. There was a goat that ⁷*looked after / had looked after* a farmer for five days. The farmer ⁸*fell / had fallen* over and he couldn't walk or get help.

c Report the statements.

1 'We can't leave the party.' *He said …*
2 'Marc has moved to a new flat.' *She told me …*
3 'I'm seeing Sarah later.' *He said …*
4 'I'll help you with the shopping.' *She said …*
5 'Michele got a great new job.' *He told me …*
6 'I'm going to get a new car.' *He said …*
7 'I don't like the hotel.' *She told me …*

2 VOCABULARY

a Complete the animal words.

1 w_ _ le
2 sp_ _ _ _ r
3 g_ r _ _ _ a
4 t_ g_ r
5 m_ _ q_ _ _ _ o
6 p_ r_ _ t

b Choose an adjective in the box to describe each person (1–8).

anxious careless funny generous
honest reliable selfish sensible

1 Jo really makes me laugh. _____
2 Manfred only thinks about himself. _____
3 Jill always tells the truth. _____
4 Shin Li always gets worried about little things. _____
5 If Ben says he'll do something, he always does it. _____
6 Steve often loses or breaks things. _____
7 Jack always gets me great presents. _____
8 Susi never makes stupid decisions. _____

3 WORDPOWER *age*

a Look at the sentences. Which is about … ?

☐ children who are almost the same age
☐ children who are different ages

1 Children who are more than **three years apart in age** play together less.
2 Children who are **of a similar age** fight less.

b Match the expressions (1–4) with the definitions (a–d)

1 ☐ **At your age**, I was studying a lot – not going out all the time.
2 ☐ I learnt to swim **at an early age**. I was only about three years old.
3 ☐ She's **about my age**, I think, because we were at university at the same time.
4 ☐ It isn't always easy to learn new things **in old age**.

a a similar age to me
b younger than expected, during childhood
c when someone is over 70
d the age you are now

c Complete the sentences with the phrases in the box.

about my age   apart in age   at an early age
at your age   early twenties   middle-aged
of a similar age   old age

1 John looks much older than Martin, but surprisingly they're _____.
2 Mozart started to write music _____ – he was only five years old.
3 _____, I never used a computer for homework. I wrote everything by hand.
4 I had a lot of fun when I was 21 – it's great to be in your _____.
5 My brother and I are only two years _____, so we played together all the time when we were little.
6 My grandparents are still really active – I think that's important in _____.
7 The person I spoke to was _____, maybe a year younger or older than me.
8 Don't say to her that she's _____ – she thinks 45 is still very young.

d 💬 Work in pairs. Use each of the phrases in 3c to describe someone you know.

⟳ REVIEW YOUR PROGRESS

How well did you do in this unit? Write 3, 2 or 1 for each objective.
3 = very well   2 = well   1 = not so well

I CAN …

Tell a story	☐
Talk about family relationships	☐
Agree and disagree in discussions	☐
Write a short story	☐

Communication Plus

3C Student C

a You are a shop assistant. Look at the photos of your products and read the descriptions.

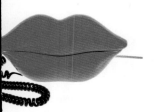

Hot lips telephone £15.50
- Fun gift: people who love to talk
- Looks great in any home
- Ringtone: choose, five fun sounds

Modern spice rack £39.99
- Perfect gift: cooks, food lovers
- 20 jars, quality herbs and spices
- Fix to wall / free standing

Football mug £4.99
- Great gift: football fans
- Fill with favourite hot drink
- Dishwasher safe

Scented candles £9.99
- Colourful gift for the home
- Three scents: vanilla, rose, pine
- Create a romantic atmosphere

Classic clock £20.00
- Stylish gift: man or woman
- Traditional design
- Batteries included

Animal slippers £15.99 one pair
SPECIAL OFFER £25.99 both designs
- Fun gift: man, woman, couple
- Fox / Rabbit design

b Students A and B are customers in your shop. Listen to their questions and describe some of your products. Ask your customers to pay for the product when they have chosen.

c ▶ Now swap roles. Go to p.130

5A

1 gardeners, 2 hairdressers, 3 nurses, 4 accountants, 5 bankers

2B Student A

a Read the text and answer the questions.
1 Where were they going?
2 How were they travelling?
3 What was the problem?
4 Who helped solve the problem? How?
5 What happened in the end?

Did you mean Capri?

Swedish tourists miss their destination by 600 km

Two Swedish tourists on holiday in Italy got a surprise after a spelling mistake on their GPS took them 600 kilometres from their destination.

The Swedish couple were travelling around Italy, and wanted to go to Capri. Capri is an island in the south of the country, famous for its beautiful coastline and a popular tourist destination. The couple put their destination into their car's GPS, but they made a spelling mistake. They accidentally typed CARPI instead of CAPRI. There is a real place called Carpi in Italy, but it is a small town in the north of the country.

The couple followed the GPS directions. Although they were travelling to an island, it didn't worry them that they didn't cross a bridge, take a boat or see the sea. When they arrived in Carpi, they went to the tourist office. They asked for directions to the Blue Grotto, a famous sea cave in Capri. But, of course, the tourist official couldn't understand. He thought they wanted to go to a restaurant called the Blue Grotto.

When the official realised that the couple thought they were in Capri, he explained their mistake. The couple got back into their car and started driving south. The official said, 'They were surprised, but not angry.'

b ▶ Now go back to p.21

10A RESULTS

0–5 points: You tell the truth to people even if they don't want to hear it. You may be the most honest person around, but you're not always the most popular.

6–13 points: You care about other people, and you don't want to upset them with the truth. Sometimes life is easier for people who aren't 100% honest. You're not hurting anyone else – that's the important thing.

14–25 points: You don't always do what other people think is the right thing. Watch out – you might cause problems for yourself one day!

11B Student A

a Read the texts about three accidental discoveries. Answer the questions.
1 Who made each discovery?
2 What exactly was the discovery?
3 How did they make the discovery?

1 Car keys were invented by an American businessman, Louis Spencer, in 1912. Until then, cars didn't have keys, because there weren't many of them and they couldn't travel very far. But one day Spencer had some important papers that he wanted to leave in his car. He had the idea for the car key.

2 Matches were invented by John Walker, a chemist in England in 1826. He was trying to find a way to start fires quickly. He didn't make much money from his idea – he wanted to share it with everyone, because he already had enough money.

3 Saccharin was invented by accident in 1878 by Constantin Fahlberg, a chemist in the USA. He was eating some bread at home, but it tasted sweeter than normal. He realised that he had some chemicals on his hands from his day at work. The chemicals were making the bread taste sweet. At work the next day, he started working on saccharin.

b Use your dictionary to check new words. You may have to explain words to your partner.

c Tell your partner about the three texts. Which one is not true? Talk about the texts and decide together.

2C Student B

a Read card 1. Think about what Student A will ask you.

> You are a platform attendant at a UK train station.
> - first train to Manchester at 7.10 am
> - trains every hour
> - prices: adult £32, student £22
> - passengers can only use their tickets on the train they book
> - no lockers in UK stations
> - the waiting room is by the station entrance

b Start the conversation with Student A. Say 'How can I help you?'

c Now look at card 2. Listen to Student A and reply. Find out the information you need.

> ② You want to visit Warwick Castle.
> - where / castle?
> - 🕐 open?
> - £ adult and child tickets?
> - where / buy tickets?
> - how often / tours?
> - take a picnic?

2B Student B

a Read the text and answer the questions.
1 Where were they going?
2 How were they travelling?
3 What was the problem?
4 Who helped solve the problem? How?
5 What happened in the end?

Coach passengers asked to get out and push

A group of coach passengers got some unexpected exercise when their coach broke down and the driver asked them to get out and push. The driver asked his 25 passengers for help after the 11.15 am coach from Heathrow airport to Norwich broke down while it was turning a corner.

A 77-year-old passenger, who was travelling back from a holiday in Italy with his wife, said, 'We heard an awful noise ... and the driver could not get the coach to move.' The coach was stopping other cars from using the road, so ten passengers got out and tried to push the coach, which weighed 14 tonnes*. The passenger said, 'It was an amazing sight ... Luckily, there were lots of strong young men on board – but a couple of women joined in as well.'

A car stopped to help and pulled the coach along with a rope while the people pushed it 200 metres to the bus station. The passengers then waited over an hour with their luggage for another coach to arrive, so they could complete their journey.

The coach company says the coach driver was wrong to ask his passengers to help and that they will give him training immediately.

* 14 tonnes = 14,000 kg

b ▶ Now go back to p.21

5B If your partner *hasn't* got a job ...

a Ask your partner about the job he/she would like to do in the future.
Do you think ... ?
- it'll be easy to find work
- you'll earn a good salary when you start
- you'll need to speak English at work
- there'll be a lot of other people who want this job
- you'll work for a company or be self-employed
- you'll move to another place for work
- you'll use your qualifications

b Then swap roles and answer your partner's questions. Give more information if you can.

c ▶ Now go back to p.51

7B

a Do the quiz. Choose the answers that are true for you. Add up your score.

Are you healthier than you used to be?

1 I used to do more sports and exercise in the past.
   a Agree (–1)   **b** Not sure (0)   **c** Disagree (+1)

2 I used to eat a healthier diet.
   a Agree (–1)   **b** Not sure (0)   **c** Disagree (+1)

3 I smoke less today than I used to.
   a Agree (+1)   **b** Not sure (0)   **c** Disagree (–1)

4 I do more housework than I used to.
   a Agree (+1)   **b** Not sure (0)   **c** Disagree (–1)

5 I used to sleep more than I do now.
   a Agree (–1)   **b** Not sure (0)   **c** Disagree (+1)

6 I used to get ill more often than I do these days.
   a Agree (+1)   **b** Not sure (0)   **c** Disagree (–1)

Scores

Below 0: You were healthier in the past than you are now.

0: You are just as healthy today as you were in the past.

More than 0: You are healthier today than you used to be.

b Compare your results with your partner. Whose health has changed the most? What are the most important differences in your health between now and the past?

1C Student B

a Read card 1. Think about what you want to say.

b Listen to Student A and reply. Use your own name.

 You are walking down the street and you see your friend.
- say hello
- listen to your friend's news and respond
- give your news:
  - you moved to a new flat last week
  - *your own idea*
- say goodbye

c Now look at card 2. Start the conversation with Student A. Use your own name.

 You meet a new colleague for the first time.
- say who you are
- listen to what they say and respond
- give some information:
  - you work in IT
  - *your own idea*
- say goodbye

10A Student A

a Take turns to ask and answer questions with Student B. Underline their answers below. If you answer *maybe*, you must explain your answer.

> If a shop assistant gave you a £20 note instead of a £10, would you tell them?

> Maybe. I'd tell them if they were young.

1 If a shop assistant gave you a £20 note instead of a £10 note, would you tell them?
   Yes 0, Maybe 3, No 4

2 If someone had food in their teeth, would you tell them?
   Yes 0, Maybe 1, No 3

3 If you found a wallet with $1,000 and an ID card in it, would you hand it in at a police station?
   Yes 0, Maybe 1, No 4

4 If you got a present you didn't like, would you wrap it up and give it to someone else?
   Yes 2, Maybe 1, No 0

5 If you dropped your friend's sandwich on the kitchen floor and they didn't see, would you throw it away and make a new one?
   Yes 0, Maybe 2, No 3

6 If someone lent you something you really liked and then forgot about it, would you give it back anyway?
   Yes 0, Maybe 1, No 3

7 If your friend was upset and wanted to come round, but you were really tired, would you tell them you were busy?
   Yes 3, Maybe 2, No 0

8 Would you tell a friend if you didn't like their new hairstyle?
   Yes 0, Maybe 1, No 2

b Add up Student B's score and check the results on p.127. Does your partner agree with their result?

11A Student A

Look at the list. Take turns describing the words to Student B, but do not say the word. How many words can you describe in two minutes?

scientist   album   laptop   novel   pilot   visa
hotel   bank account   Greece   Brad Pitt

It's a thing that …
It's a place where …
It's a person who …

▶ Now go back to p.109

3C Students A and B

a You want to buy a present for a friend. Choose someone you both know.

b Student C is a shop assistant. Ask about the products in the shop. Choose the best product for your friend and buy it.

c Now swap roles. Student B: You are the shop assistant – go to p.127. Student A: Stay on this page.

3B RESULTS

Mostly 'a': You are a big spender. You spend a lot of money without thinking. Maybe you need to start to plan your spending a bit better.

Mostly 'b': You are a smart spender. You spend money, but you are clever when you do it. You find all the special offers. But don't buy things that you don't need!

Mostly 'c': You are a non spender. You don't like spending and you only do it when you really have to.

▶ Now go back to p.30

5B If your partner *has* got a job …

a Ask your partner about their future in their job.
Do you think … ?
- you'll work longer hours
- you'll earn more money
- you'll need new skills
- you'll go to more meetings
- you'll travel abroad for work
- you'll need to speak English at work
- you'll become a boss

b Then swap roles and answer your partner's questions. Give more information if you can.

c ▶ Now go back to p.51

6A Student A

a Read the advice for people who are always late.

No one wants to be the person who always arrives last. Here's some advice to help you get there on time, whatever the occasion.

I'm always late

Imagine the worst. Don't think that everything will go perfectly and you will arrive at a place in the shortest time possible. Leave earlier than you need to. Then, when you can't find a parking place, or there's a long queue, it won't make you late.

Tell people how much time you have. When someone starts talking to you, and you don't have much time, say 'I only have five minutes.' Then, after five minutes, make sure you leave. Say 'I'm sorry but I have to go.' Nobody will think you are rude.

Find things to do while you wait. Some people are always late, because they hate waiting for other people. If this is you, you should take something with you to do while you are waiting. Don't try to do 'just one more thing' before you leave for an appointment.

b Cover the text. Tell Student B about the advice.

c Listen to Student B's advice for the same problem.

d Answer the questions with Student B.
1 Which of the six pieces of advice is the most useful?
2 Do you know anyone who needs this advice?

e ▶ Now go back to p.59

4B Student A

a Read the sentences to Student B. Listen to their reply.
1 My flight arrives at 5 pm.
2 I'd like to buy some clothes.
3 I don't understand the menu.
4 I don't like crowds.
5 I'd love to see some art.

b Listen to Student B's sentences. Choose the best reply.
I'll take you to the airport soon.
Shall we visit the castle?
Shall I come and pick you up?
I'll take you to a nice park.
I'll find a good place to eat nearby.

c ▶ Now go back to p.41

12B

a Read the facts. Did you complete them correctly?

BROTHERS AND SISTERS
THE FACTS

1 **80%** of fights between brothers and sisters are about possessions.
2 Children who are of a similar age **fight less**.
3 Children who are more than three years apart in age **play together** less.
4 When sisters are together, they prefer to **talk** than do anything else.
5 When brothers, or brothers and sisters, are together, they prefer to **do activities**.
6 Children with no brothers and sisters **do better at school** and get better jobs.
7 The oldest child in a family is normally more intelligent and usually **earns a higher salary** than younger brothers and sisters.
8 Younger brothers and sisters **are more sociable** when they become adults.
9 Boys with older sisters find it easier to **get on with women** when they are adults.
10 Older brothers and sisters have more allergies, but more of them **live to over 100**!

b Work in pairs. Talk about the facts. Do you think they are true? Use examples from your own family or other people you know.

c Have a class vote on each fact. How many of the facts do your class agree with?

11B ANSWERS

Student A: story one is not true.

Student B: story three is not true.

10A Student B

a Take turns to ask and answer questions with Student A. <u>Underline</u> their answers below. If you answer *maybe*, you must explain your answer.

> If a friend cooked dinner for you and you didn't like it, would you eat it?

> Maybe. I'd eat it if it was something really expensive.

1 If a friend cooked dinner for you and you didn't like it, would you eat it?
Yes 2, Maybe 1, No 0

2 If you were at a cash machine and the person in front of you forgot to take their cash, would you run after them?
Yes 0, Maybe 2, No 4

3 If you wanted to see a film that didn't come out at the cinema in your country for three months, would you download it?
Yes 3, Maybe 2, No 0

4 If you were looking after a friend's pet fish and it died, would you replace it before they came back?
Yes 2, Maybe 1, No 0

5 If you hit a parked car and no one saw you, would you carry on driving?
Yes 4, Maybe 3, No 0

6 If you saw a job advert that was perfect for your friend, but you also wanted to apply, would you pass on the information?
Yes 0, Maybe 1, No 3

7 If you spilt some water on someone's mobile phone, would you tell them?
Yes 0, Maybe 1, No 3

8 If your friend offered you a free ticket to a concert, but you were working that day, would you tell your boss you were sick and go along?
Yes 4, Maybe 2, No 0

b Add up Student A's score and check the results on p.127. Does your partner agree with the result?

11A Student B

Look at the list. Take turns describing the words to Student A, but do not say the word. How many words can you describe in two minutes?

dentist	airport	freezer	MP3 player	plumber
luggage	fiction	Japan	*Thriller*	tourist

It's a thing that …
It's a place where …
It's a person who …

▶ Now go back to p.109

131

4C Student B

a Student A is going to invite you to dinner. Complete your diary with plans for three days.

Wednesday:
Thursday:
Friday:
Saturday:
Sunday:

b Answer Student A's call. Arrange an evening for dinner. Offer to bring something.

6A Student B

a Read the advice for people who are always late.

No one wants to be the person who always arrives last. Here's some advice to help you get there on time, whatever the occasion.

Make a list of everything you need to do the day before an important event. Do you need to wear smart clothes? Buy a gift? Find out train times? Then do all the jobs on your list and you'll be ready to go the next day.

I'm always late

Do only the things you need to do. Use your time carefully before an appointment. Don't try to be perfect. Think about each action. Do you really need to print that document? If it's not necessary, don't do it.

Think about how other people feel. Being late tells other people, 'My time is more important than yours.' People who are often late don't usually understand how rude it is. Remember this and you will have another reason to arrive on time.

b Listen to Student A's advice about the same problem.

c Cover the text. Tell Student A about the advice you read.

d Answer the questions with Student A.
1 Which of the six pieces of advice is the most useful?
2 Do you know anyone who needs this advice?

e ▶ Now go back to p.59

4B Student B

a Listen to Student A's sentences. Choose the correct reply.
- Shall I read it for you in English?
- Shall we go to a gallery?
- OK – so we won't go to the market.
- I'll meet you at the airport.
- Shall we go to a shopping centre?

b Read the sentences to Student A. Listen to their reply.
1 My hotel doesn't have a restaurant.
2 I'd like to go for a walk.
3 My flight leaves in three hours.
4 I'm interested in history.
5 There's a long queue for taxis.

▶ Now go back to p.41

11B Student B

a Read the texts about three accidental discoveries. Answer the questions.
1 Who made each discovery?
2 What exactly was the discovery?
3 How did they make the discovery?

1 Coca-Cola was invented by John Pemberton, a chemist in the USA. He was trying to make a medicine for headaches. For the first eight years, the drink was only sold in chemists, as a medicine, not in normal shops as a soft drink.

2 Velcro was invented by George De Mestral, a Swiss engineer, in 1941. One day, after a day's walk in the Alps with his dog, he noticed that there were lots of seeds in his dog's fur. The seeds were difficult to remove and he looked at them using a microscope to see what was happening. From this, he had the idea for Velcro.

3 Exercise bikes were invented by the Austrian cyclist Hans Weger in 1854. He was trying to fix a problem with his bike, so he put the front wheel between two piles of books to look at what was happening. Then he realised that a bike like this would be perfect for exercise at home. The exercise bike was invented.

b Use your dictionary to check new words. You may have to explain words to your partner.

c Tell your partner about the three texts. Which one is not true? Talk about the texts and decide together.

d When you have decided which stories in each set are not true, check your answers on p.131.

Vocabulary Focus

1A Common adjectives

a ▶1.4 Listen to the conversations and look at the pictures. <u>Underline</u> the adjectives.

b Look at these adjectives and answer the questions. Use the conversations in **a** to help you.

> delicious /dɪlɪʃəs/ ugly /ʌgli/ serious /sɪəriəs/
> rude /ruːd/ alright /ɔːlraɪt/ silly /sɪli/
> boring /bɔːrɪŋ/ strange /streɪndʒ/

Which adjective means … ?
1 OK _____
2 not normal _____
3 not beautiful _____
4 not polite _____
5 the food is good _____
6 stupid _____
7 bad (for a problem) _____
8 not interesting _____

c Now look at these adjectives.

> gorgeous /gɔːdʒəs/ horrible /hɒrɪbəl/ lovely /lʌvli/
> amazing /əmeɪzɪŋ/ awful /ɔːfəl/ perfect /pɜːfekt/

Which adjective means … ?
- very nice/good _____ _____ _____ _____
- very bad _____ _____

d ▶1.5 Listen to the adjectives in **b** and **c**. How many syllables are there in each word? <u>Underline</u> the stressed syllable in each word.

e Practise the conversations with a partner.

f ▶ Now go back to p.8

1 What a silly game!
Don't be boring! Join in.

2 Perhaps he had a serious problem.
It's very rude to arrive so late.

3 The food here is delicious.
Yes. The fruit salad is gorgeous!

4 The weather's awful today.
Yes, it's horrible outside.

5 The weather's lovely today!
It's a perfect day for a BBQ.

6 Yes, but the music's alright.
It's a strange band to have at a wedding.

7 The room looks amazing.
I think the carpet's a bit ugly.

2A Tourism

a ▶1.29 Match the holiday items with the pictures. Listen and check. Repeat the words.

- [ ] backpack /ˈbækpæk/
- [ ] foreign currency /fɒrən ˈkʌrənsi/
- [ ] guidebook /ˈgaɪdbʊk/
- [ ] map /mæp/
- [ ] passport /ˈpɑːspɔːt/
- [ ] suitcase /ˈsuːtkeɪs/
- [ ] sunglasses /ˈsʌnglɑːsɪz/
- [ ] suntan lotion /ˈsʌntæn ləʊʃən/

b 💬 Which of the items in **a** do you always take on holiday?

c ▶1.30 Complete the travel phrases with the words in the box. Listen and check.

> ~~holiday~~ sightseeing /ˈsaɪtsiːɪŋ/ visa /ˈviːzə/
> campsite /ˈkæmpsaɪt/ souvenirs /suːvənˈɪəz/
> money accommodation /əkɒməˈdeɪʃən/
> hotel hostel /ˈhɒstəl/ adventure /ədˈventʃə/
> luggage /ˈlʌgɪdʒ/

1 We **went away on** _holiday_ for three weeks.
2 We needed to **get** a _____ from the embassy, before we travelled.
3 We also **exchanged** some _____ at the bank.
4 We **booked** all of our _____ online.
5 When we arrived, we **checked into** our luxury _____ and **unpacked** our _____.
6 We **did** some _____. The castles and gardens were gorgeous!
7 We **bought** _____ for our friends and family.
8 The second week, we **checked out of** our hotel and **stayed in** a _____. It was cheap and friendly!
9 The third week we **stayed on** a _____ by the beach.
10 We **had** a great _____ and we didn't want to come home.

d 💬 Work in pairs. Think of your last holiday. Which of the things in **c** did you do? Tell your partner.

e ▶ Now go back to p.19

2B Travel collocations

a ▶ **1.31** Listen to sentences 1–9 and look at the journey on the map. Match the words in **bold** with their definitions a–i.

1 ☐ We **travelled around** Europe last year.
2 ☐ We **set off** in June.
3 ☐ We **took off** late but …
4 ☐ … we **landed** on time in Berlin.
5 ☐ We **hitchhiked** across Germany.
6 ☐ A kind man **gave us a lift** to Frankfurt.
7 ☐ We **boarded a train** to Paris.
8 ☐ We **changed** at Strasbourg
9 ☐ We **got to** Paris at seven thirty.

a get on a bus/train/plane
b get off one train and get on a different train
c drive another person to their destination
d leave an airport by plane
e stand by the road and ask for free rides
f arrive at a place
g arrive at an airport by plane
h visit many different places in a large area
i start a journey

b 💬 Cover the sentences 1–9 and use the map to retell the story in **a**.

c Match the travel problems with the pictures.

1 ☐ They **missed** their train.
2 ☐ My car **broke down** on the motorway.
3 ☐ There was a lot of **turbulence** /ˈtɜːbjʊləns/ during the flight.
4 ☐ I **had a crash** on the drive to work.
5 ☐ The **traffic jam** went on for miles down the road.
6 ☐ There was **something wrong with** the plane.
7 ☐ There was a **strike** so there were no buses.
8 ☐ We **got lost** in the city centre.
9 ☐ There was a **long queue** /kjuː/ at the ticket office.
10 ☐ There was a **delay** at the station.

d ▶ **1.32** Listen and check. Then listen and repeat.

e 💬 Cover the sentences in **c** and try to remember them. Use the pictures to help you.

f 💬 Ask and answer the questions.

1 Which of the problems in the pictures have you had on journeys this year?
2 Is there a country you'd like to travel around?
3 When was the last time someone gave you a lift?
4 How do you feel when a plane takes off and lands?
5 Do you know anyone who hitchhikes? Do you think it's a good idea?

g ▶ Now go back to p.20

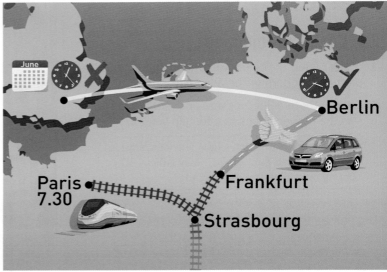

DUE 12:15 EXPECTED 14:15

3B Money

a ▶**1.50** Match each sentence with a picture to tell two stories. Listen and check.

- ☐ Carol now **owed** Fay £700. So she **got a loan** for £1000 from the bank.
- ☐ Fay offered to **lend** her some money, so she **borrowed** £100.
- ☐ Carol saw some shoes she loved, but she didn't have any **cash**.
- ☐ One day Carol and Fay went shopping in **the sales**.
- ☐ She **paid back** the £700 pounds (and spent the rest on shoes!)
- ☐ Carol had a problem. She **spent** a lot of money on shoes.

- ☐ When Brian got home he found a **special offer** online.
- ☐ Brian was **saving up for** a camera.
- ☐ He saw a great camera but it **cost** £499.
- ☐ He asked the shop assistant for a **discount** but she said no.
- ☐ So he got the cameral for £399! He was very happy!
- ☐ Brian **couldn't afford** it. He only had £400 in his **bank account**.

b 💬 Cover the sentences and use the words in the box to tell the stories.

Carol spend money on the sales cash lend
borrow /ˈbɒrəʊ/ owe /əʊ/ get a loan /ləʊn/ pay back

Brian save up for cost afford /əˈfɔːd/
bank account /əˈkaʊnt/ discount /ˈdɪskaʊnt/
special offer

c ▶ Now go back to p.30

4A Clothes and appearance

a 💬 Read the lists of words. Which words do you already know?

Small clothes: socks, shorts, underwear /ˈʌndəweə/, tights /taɪts/

Accessories: necklace, sunglasses, belt, scarf, handbag, bracelet /ˈbreɪslət/, earrings /ˈɪərɪŋz/, tie /taɪ/, gloves /glʌvz/

Footwear: trainers, boots, flat shoes, high heels, sandals /ˈsændəlz/

Clothing: jumper, suit, raincoat, top, tracksuit /ˈtræksuːt/, sweatshirt /ˈswetʃɜːt/

b Write the correct word from **a** next to each picture.

①   ②  ③  ④

⑤  ⑥   ⑦  ⑧

⑨   ⑩   ⑪  ⑫

c ▶**1.63** Listen and check your answers in **b**. Repeat the words.

d Cover the words. Can you remember the names of all the things in the pictures?

e Match the sentence halves.
1 ☐ I need a haircut so I'm **go**ing
2 ☐ I'm going to go shopping and **get**
3 ☐ I want to **look**
4 ☐ He should **have**
5 ☐ It's an expensive restaurant so please **wear**
6 ☐ She has very long nails so she often **go**es

a **a new outfit** for the party.
b **something nice**.
c **to the hairdresser's** this afternoon.
d **a shave** before he grows a beard.
e **my best** because all my family is coming.
f **to the beautician's**.

f ▶**1.64** Listen and check your answers to **e**.

g 💬 Work in pairs. Ask and answer the questions.
- When was the last time you wanted to look your best?
- What did you wear? Did you get a new outfit?
- Did you have a shave / go to the hairdresser's / the beautician's?

h ▶ Now go back to p.38

5A Work

a ▶ 2.3 Match the jobs with the pictures. Listen and check.

1 ☐ gardener /'gɑːdnə/
2 ☐ hairdresser /'heədresə/
3 ☐ plumber /'plʌmə/
4 ☐ scientist /'saɪəntɪst/
5 ☐ lawyer /'lɔɪə/
6 ☐ accountant /ə'kaʊntənt/
7 ☐ electrician /ɪlek'trɪʃən/
8 ☐ banker /'bæŋkə/
9 ☐ IT worker

We normally say *I work in IT* not *I'm an IT worker.*

b ▶ 2.3 Listen to the words in **a**. Which syllables are stressed? Add **1–8** to the table.

X x	X x x	x X x	x x X x
gardener			

c ▶ 2.4 Choose the correct verbs to complete the sentences. Then listen and check. Repeat the sentences.

'm   deal   with   earn   ~~have~~   make   need   work

1 They ___have___ ⟨ a nice working environment. /ɪn'vaɪrənmənt/
   a lot of skills.

2 I _____ ⟨ long hours.
   weekends.
   in a team.

3 You _____ ⟨ several years of training.
   good qualifications. /kwɒlɪfɪ'keɪʃənz/
   a university degree. /juːnɪ'vɜːsɪti dɪgriː/

4 I _____ ⟨ serious problems.
   people every day.

5 I _____ a good salary. /'sæləri/

6 I _____ self-employed. /ɪm'plɔɪd/

7 I _____ important decisions. /dɪ'sɪʒənz/

d 💬 Name one job for each description in **c**.

> Plumbers have a lot of skills.

e ▶ Now go back to p.48

5B Jobs

a Match the jobs with the pictures.

1 ☐ shop assistant /'ʃɒp əsɪstənt/
2 ☐ postman / postwoman /'pəʊstmən/ /'pəʊstwʊmən/
3 ☐ computer programmer /kəmpjuːtə 'prəʊgræmə/
4 ☐ actor / actress /'æktə/ /'æktrəs/
5 ☐ musician /mjuː'zɪʃən/
6 ☐ politician /pɒlɪ'tɪʃən/
7 ☐ builder /'bɪldə/
8 ☐ journalist /'dʒɜːnəlɪst/
9 ☐ architect /'ɑːkɪtekt/
10 ☐ designer /dɪ'zaɪnə/
11 ☐ vet /vet/
12 ☐ carer /'keərə/

b ▶ 2.12 Listen and check. Repeat the words.

c 💬 Which of the jobs are popular in your country? Which would you like to do?

d ▶ Now go back to p.51

6B -ed and -ing adjectives

a ▶**2.26** Look at the pictures. Complete the sentences with the pairs of words. Listen and check.

annoying / annoyed
1 a Magda was _____ by the music from the neighbour's flat.
   b The music from the neighbour's flat was really _____ .

disappointing / disappointed
2 a Will's birthday present was very _____ .
   b Will was very _____ by his present.

confusing / confused
3 a Andreas was very _____ by the road signs.
   b The road signs were really _____ .

tiring / tired
4 a Sara was _____ after a long day at work.
   b Sara had a really _____ day at work.

frightening / frightened
5 a Mehmet thought the animals were _____ .
   b Mehmet was _____ of the animals.

amazing / amazed
6 a The fireworks looked _____ .
   b Everyone was _____ by the fireworks.

embarrassing / embarrassed
7 a Liza was _____ by her boyfriend's dancing.
   b Liza's boyfriend's dancing was _____ .

surprising / surprised
8 a Anita was _____ to get the news from her sister.
   b Anita got some _____ news from her sister.

shocking / shocked
9 a The price of the meal was _____ .
   b They were _____ when they got the bill for the meal.

b ▶**2.27** Listen to the -ed adjectives. How many syllables are there? Then listen again and repeat.

amazed /əˈmeɪzd/
excited /ɪkˈsaɪtɪd/
annoyed /əˈnɔɪd/
confused /kənˈfjuːzd/
disappointed /dɪsəˈpɔɪntɪd/
embarrassed /ɪmˈbærəst/
frightened /ˈfraɪtənd/
interested /ˈɪntrəstɪd/
shocked /ʃɒkt/
surprised /səˈpraɪzd/
tired /taɪəd/

c 💬 Talk to a partner. Which word(s) could describe your feelings in these situations?
1 You can't understand the instructions for your new phone.
2 You are walking alone in a forest at night.
3 You hear some very bad news that you can't believe is true.
4 You have just broken a box of eggs in the supermarket.
5 Your boss has forgotten to tell you where the meeting is.
6 You have just run 10 km.
7 The weather on holiday was terrible every day.
8 You suddenly get a big pay rise.

d Write a sentence about each situation in c using an -ed or an -ing adjective.
My new phone is very confusing.

e 💬 Compare your sentences with a partner. Are they similar?

f ▶ Now go back to p.60

137

7A *get* collocations

a ▶ **2.44** Complete the sentences with the phrases in the box. Then listen and check.

> get better   get a job   get paid
> get on well   get ill   get an offer

A I would love to ¹ _____ as a designer. But for now I'll take any work.

B You could work as a waiter until you ² _____ from a design company.

A I've got a terrible cold at the moment. It's strange – I hardly ever ³ _____ .

B Oh dear. I hope you ⁴ _____ soon.

A How's the new job?

B It's great. I really ⁵ _____ with my new colleagues. But I don't ⁶ _____ for the first month so I can't afford to go out for a while.

b 💬 Practise the conversations in **a** with a partner.

c ▶ **2.45** Complete Ted's story with the phrases in the box. Use the correct form of *get*. Listen and check.

> get to know   get engaged   get together
> get a place   get divorced   get in touch

Ted studied hard at school and ¹_____ at university. While he was there he ²_____ Sylvia, another student on his course. They didn't see each other after university, but one day Ted saw Sylvia's photo in a newspaper and decided to ³_____ with her again. They soon ⁴_____ and were a very happy couple. Just six months later they decided they wanted to spend their lives together, so they ⁵_____. But the story didn't end well. Only a year after the wedding, they ⁶_____ .

d Work in pairs. Write your own definitions for these phrases.

> get divorced   get on well   get together
> get engaged   get in touch   get to know

e Check your definitions in a dictionary or with your teacher. Were you right?

f ▶ Now go back to p.69

8B Sports and activities

a Match the sports and activities with the pictures.

1 ☑ surfing /sɜːfɪŋ/	6 ☐ rock climbing /klaɪmɪŋ/	11 ☐ windsurfing /wɪndsɜːfɪŋ/
2 ☐ snowboarding /snəʊbɔːdɪŋ/	7 ☐ gymnastics /dʒɪmnæstɪks/	12 ☐ athletics /æθletɪks/
3 ☐ golf /gɒlf/	8 ☐ (scuba) diving /(skuːbə) daɪvɪŋ/	13 ☐ ice hockey /aɪs hɒki/
4 ☐ volleyball /vɒlibɔːl/	9 ☐ yoga /jəʊgə/	14 ☐ squash /skwɒʃ/
5 ☐ skateboarding /skeɪtbɔːdɪŋ/	10 ☐ jogging /dʒɒgɪŋ/	15 ☐ ice skating /aɪs skeɪtɪŋ/

b ▶ **2.67** Listen and check. Underline the stressed syllable on each word in **a**. Then listen and repeat.

c Read the note below. Which verb do we use with the sports in **a**: *play*, *do* or *go*?

> We normally use the verb *play* with sports that use a ball: *play volleyball / squash*
>
> We normally use *go* with -*ing* forms: *go surfing / skateboarding*
>
> We use *do* with other activities: *do yoga / athletics*

d Write one sport or activity for each adjective. Use the sports and activities in **a** or your own ideas.

- relaxing
- exciting
- tiring
- boring
- frightening
- fun

e 💬 Work in pairs. Compare your answers to **d**.

f ▶ Now go back to p.81

9A Education collocations

a Match the phrases 1–5 in **bold** with the definitions a–e.

1. [ ] **fail an exam**
2. [ ] **hand in an essay**
3. [ ] **get into university**
4. [ ] **do a degree in** maths
5. [ ] **revise** for an exam
6. [ ] **take notes**
7. [ ] **get good marks**

a get a place at university
b study on a three- or four-year course at university
c give a finished essay to a teacher
d study for an exam
e not pass an exam
f receive a high grade in an exam or on an essay
g write down main ideas

b Choose the correct word to complete the text.

My brother was always the ambitious one in the family and he really wanted to *get into / get onto*[1] university. His dream was to *make / do*[2] a degree in physics because he wanted to become a scientist. He studied hard at school and he managed to *get / go*[3] a place at a top university – St Andrews!

University was hard but he enjoyed it. He had to *take / write*[4] a lot of essays but he was a good student. He always *did / took*[5] a lot of notes during his classes and he only *handed / put*[6] an essay in late once because he had a broken leg and was in hospital! Because of his hard work, he *got / made*[7] good marks for all his courses and he never *failed / lost*[8] an exam. He was an A+ student. And what about me? Well, that's a different story …

c ▶ **3.4** Listen and check.

d Complete the sentences with the words below.

notes	mark	degree	university	essay	place	exam

1. She's doing a _____ in business management.
2. He handed in his _____ late because he was ill.
3. I need to revise for my _____ next week.
4. She got a very good _____ for her essay: A+.
5. I took a lot of _____ during the lecture. You can read them if you want.
6. She's very intelligent. She's got a _____ at Tokyo University. She starts this year.
7. He got into _____ last year. He's studying law.

e ▶ Now go back to p.89

9B Verbs followed by *to* + infinitive / verb + -*ing*

a Match the sentences 1–12 with the things the people said, below.

1. She **refused** to discuss the matter.
2. They **arranged** to meet in the evening.
3. He **forgot** to go to the supermarket.
4. He **recommended** ordering the cake.
5. He **imagined** being somewhere warmer.
6. She **missed** living by the sea.
7. He really **disliked** travelling by train.
8. The shop **seemed** to be closed.
9. They **agreed** to change tables.
10. She **managed** to make the sauce.
11. He **regretted** wearing a suit.
12. She **avoids** eating spicy food.

[ ] "OK, so see you tomorrow evening at 7 pm."
[ ] "Making the sauce was really difficult, but it tastes alright."
[ ] "I didn't remember to go to the supermarket. Sorry. I was really busy."
[ ] **"You should try the cake. It's delicious."**
[ ] "I loved living by the sea. I used to go swimming every morning."
[ ] **"Sorry, I'm not going to talk about this. I've made my decision."**
[ ] "I hate trains. They're so noisy."
[ ] **"I'd love to be on the beach in Greece right now. The sun, the sea ..."**
[ ] **"It looks like the shop's closed."**
[ ] "I look so silly in this suit!"
[ ] **"OK, let's move to that table over there."**
[ ] "No, thanks. I don't eat curry. It gives me a bad stomach."

b Complete the table with the verbs in **bold** from **a**.

Verbs followed by *to* + infinitive	Verbs followed by verb + -*ing*
refuse	

c ▶ **3.11** Listen to the sentences **a 1–12**. <u>Underline</u> the stressed syllable in the words in **bold**. Practise saying the sentences.

d Complete the sentences using the verbs in the tables in **b**.

1. *This computer is terrible. Buying it was a big mistake!*
   He _____ buying the computer.
2. *I hate doing exams. I get so nervous!*
   He really _____ doing exams.
3. *Oh, no! It's my mother's birthday. I haven't sent her a card.*
   He _____ to send his mother a birthday card.
4. *It would be lovely to live in Paris! I could eat great food every day!*
   He _____ living in Paris.
5. *No, I won't pay more money.*
   She _____ to pay more money.
6. *OK, so let's talk tomorrow. I'll call you.*
   They _____ to talk on the phone.
7. *I try not to leave work at 5 pm. The traffic is terrible.*
   She _____ leaving work at 5 pm.
8. *You should read this book on Italy. It's great.*
   He _____ reading a book on Italy.
9. *I want to play with my cat but he's at my parents' house.*
   She _____ playing with her cat.
10. *Fine with me, I'm happy to share a dessert.*
    They _____ to share one dessert between two.
11. *I've finished my essay just in time to hand it in.*
    She _____ to finish her work on time.
12. *You look upset. Are you OK?*
    She _____ to be upset.

e ▶ Now go back to p.91

10A Multi-word verbs

a Read the sentences. Which multi-word verb in the box can replace the words in **bold**?

> passed on   put off   carried on   came round
> looked after   handed in   broke up
> turned down   joined in   felt like

1 I asked him to be quiet, but he just **continued** talking. _____
2 It was a really sunny day and he really **wanted** an ice cream. _____
3 She **came to my house** to ask for some advice. _____
4 I **took care of** my friend's cat while he was on holiday. _____
5 They used to go out with each other, but they **ended their relationship**. _____
6 He **said 'no' to** the invitation, because he had too much work. _____
7 The game looked like fun, so I **did it with them**. _____
8 They **delayed** the meeting, because Bob was ill. _____
9 I **took** the keys I found to the receptionist. _____
10 He **told her** the message as soon as he saw her. _____

b Complete the sentences with the correct form of a multi-word verb from **a**.

1 My friend _____ for dinner last night. I cooked her spaghetti.
2 She's ill, so we've _____ the party until she gets better.
3 Can you _____ my new number to Bob? It's 07806 540 234.
4 Mike and I were together for a year but we _____ two months ago.
5 Tom started singing a song and then we all _____. It was pretty noisy!
6 Somebody _____ my wallet at the police station.
7 She _____ the job offer because the pay was too low.
8 "Do you _____ a pizza tonight?" "Yes, that sounds nice."
9 I'm _____ my niece this evening. She's only 7 years old.
10 We were all tired and wanted to stop running but our teacher told us to _____ .

> 🗨 **Tip**
>
> Multi-word verbs have different kinds of grammar. Some transitive multi-word verbs (*hand in, pass on, put off*) can be separated by an object:
>
> We **put off** the match. ✓   We **put** the match **off**. ✓
>
> If the object of these multi-word verbs is a pronoun, they must be separated:
>
> I **handed** it **in**. ✓   ~~I **handed in** it~~. ✗
>
> Other multi-word verbs (*feel like, look after*) can never be separated:
>
> He **felt like** an ice cream. ✓   ~~He **felt** an ice cream **like**~~. ✗

c ▶ Now go back to p.99

11A Compound nouns

a Write the compound nouns. Use the words in the sentences to help you.

1 A shop that sells shoes is a *shoe shop* .
2 A book with addresses in it is an _____ .
3 A shelf you put books on is a _____ .
4 An office where you buy tickets is a _____ .
5 A ring you put keys on is a _____ .
6 A programme on the television is a _____ .
7 Lights on a street to help you see when it's dark are _____ .
8 A sign by the road is a _____ .
9 A machine you can get cash from is a _____ .
10 Fiction which describes a new kind of science is _____ .

> 🗨 **Tip**
>
> • The first word in a compound noun is normally singular:
> a ~~books~~ shop ✗   a book shop ✓
> This is also true if the compound noun is plural:
> There are three ~~tickets~~ offices in the station. ✗
> There are three ticket offices in the station. ✓
>
> • When a compound noun is used for many years, it sometimes becomes one word, not two. For example, *Cambridge Advanced Learner's Dictionary* says:
> streetlights ✓   NOT ~~street lights~~ ✗
> But not all compounds can be joined together.
> road sign ✓   NOT ~~roadsign~~ ✗
> Check the punctuation in a recent dictionary to be sure.

b ▶3.36 Listen to the compound nouns in **a**. <u>Underline</u> the main stressed syllable. Answer the questions.
1 Which word in compound nouns is normally stressed?
2 Which compound noun is stressed differently from the others?

c Practise saying the compund nouns in **a**.

d Make compound nouns with one word from box A followed by one word from box B. How many can you make?

> **A**
> mountain   TV   bread   coffee   shopping   city
> kitchen   computer   tea   rock   car   bottle

> **B**
> knife   top   park   door   bag   climbing
> star   screen   cup   centre   game

e Complete the questions using a compound noun from **d**. There is usually more than one possible answer.
1 Do you like playing _____?
2 How long do you spend looking at a _____ every day?
3 Have you ever gone _____?
4 Would you like to be a _____?
5 Who is your favourite _____?
6 What is your favourite _____?

f 🗨 Ask and answer the questions in **e**.

g ▶ Now go back to p.109

12B Personality adjectives

a Read the sentences and match the people who are opposites.

1 ☐ Sara's so **serious** – she doesn't laugh much and she never makes jokes.
2 ☐ Maria always pays for me and helps me with stuff. She's really **generous**.
3 ☐ Andrew is always so **anxious** – he worries about everything.
4 ☐ Mai-Li is quite **shy** and doesn't like meeting new people.

a My sister Yasmin hardly ever worries about anything – I'd love to be as **easygoing** as she is.
b Rea is so **selfish** – she only thinks about what she wants, never other people.
c Ros is a very **sociable** person – she's always out with friends or at parties.
d Jon's a really **fun** person and I always have a good time when I see him.

b Complete the sentences with the words in the box.

generous   sensible   funny   strict   reliable
creative   careless   confident   honest
patient   fair

1 People who make good decisions and don't do stupid things are _____ .
2 People who know they are good at certain things are _____ .
3 People who always keep their promises, arrive on time etc. are _____ .
4 People who make a lot of rules for children are _____ .
5 People who make mistakes because they are not careful are _____ .
6 People who don't get angry when something takes a long time are _____ .
7 People who give a lot to other people are _____ .
8 People who treat everyone equally are _____ .
9 People who are good at thinking of new ideas are _____ .
10 People who always tell the truth are _____ .
11 People who make other people laugh are _____ .

c ▶ **3.58** Listen to the adjectives. <u>Underline</u> the stressed syllable in each. The first has been done for you. Practise saying the words.

<u>anx</u>ious /æŋkʃəs/	fun /fʌn/	selfish /selfɪʃ/
careless /keələs/	funny /fʌni/	sensible /sensɪbəl/
confident /kɒnfɪdənt/	generous /dʒenərəs/	shy /ʃaɪ/
creative /krieɪtɪv/	honest /ɒnɪst/	sociable /səʊʃəbəl/
easygoing /iːzigəʊɪŋ/	patient /peɪʃənt/	strict /strɪkt/
fair /feə/	reliable /rɪlaɪəbəl/	

d Which of the adjectives in **c** are negative?

e 💬 Ask and answer the questions.
1 Which of the adjectives do you think describe your personality?
2 Which qualities would you like to have (but don't)?

I think I'm sociable and easygoing.

I'd like to be more patient.

f ▶ Now go back to p.121

> 💬 **Tip**
> *fun* and *funny* have different meanings.
> She's **funny**. = She makes you laugh.
> She's **fun**. = She isn't serious or boring.

Grammar Focus

1A Question forms

Questions with *be*
In questions with *be*, the verb *be* goes before the subject. We don't add an auxiliary verb.

▶ **1.6**

Question word	*be*	Subject	
How	**'s**	the food?	–
What	**was**	the party	like yesterday?
–	**Are**	you	a teacher?
–	**Were**	they	late?

> 💬 **Tip** When we want to ask for a description or an opinion we can use:
>
> **be like**   **How ...** with the verb *be*
> **A** *What* **was** *the film* **like**?   **A** **How was** *your holiday?*
> **B** *It was alright.*   **B** *Fantastic!*

Questions with other main verbs
In questions with other verbs, we add an auxiliary verb to form questions. The auxiliary verb goes before the subject.

▶ **1.7**

Question word	Auxiliary verb	Subject	Main verb	
Where	**do**	you	live?	–
What time	**did**	they	arrive	at the party?
–	**Does**	the film	have	a happy ending?
–	**Did**	you	make	the food?

In questions with *do* or *did*, the main verb is in the infinitive:
Does *she* **live** *here?* NOT ~~**Does** she **lives** here?~~
Did *you* **come** *by taxi?* NOT ~~**Did** you **came** by taxi?~~
Modal verbs like *can* are also auxiliary verbs:
What **can** *you see?*

Wh- questions start with a question word: *Who, What, Where, When, Why, Which, Whose, How;*
How much, How many, What time, What colour, What kind of car, etc.

1B Present simple and present continuous

Present simple
We use the present simple to describe:
- routines and habits
  I **send** a lot of emails.
- situations which are generally true or stay the same for a long time:
  He **doesn't work** very hard.

We use adverbs of frequency with the present simple:
I **always** / **sometimes** / **rarely** / **never** write letters.
I write letters **once** / **ten times** a week / year.

The verb *be* doesn't have the same form as other verbs:
I **am** a student.   They **are** not here.
Is she always friendly? Yes, she **is**.

Present continuous
We use the present continuous to describe:
- actions right now, at the moment of speaking:
  He **'s not cooking** dinner, he **'s watching** TV.
- temporary actions around the present time:
  They **'re travelling** around Asia this year.

We often use these time expressions with the present continuous:
I'm working at a supermarket **right now** / **these days** / **at the moment** / **today** / **this summer** etc.

▶ **1.13**

	I / You / We / They	He / She / It
+	We **live** next door.	He **lives** here.
–	I **don't work** here.	She **doesn't work** here.
Y/N?	**Do** your friends **write** emails? Yes, they **do**. / No, they **don't**.	**Does** your sister **write** a blog? Yes, she **does**. / No, she **doesn't**.

> 💬 **Tip** Some verbs, which describe feelings and states, are not usually used in continuous tenses:
> *be like love hate prefer know understand remember forget want own need*
> I **need** a new computer. NOT ~~I'm needing a new computer.~~
> He **doesn't understand** you. NOT ~~He isn't understanding you.~~

▶ **1.14**

	I	He / She / It	You / We / They
+	I **'m watching** TV.	She **'s helping**.	We **'re working** hard.
–	I **'m not feeling** well.	It **'s not raining**.	They **'re not sleeping**.
Y/N?	**Am** I **looking** alright? Yes, I **am**. / No, I **'m not**.	**Is** he **working** late? Yes, he **is**. / No he **isn't**.	**Are** they **enjoying** the party? Yes, they **are**. / No, they **aren't**.

SPELLING: verb + -*ing*

Most verbs	+ -*ing*
sleep watch say	*sleeping watching saying*
Stressed vowel + one consonant (not w, x, y)	**2× consonant + -*ing***
stop run get	*stopping running getting*
Consonant + -*e*	**– -*e* and + -*ing***
live make have	*living making having*

> 💬 **Tip** *is not* and *are not* can be contracted two different ways:
> *is not = isn't = 's not*
> *are not = aren't = 're not*

1A Question forms

a <u>Underline</u> the main verb in each question.

1 Where do you <u>live</u>?
2 How are you today?
3 Did you see the football match yesterday?
4 Who do you know at this party?
5 What did you do at the weekend?
6 What kind of food do you like?
7 What's the food like?
8 Can I sit here?

b Look at the questions in **a** again. Tick (✓) the questions which have an auxiliary verb.

c Add the word at the end of the line to form a correct question. Sometimes you also need to change the punctuation.

1 What kind of books you usually read?   *do*
   <u>What kind of books do you usually read?</u>
2 You watch the Olympics on TV?   *did*
   _____
3 What the food like in India?   *was*
   _____
4 You go to the gym?   *do*
   _____
5 How much she earn?   *does*
   _____
6 It cold today?   *is*
   _____
7 Where they go on holiday?   *did*
   _____
8 I late?   *am*
   _____

d Correct the mistake in each question.

1 **A** Why do want you to go home?
   B Because I'm tired.
2 **A** What did you meet at the party?
   B Rashid and Fran.
3 **A** How much your car was?
   B I paid £500.
4 **A** Which did you see film?
   B The new James Bond film.
5 **A** Who key is this?
   B Mine.
6 **A** How many people you did invite?
   B About 20.
7 **A** Was the film like?
   B It was pretty good.
8 **A** What kind music do you like?
   B I like dance music.

e ▶ Now go to back to p.9

How's the food?

It's wonderful! Did you make it?

1B Present simple and present continuous

a Choose the best ending for each sentence from each pair. Write the number in the box.

1 a ☐ I work in a bank …   1 but I don't enjoy it.
  b ☐ I'm working in a café …   2 but it's only a summer job.

2 a ☐ She drives to work every day …   1 so she can't answer the phone,
  b ☐ She's driving right now …   2 so she spends a lot on petrol.

3 a ☐ I write to my parents …   1 because their phone's broken.
  b ☐ I'm writing to my parents …   2 once a month.

4 a ☐ We're not eating there …   1 today because it's full.
  b ☐ We don't eat there …   2 because the food is awful.

b Choose the correct answer.

1 *I eat / I'm eating* my lunch at the moment. Can you wait?
2 Look at that man! He *doesn't wear / isn't wearing* any shoes.
3 *She normally goes / She's normally going* to the cinema on Tuesday nights.
4 *I study / I'm studying* hard, because I've got an exam next week.
5 Some of my friends *look / are looking* at their phones every five minutes.
6 My grandparents *hardly ever visit / are hardly ever visiting* us because they live in Australia.
7 We want to finish the project tonight, so *we work / we're working* late.
8 *Is your brother liking / Does your brother like* computer games?

c Complete the conversation with the present simple or present continuous.

A What [1] <u>are you doing</u> (you / do)?
B [2] _____ (I / check) Facebook.
A Really? But you checked it about 20 minutes ago. How often [3] _____ (you / check) your account?
B Well, [4] _____ (I / usually check) my account once a day. But today's different. [5] _____ (my sister / travel) around Africa at the moment, and I'm worried about her.
[6] _____ (she / usually send) me a message on Facebook two or three times a day, but the last time she wrote was a week ago.
A Maybe [7] _____ (she / travel) right now, and she can't use the Internet.
[8] _____ (she / go) on safari?
B No, I don't think so. [9] _____ (she / not like) the countryside. [10] _____ (she / prefer) cities. Oh … look! Here's a message from her. You were right! [11] _____ (she / drive) through the Masai Mara National Park at the moment.
A Where's that?
B [12] _____ (it / be) in Kenya.
[13] _____ (there / be) lots of wild animals there.
A Cool … that's amazing. So why [14] _____ (she / spend) her time on Facebook?

d ▶ Now go to back to p.11

2A Past simple

We use the past simple to talk about completed actions and situations in the past.
*I **went** to Greece last summer. It **was** amazing.*
*I **didn't want** to leave.*
*Where **did** you **stay**?*

The form of the past simple is the same for all persons.

(▶) **1.25** In positive statements, regular verbs have *ed* endings:
*I **decided** yesterday.*
*We **played** volleyball on the beach.*

However, many common verbs are irregular:
go > *I **went** there last year.*
have > *We **had** a lot of fun.*
see > *She **saw** the Taj Mahal.*

There is a list of irregular verbs on p.176

*I didn't **want** to go water skiing but when I **tried** it, it **was** brilliant*

To form negative statements and questions, we use the auxiliary verb *did*.

	I / You / We / They / He / She / It
–	*I **didn't go** there.*
Y/N?	***Did** you **have** fun?* *Yes, I **did**. / No, I **didn't**.*

(▶) **1.26** *be* doesn't have the same form as other verbs:

	I / He / She / It	You / We / They
+	*The weather **was** great.*	*The shops **were** near the beach.*
–	*I **wasn't** very happy.*	*We **weren't** tired.*
Y/N?	***Was** your tour guide good?* *Yes, she **was**. / No, she **wasn't**.*	***Were** you late for your flight?* *Yes, we **were**. / No, we **weren't**.*

We often use these time expressions with the past simple:
I drove to London   ***last** week / year.*
           *two days **ago**.*
           ***when** I was a child.*

They come at the beginning or the end of a sentence:
***When I finished school**, I went to university.*
*I went to Greece **two years ago**.*

SPELLING: verb + -ed

Most verbs *play watch show*	**+ -ed** *play**ed** watch**ed** show**ed***
Ending in -e *liv**e** phon**e** agre**e** lov**e***	**+ -d** *liv**ed** phon**ed** agre**ed** lov**ed***
Stressed vowel + consonant **(not w, x, y)** *stop plan prefer*	**2× consonant and + -ed** *stop**ped** plan**ned** prefer**red***
Consonant -y *marry study try*	**– -y, + -ied** *marr**ied** stud**ied** tr**ied** worr**ied***

2B Past continuous

We use the past continuous to describe something in progress at a particular time in the past.
*In 2010, I **was living** in Poland.*
*At 11 o'clock, he **was waiting** by the fountain.*
*When they arrived, I **was cooking** dinner.*

Use the past continuous with the past simple:

- to describe long and short actions together:
  *I **was reading** my book when the plane took off.*

- to describe a longer action that stopped suddenly because something else happened:
  *When I **was driving** to work, my car broke down.*

We can use *when* to join the two parts of a sentence:
***When** my car broke down, I was driving to work.*
*My car broke down **when** I was driving to work.*

> 💬 **Tip**
> We often use the past continuous to describe the situation at the beginning of a story.
> *In 2010, we **were travelling** across Russia.*
> *John **was driving** too fast down the motorway.*

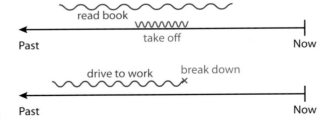

(▶) **1.35**

	I / He / She / It	You / We / They
+	*I **was driving** to work.*	*You **were standing** on the platform.*
–	*He **wasn't listening**.*	*We **weren't watching**.*
Y/N?	***Was** she **waiting** for you?* *Yes, she **was**. / No, she **wasn't**.*	***Were** they **travelling** by train?* *Yes, they **were**. / No, they **weren't**.*

2A Past simple

a Write the past simple form of the verbs. Some of them are irregular.

1 ask _____   6 forget _____   11 offer _____
2 buy _____   7 know _____   12 prefer _____
3 dance _____   8 learn _____   13 relax _____
4 enjoy _____   9 hurry _____   14 say _____
5 find _____   10 meet _____   15 wear _____

b Last week, Elliot's holiday was very good. Victoria's was very bad. Complete each sentence with the positive or negative form of the verb at the beginning of the line.

ELLIOT

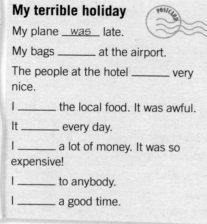

My fantastic holiday

be 1 My plane <u>wasn't</u> late.

arrive 2 My bags _____ at the airport.

be 3 The people at the hotel _____ very nice.

eat 4 I _____ the local food. It was great!

rain 5 It _____.

spend 6 I _____ a lot of money. It was so cheap!

speak 7 I _____ to a lot of people.

have 8 I _____ a good time.

VICTORIA

My terrible holiday

My plane _<u>was</u>_ late.

My bags _____ at the airport.

The people at the hotel _____ very nice.

I _____ the local food. It was awful.

It _____ every day.

I _____ a lot of money. It was so expensive!

I _____ to anybody.

I _____ a good time.

c Elliot asked Victoria about her holiday. Write Elliot's questions in the past simple.

1 **E** why / your plane / be late
   <u>Why was your plane late?</u>
   V I think there was a problem with the engine.

2 **E** when / your bags / arrive
   _____?
   V On the last day of my holiday.

3 **E** what / you / wear?
   _____?
   V I bought some new clothes.

4 **E** the people / be friendly
   _____?
   V No, they were rude.

5 **E** what / weather / be like
   _____?
   V It rained every day.

6 **E** what kind of food / you eat
   _____?
   V Nothing special.

7 **E** you / have / a good time
   _____?
   V No!

d ▶ Now go back to p.19

2B Past continuous

a Complete the sentences with the past continuous forms of the verbs.

1 A year ago, _____ (I / live) with my parents.
2 At nine last night, _____ (we / sleep).
3 **A** What _____ (you / do) at midnight on New Year's Eve?
   B We _____ (watch) the celebrations on TV.
4 _____ (she / not study) when I got home, _____ (she / chat) to her friends online.
5 **A** _____ (Most people / not wear) suits for the job interview.
   B What _____ (they / wear)?

b Choose the best form for each verb. There is one past simple verb and one past continuous verb in each sentence.

1 The Internet *stopped / was stopping* when I *watched / was watching* a film.
2 She *walked / was walking* down the street when she *saw / was seeing* her friend.
3 He *left / was leaving* his job when he *studied / was studying* for his exams.
4 I *did / was doing* some cleaning when I *heard / was hearing* the news on the radio.
5 We *felt / were feeling* tired when we *got / were getting* home.
6 I *didn't visit / wasn't visiting* Cancún when I *worked / was working* in Mexico.
7 I *wasn't looking / didn't look* when I *crashed / was crashing* my bicycle into a tree.

c Use the past continuous and the past simple of the verbs in brackets to complete the sentences about each picture.

1

When I _____ down the street, I _____ ten pounds. (walk, find)

2

It _____ when she _____ the house. (rain, leave)

3

When you _____ me, I _____ dinner. (call, cook)

4

They _____ quietly when the teacher _____ back. (not work, come)

d ▶ Now go back to p.21

3A Present perfect or past simple

We use the present perfect to talk about past experiences.

The present perfect refers to the whole past, not a particular time.

1.47

	I / You / We / They **have** + past participle	He / She / It **has** + past participle
+	*I've given* a stranger a lift.	He***'s given*** a stranger a lift.
–	We **haven't done** any charity work.	He **hasn't done** any charity work.
Y/N?	**Have** you ever helped a stranger? Yes, I **have**. / No, I **haven't**.	**Has** she ever helped a stranger? Yes, she **has**. / No, she **hasn't**.

Regular past participles end in -ed, e.g. *I have* **worked**...
Many past participles are irregular, e.g. *I have* **bought**...

The past simple and the past participle are often different, e.g. *I* **drove**; *I have* **driven**.
See p.176 for a list of irregular verbs.

> 💬 **Tip**
>
> **The verb *go* in the present perfect**
> We use *been* instead of *gone* for a past experience:
> *I've* **been** *to China.* (= I went there and came back home.)
> We use *gone* to say where other people are now:
> *She's* **gone** *to China.* (= She's there now.)

We often use *ever* and *never* with the present perfect to talk about our whole life experience. *ever* and *never* come before the past participle in the sentence.
We can also use *once / twice / three times* etc. at the end of a sentence to say how many times we have had an experience.

A *I've* **never** *visited the UK. Have you* **ever** *been there?* ⎱ Present perfect
B *Yes, I have. I've been there* **three times**. ⎰ for experiences in general

When we ask or talk about specific past times we use the past simple.

A *When was* **the last time** *you went?* ⎱ Past simple for
B **Two years ago**. *I rented a car and drove to Scotland.* ⎰ specific events

---

3B Present perfect with *just*, *already* and *yet*

1.53 We can use the present perfect to talk about the recent past.

Use present perfect with *just* in positive statements to say that something happened a very short time ago.
just comes before the past participle in the sentence.
We also use *just* in present perfect questions.
A **Has** *she* **just left**? B *No, she went a few hours ago.*

The present perfect with *already* in positive statements shows that something is complete, often before we expected.

already usually comes before the past participle.
We also use *already* in present perfect questions to show surprise.
Have *you* **already done** *all your work?*

Use present perfect with *yet*:
• in a negative statement to show that something is not complete.
• in a question to ask if something is complete.
yet comes at the end of the sentence.

> 💬 **Tip**
>
> Don't use a past time expression (e.g. *five minutes ago, last week*) with the present perfect. Change to the past simple to talk about the time when something happened:
> *I've* **already seen** *this film. I* **saw** *it* **last week**.
> NOT *I've already seen this film last week.*

3A Present perfect or past simple

a Write the past participles of the verbs.

1	buy	_bought_	6	lend	_____
2	do	_____	7	ride	_____
3	drive	_____	8	save	_____
4	give	_____	9	see	_____
5	make	_____	10	sell	_____

11	smile	_____
12	spend	_____
13	take	_____
14	want	_____
15	write	_____

b Complete the sentences with the present perfect form of the verbs in brackets. Use contractions where they are natural.

1 I _'ve never given_ (never / give) money to charity.
2 **A** _____ (you / ever / sell) anything on eBay?
  B Yes, I have. Several times.
3 She _____ (live) in lots of different countries.
4 I know that restaurant – we _____ (eat) there before. The food's excellent.
5 I _____ (never / sing) in front of a large group of people – and I never want to!
6 **A** _____ (he / ever / cook) for more than ten people?
  B No, he hasn't. What about you?
7 She _____ (help) me several times – she's very kind.
8 My car _____ (never / break) down and it's more than ten years old.
9 How many times _____ (the children / see) this film?
10 We _____ (never / try) this, so it'll be new experience.

c Correct the mistakes in these sentences.

1 Have you ever ~~climb~~ a mountain?
  Have you ever climbed a mountain?
2 I never saw that film.
  _____
3 Have you ever gone to Canada?
  _____
4 Where have you been on holiday last year?
  _____
5 She's broken her leg two times.
  _____
6 I've worked in a hospital a long time ago.
  _____
7 In your life, how many times did you move house?
  _____
8 When we went to London we've visited Kew Gardens.
  _____

d ▶ Now go back to p.29

3B Present perfect with *just*, *already* and *yet*

a Match the questions and answers.

1 [g] Would you like some food?
2 [ ] Did you like the movie?
3 [ ] Has Junko called yet?
4 [ ] Where's Liza?
5 [ ] Would you like to go for a walk?
6 [ ] Can you email Marc about the meeting?
7 [ ] Have you written your essay yet?
8 [ ] What did you think of the report?

a Yes, I've just spoken to her.
b I've already emailed him.
c She's just gone out. She'll be back soon.
d I'm afraid I haven't read it yet.
e No, thanks. I've already been out.
f We haven't seen it yet.
g No, thanks. I've already had lunch.
h Not yet. I've just finished the introduction.

b Put the words in the correct order to make sentences or questions.

1 they / have / us / yet? / paid
  Have they paid us yet?
2 already / I've / money / all / spent / my
  _____
3 arrived / our visitors / have / just
  _____
4 shops / I / yet / haven't / to / the / been
  _____
5 raining / just / started / it / has
  _____
6 he / yet? / any / has / money / saved
  _____

c Look at Jeff's list of things to do. Write sentences about what he has already done (✓), and what he hasn't done yet. Use *already* / *yet* and the present perfect.

1 _He hasn't done the shopping yet._
2 _____
3 _____
4 _____
5 _____
6 _____
7 _____
8 _____
9 _____
10 _____

Jeff To Do – Wednesday

1 do shopping
2 pay Mark back
3 buy paper for the printer ✓
4 check my emails ✓
5 ask Dad for some money
6 write to Daniel ✓
7 finish writing my project ✓
8 clean the flat
9 take out rubbish
10 have a haircut ✓

d ▶ Now go back to p.31

4A Present continuous and *going to*

I'm meeting Mary at the library to study tomorrow. After the exams, we're going to celebrate!

We use both the present continuous and *going to* + infinitive to talk about future plans – things we have decided to do in the future. In most situations, both forms are possible.

*I'm **taking** an English exam next year.* ✓
*I'm **going to take** an English exam next year.* ✓

Present continuous

The present continuous is more natural to talk about **arrangements** – when you have agreed something with other people or you have already spent money.

*I'm **getting** married next week.* (We have arranged and paid for everything.)
*I'm **meeting** Mary at the library tomorrow.* (We have arranged a time and place for the meeting.)

> 💬 **Tip**
>
> When we use the present continuous with a future meaning, we usually mention the time (e.g. *tomorrow, next week*)
> We don't need to mention the time with *be going to*:
> *She's leaving **tomorrow**.* (future arrangement)
> *She's leaving.* (right now)
> *She's going to leave.* (future plan)

(For the form of the present continuous see Grammar reference 1B.)

going to

be going to + infinitive tells people about a **plan** or **intention** – when you have already decided to do something in the future.

*We're **going to get** married next year.* (We have decided this, but we haven't booked anything yet.)
*After the exams, **we're going to celebrate**.* (But we don't know exactly where or what time.)

▶ **1.66** *be going to* + infinitve

	I	He / She / It	You / We / They
+	*I'm going to watch TV.*	*She's going to help.*	*We're going to work hard.*
−	*I'm not going to play.*	*It's not going to arrive today.*	*They're not going to sleep.*
Y/N?	*Am I going to pick him up? Yes, I am. / No, I'm not.*	*Is he going to work late? Yes, he is. / No, he isn't.*	*Are they going to bring anything? Yes, they are. / No, they aren't.*

4B *will / won't / shall*

We use *will* to show we are deciding something while we are speaking:
A *Would you like tea or coffee?*
B *Er … **I'll have** tea, please.*

This is often to make **offers** and **promises**:
A *Oh no – I've left my money at home!*
B *Don't worry – **I'll pay**.*
A *Can I tell you a secret?*
B *Of course. I promise **I won't tell** anyone else.*

We can make a **request** with *will*:
*Will you **take** a photograph?*
*Will you **give** me a lift to the cinema tomorrow?*

We use *shall* in questions to make **offers** and **suggestions**:
*Shall I **pay** for your food?* (= I'm offering to pay.)
*Shall we **go** to the cinema this weekend?* (= I'm suggesting this.)

We can also use *shall* to **ask for a suggestion**:
A *What **shall we do** this evening?*
We often reply to these questions with *Let's* + infinitive:
B *Let's **go** to a nice restaurant.*

> 💬 **Tip**
>
> Reply to offers with *shall* with *Yes, please. / No, thanks.*
> NOT ~~Yes, you shall. / No, you shan't.~~

will and *shall* are modal auxiliary verbs. They are the same for all persons.

▶ **1.70**

	I / You / We / They / He / She / It
+	*I'll **pay** for dinner.*
−	*We **won't be** late.*
Y/N?	*Will you **help** me? Yes, I **will**. / No I **won't**.*

Short forms: *will* = 'll, *will not* = *won't*

▶ **1.71**

I / You / We / They / He / She / It
*Shall I **pay** for dinner?*
*Shall we **leave** soon?*
*What **shall** I wear?*

4A Present continuous and *going to*

a Complete the sentences with the correct form of the present continuous, using the verbs in brackets.

1 My parents _are buying_ (buy) me a computer for my birthday.
2 He _____ (study) French next year.
3 _____ (I / not walk) home tonight.
4 '_____ (you / wear) a suit to the interview?' 'No, _____.'
5 'When _____ (your sister / move) to Italy?' 'In about 2 weeks.'
6 _____ (we / go) to the cinema after work.
7 _____ (I / not come) into the office on Friday morning because _____ (I / go) to the doctor's.

b Look at the sentences in **a** again. What arrangements have the people made for each plan?

1 *The parents have already ordered the computer.*

c Martina and Anna are planning a party. Complete the conversation with the correct form of *going to*.

A So, how's the party planning going?
M Well … We've made a list of what we need to do. And I [1] _'m going to invite_ (invite) everybody on Facebook today.
A What [2] _____ (you / do) about music?
M I [3] _____ (not play) my music. We [4] _____ (ask) Graeme to deal with that. He's a DJ, you know! But [5] _____ (we / write) a list of our favourites for him.
A Brilliant! [6] _____ (there / be) a lot of food?
M Yes, quite a lot. Rachael loves cooking so [7] _____ (she / make) the food the day before the party.
A Cool …
M But [8] _____ (she / not pay) for it all! We [9] _____ (pay) her back for the ingredients.
A So what [10] _____ (I / do)?
M [11] _____ (you / clean) the house!
A Oh fantastic … I get all the best jobs …

d Choose the most natural sentence to follow sentences a and b in each pair.

1 a ☐ I'm going to have a party.
  b ☐ I'm having a party.
  1 It's this Saturday. Do you want to come?
  2 I don't know how many people to invite. What do you think?

2 a ☐ They're going to arrive in the afternoon.
  b ☐ They're arriving in the afternoon.
  1 They're not sure what time yet.
  2 They've arranged for a taxi to meet them at the station.

3 a ☐ Are we going to play tennis on Saturday?
  b ☐ Are we playing tennis on Saturday?
  1 Yes, I've booked the court for 2 o'clock.
  2 Yes, what time do you want to play?

4 a ☐ She's going to study all day tomorrow.
  b ☐ She's studying all day tomorrow.
  1 She's got an exam next week, and she wants to pass.
  2 She's got classes at university from 9 am to 6 pm.

5 a ☐ I'm going to fly from Denver to Boston.
  b ☐ I'm flying from Denver to Boston.
  1 Which airline do you recommend?
  2 My plane leaves at 8 am.

e ▶ Now go back to p.38

4B *will / won't / shall*

a Look at the sentences. Is each sentence a promise (*P*), an offer (*O*), a decision (*D*), or a suggestion (*S*)?

1 Shall I help you carry that box? ____
2 Shall we go for a walk? ____
3 I'll drive you to the station if you like. ____
4 I think I'll have spaghetti. ____
5 Don't worry. I'll call you later. ____
6 Let's go to the beach. ____
7 I won't be late for the meeting. ____
8 Shall we have chicken for dinner? ____

b Choose the correct word in *italics* to complete the sentence.

1 **A** I need to go to the station.
  B *I'll / I shall* call a taxi for you.
2 **A** This document is secret.
  B Don't worry – I *won't / shall not* show it to anyone.
3 **A** This box is really heavy!
  B *Shall / Will* I help you carry it?
4 **A** Those shoes are in the sale, madam. They're only £20.
  B Great! *I'll / I shall* take them.
5 **A** *Shall / Will* we go out this evening?
  B Good idea. Let's go to the cinema.
6 **A** I'm working late tonight. *Will / Shall* you cook dinner?
  B Of course.

c Complete the conversation with *will* or *shall* and the correct form of the verbs in brackets.

A [1] _Shall we go_ (we / go) out for dinner tonight?
B Er … well, I haven't got much money. [2] _____ (I / cook) something for you at my flat?
A Don't worry. [3] _____ (I / pay) for the meal.
B Really? Thank you! That sounds great. Where [4] _____ (we / eat)?
A Let's go for a curry. [5] _____ (I / book) a table?
B No, it's OK. [6] _____ (I / do) it. I know a good place near here. [7] _____ (I / call) them now.
A OK. [8] _____ (you / call) me after you make the booking? I'd like to know what time we're going to meet.
B Yes, [9] _____ (I / call) you later. I promise [10] _____ (I / forget).
A Great. Talk to you later then. Bye.

d ▶ Now go back to p.40

5A must / have to / can

Necessary, a rule	Not allowed, a rule
Visitors **must** wash their hands. We **have to** wash our hands.	You **mustn't** smoke in the building. We **can't** smoke here.
Allowed	Not necessary
You **can** smoke outside.	You **don't have to** wear a uniform.

must and *have to* have very similar meanings.

must is often used in written rules:
*All patients **must wash** their hands.*

People in authority use *must* when they are speaking, for example, teachers, parents etc.:
*You **must switch** off your mobile phone.*

We use *have to* when we say what is necessary. It is very common in spoken English:
*Doctors **have to work** very long hours.*
*I **have to leave** for work at 7.00 am.*

must not and *don't have to* have very different meanings.

must not means something is not allowed – it is important **not** to do something:
*Students **must not talk** in the exam room.*
*You **mustn't smoke** in here.*

don't have to means something is unnecessary:
*Teachers **don't have to wear** a uniform.*
*He **doesn't have to work** because he's rich.*

can means something is allowed:
*You **can take** a one-hour lunch break.*
*You **can borrow** up to five books from the library.*

can't is similar to *mustn't*.
It means not allowed / not possible:
*You **can't smoke** here.*
*Bankers **can't relax** for a minute.*

▶ **2.6** *have to + infinitive*

	I / You / We / They	He / She / It
+	We **have to work** hard.	She **has to leave** early today.
–	They **don't have to** play.	He **doesn't have to work**.
Y/N?	**Do** nurses **have to have** a degree? Yes, they **do**. / No, they **don't**.	**Does** he have to wear a uniform? Yes, he **does**. / No, he **doesn't**.

can and *must* are modal auxiliary verbs. They are the same for all persons.

▶ **2.7** *must + infinitive*

	I / You / We / They / He / She / It
+	You **must arrive** on time.
–	Teachers **mustn't be** late.

Questions with *must* are rarely used in modern English.

▶ **2.8** *can + infinitive*

	I / You / We / They / He / She / It
+	You **can leave** work early today.
–	The children **can't go** outside alone.
Y/N?	**Can** I smoke here? Yes, you **can**. / No, you **can't**.

5B will and might for predictions

We use *will* and *might* to make predictions about what we expect to happen in the future.
will shows that we are very sure:
*I'**ll say** something silly. They **won't give** me the job.*

might shows we are less sure:
*They **might ask** difficult questions. I **might not get** the job.*

will and *might* are modal auxiliary verbs. They are the same for all persons.

▶ **2.10**

	I / You / We / They / He / She / It
+	You**'ll get** the job. You **might get** the job.
–	He **won't get** the job. He **might not get** the job.

Short forms: *will = 'll, will not = won't*

We usually use phrases like *I think ... , I don't think ...* and *Do you think ... ?* to introduce predictions when we speak.

▶ **2.11**

	I / You / We / They / He / She / It
+	**I think** you**'ll get** the job. **I think** he **might get** the job
–	**I don't think** I**'ll get** the job.
Y/N?	**Do you think** we**'ll get** the job? **I think so.** / **I don't think so.** **Do you think** we **might get** the job? We **might.** / We **might not.**

We can also use *I'm sure ...* before predictions with *will*:
I'm sure I'll say something silly.

5A must / have to / can

a Flavia works in a call centre. Read her office rules. Complete Flavia's description of her work with *have to*, *can* or *can't* and the words in brackets.

> **Office Rules**
> • Employees must wear a uniform at all times.
> • Employees must not check emails during working hours.
> • You must not talk to other employees during working hours.
> • You must answer the phone within 5 seconds.
> • Employees must always be polite to customers.

I'm telling you, Jo, it's a terrible place to work! The customers can't see you, but we still ¹ _have to_ wear a uniform all the time. You ² _____ (wear) your normal clothes.
I ³ _____ (check) my emails – it's not allowed – and I ⁴ _____ (speak) to my colleagues during the day! Fortunately, we ⁵ _____ (talk) to each other during our breaks!
When the phone rings, we ⁶ _____ (answer) it very quickly – within 5 seconds. And we always ⁷ _____ (be) polite to customers, but they're often incredibly rude to us! I really ⁸ _____ (find) a new job!

b Choose the correct option.
1 Visitors *must not* / *don't have to* smoke in the building.
2 It's a relaxed office – you *must not* / *don't have to* wear a tie.
3 I start at 10 am, so I *mustn't* / *don't have to* get up early.
4 Employees *must not* / *don't have to* park in the customer car park. It is for customers only.
5 If there is a fire, you *must not* / *don't have to* use the lift. You must use the stairs.

c Complete the sentences with one of the expressions from the box. Use each expression once.

can	can't	doesn't have to	has to	must	must not

1 In my office, we _____ eat or drink at our desks. We have to go to the canteen.
2 My job's really nice. I _____ start work when I want and finish when I want.
3 She works from home so she _____ drive to work.
4 Warning! Dangerous work area. Visitors _____ enter without permission.
5 Important! You _____ keep your visitor card with you at all times.
6. He _____ travel a lot in his job. Sometimes he goes to three or four countries in a month.

d ▶ Now go back to p.49

5B will and might for predictions

a Duncan is planning to move to China for a year. Look at his predictions and complete his sentences with *will* / *won't*, *might* / *might not*.

	100% sure	50% sure ???
Good	learn about China	learn to speak Chinese?
	meet new people	travel around China?
	try new things	stay more than a year?
Bad	difficult language	tiring job?
	not much money	miss family?
	no friends	not like food?

1 I'm sure I ___'ll___ learn a lot about China.
2 They have different food in China, and I _____ like it.
3 I'm sure Chinese _____ be really difficult, but I _____ learn to speak a bit.
4 I _____ have any friends at first, but I _____ meet new people.
5 My job _____ be tiring and I _____ have much money!
6 I _____ try new things and I _____ travel around the country.
7 I _____ want to stay more than a year – I _____ want to come back!

b Correct the mistakes in the sentences below. Sometimes there is more than one possible answer.
1 She thinks she might to go to Spain for her holiday.
2 Which sights do you think you visit?
3 I sure the restaurant will be busy.
4 I'm sure it won't raining today – the sky's blue.
5 Do you think you might buying a new computer?
6 I'm sure I might change jobs next year.
7 He might not to arrive on time. The traffic's bad.
8 I won't think I pass my exam.

c Write questions using *will* and the words in brackets.
1 **A** Are you sure (you / enjoy) it?
  B Yes, I'm sure I will.
2 **A** Do you think (she / leave)?
  B She might.
3 **A** How much do you think (it / cost)?
  B About fifty pounds.
4 **A** When do you think (they / tell) us?
  B I don't know.
5 **A** Are you sure (we / finish) on time?
  B No. We might not.
6 **A** Do you think (I / get) an interview?
  B I think so!

d In which questions in **c** can you replace *will* with *might*?

e ▶ Now go back to p.50

6A Imperative; should

We use the imperative and *should* to give advice – to tell other people what we think is the best or the right thing to do.

▶ 2.21 Imperative

The imperative is stronger than *should*. It tells somebody exactly what to do.

We can use it to give…

- advice:
  Try to get a good
  night's sleep.
  Don't stay up late.
- instructions:
  Don't turn right! **Turn** left!
  Come here!

- warnings:
  Be careful!

The imperative is the infinitive of the verb with no subject. For negative imperatives, use *don't* + infinitive:

▶ 2.22 should

should is a bit less strong than the imperative. It shows that what we are saying is advice, not an instruction.

should is a modal auxiliary verb. It is the same for all persons.

	I / You / We / They / He / She / It
+	You **should get up** early.
−	Children **shouldn't eat** a lot of sweets.
Y/N?	**Should** I **stop** eating sweets? Yes, you **should**. / No, you **shouldn't**.

We often use phrases like *I think …*, *I don't think …* and *Do you think … ?* to introduce advice with *should*:
I think / **I don't think** you should go to bed.
A **Do you think** I should say sorry?
B Yes, **I think so**. / No, **I don't think so**.

> 💭 **Tip**
>
> Adding *I think … I don't think …* before *should* is more polite because it shows you are talking about opinion, not fact.

6B Uses of to + infinitive

The infinitive is the dictionary form of the verb (*go, swim, be, have* etc.).

We use *to* + infinitive (*to go, to swim, to be*, etc.) in many different patterns.
The negative is *not* + *to* + infinitive (*not to go, not to swim, not to be* etc.).

▶ 2.30

1 **Infinitive of purpose**
   Use *to* + infinitive to give a reason:
   A *Why did you go to Egypt?*
   B **To see** the sharks.
   I looked in the mirror **to check** *my hair.*
   Read a book **to relax**.

2 **verb + to + infinitive**
   When two verbs go together in a sentence, certain verbs are followed by *to* + infinitive:
   I **wanted to visit** *Australia.*
   I **decided not to go** *home.*
   Some of the verbs that follow this pattern are: *choose, decide, want, would like, try, promise, expect, remember, forget, need, plan, learn, offer.*

3 **adjective + to + infinitive**
   Many adjectives can be followed by *to* + infinitive:
   I was **surprised to get** *the job.*
   It's **important not to forget** *people's names at work.*

4 **verb + question word + to + infinitive**
   Some verbs can be followed by a question word + *to* + infinitive:
   I **forgot what to do**.
   I don't **know who to ask**.
   Can you **tell** *me* **where to go**?
   I can't **decide what to wear**.

   Some of the verbs that follow this pattern are: *ask, decide, explain, forget, know, show, tell, understand*

6A Imperative; *should*

Tony gets up late every morning and has to get ready for work very quickly. He doesn't have breakfast – he just drinks a cup of strong coffee. He drives to work – it's only about 2 kilometres, but the traffic is terrible. He checks his messages while he's waiting. At work, he drinks coffee all day and he doesn't stop for lunch – he eats a takeaway pizza at his desk. When he gets home after work, he watches TV until about 1 am. Then the next day he does the same all over again.

a Read about Tony's normal daily routine. Write advice for him using *should / shouldn't* and the words in brackets.

1 (get up earlier)
   He should get up earlier.
2 (have breakfast)
   _____
3 (drink less coffee)
   _____
4 (drive to work)
   _____
5 (use his phone in the car)
   _____
6 (stop for lunch)
   _____
7 (eat at his desk)
   _____
8 (go to bed earlier)
   _____

b Tony's friend Andy is giving him advice. Complete Andy's advice with the imperative form of the verbs from the box. Be careful – two verbs need to be negative.

| drink eat get go |
| set spend ~~start~~ wake |

T I'm always tired these days. What should I do?
A That's easy. ¹__Start__ the day with a good breakfast. ²_____ about half an hour on breakfast – it's really important.
T Half an hour? I don't have time in the morning.
A So ³_____ up earlier. ⁴_____ your alarm for six thirty. And then ⁵_____ back to sleep – ⁶_____ out of bed straight away.
T Six thirty? Are you joking?
A No, I'm serious. Get up early, ⁷_____ breakfast and ⁸_____ coffee. It's really bad for you.

c Correct one mistake in each sentence.

1 Everybody should to bring warm clothes.
2 How much money do I should take?
3 Don't to be late for the party!
4 He shoulds be more careful.
5 Not spend so much money on the Internet.
6 You don't should check your email every five minutes.
7 What you think I should do to get fit?

d ▶ Now go back to p.58

6B Uses of *to* + infinitive

a Match the sentence halves 1–7 with the best ending.

1 [e] It's dangerous
2 [ ] They went to the gym
3 [ ] He drove to the shops
4 [ ] It will be great
5 [ ] I'm going to bed
6 [ ] She was disappointed
7 [ ] She emailed the company

a to get some sleep.
b to buy some food.
c to visit Paris!
d to apply for the job.
e to text and drive.
f to do some exercise.
g not to pass her exam.

b Complete the sentences with the correct question word + *to* + infinitive.

| which to buy   what to watch   where to go |
| how to use   ~~what to do~~   how to get   who to speak to |

1 I don't know _what to do_ about my problem.
2 Can you show me _____ this computer?
3 I can't decide _____ for my holiday.
4 Do you know _____ to the station?
5 I'm not sure _____ on TV tonight.
6 I like both these dresses. I can't decide _____ .
7 Can you tell me _____ about getting a refund?

c Use the verbs in the box to complete the sentences with a positive or negative *to* + infinitive.

| ~~read~~ eat break listen wear receive go arrive |

1 I bought this book _to read_ about sharks.
2 It's expensive _____ in restaurants every day.
3 I was annoyed _____ a reply to my email.
4 It's rude _____ when she's talking.
5 We promise _____ anything.
6 I don't know what _____ to the wedding.
7 You should leave now _____ on time.
8 I decided _____ to the party. I was too tired.

d ▶ Now go back to p.61

7A Comparatives and superlatives

▶ 2.40

We use comparative adjectives and adverbs to compare two things or actions, usually with *than*:
*John's **more interesting than** Michael.*
*He's **richer than** he was.*
*She drives **more carefully than** all my friends.*

We use superlative adjectives and adverbs to talk about extremes, usually with *the*:
*He's **the worst** guitar player in the world!*
*Who can run **the furthest**?*
*He played **the best** I've ever seen him play.*

less / least is the opposite of *more / most*. We can use it with all adjectives and adverbs:
*I'm **less happy** than I was.*
*She drives **less slowly** than me.*
*It was **the least interesting** meeting ever!*

We can use *as ... as* to show that two things are equal:
*He's **as tall as** me.*
*She drives **as carefully as** me.*

We can use *not as ... as* to mean *less than*:
*He is**n't as clever as** me.* (= He is less clever than me. I am cleverer than him.)
*She does**n't** drive **as carefully as** me.* (= She drives less carefully than me. I drive more carefully than her.)

We often use comparatives or *as ... as* to compare past with present:
*He's much **better than** he was.*
*He's **not as bad as** last time.*

We often use superlatives with *ever* and the present perfect:
*This is **the best** meal **I've ever eaten**.*
*It was **the least interesting** book **I've ever read**.*

Adjectives

One syllable	*rich* → *richer, **the** richest*
	big → *bigger, **the** biggest*
Ending in -y	*easy* → *easier, the easiest*
	friendly → *friendlier, the friendliest*
Two or more syllables	*careful* → **more** *careful, **the most** careful*
	interesting → **more** *interesting, **the most** interesting*
Irregular adjectives	*good* → **better**, *the best*
	bad → **worse**, *the worst*
	far → **further**, *the furthest*
	clever → *cleverer / the cleverest*
	quiet → *quieter / **the** quietest*
	bored / tired / ill → **more / the most** *bored / tired / ill*

Adverbs

One syllable	*hard* → *harder, **the** hardest*
	late → *later, **the** latest*
Two or more syllables	*often* → **more** *often, **the most** often*
	carefully → **more** *carefully, **the most** carefully*
Irregular adverbs	*well* → **better**, *the best*
	badly → **worse**, *the worst*
	far → **farther**, *the farthest*
	early → **earlier**, *the earliest*

7B used to

We use *used to* + infinitive to talk about past situations and habits which have now changed. *Used to* tells us something was different in the past.
*I **used to be** very thin.* (= I was thin in the past, but I'm not thin now.)
*He **didn't use to go** to the gym.* (= He didn't go to the gym in the past, but now he goes to the gym.)
used to has the same form for all persons.

▶ 2.48

	I / You / We / They / He / She / It
+	*I **used to hate** tomatoes.*
–	*She **didn't use to wear** high heels.*
Y/N?	***Did** you **use to be** good at sport?*
	*Yes, I **did**. / No, I **didn't**.*

There is no present form of *used to*. Use the present simple.
*I **play** tennis three times a week.*
NOT *I use to play tennis three times a week.*

I **used to be** very thin.

Now I'm much **stronger!**

> 💬 **Tip**
>
> **used to and the past simple**
> We can usually use the past simple to talk about these situations/habits, if we make it clear that we are talking about a particular period of past time:
> *He **was** very fit **when he was younger**.*
> ***When I was a student**, I **went** running three times a week.*
>
> It's natural to use a mixture of *used to* and the past simple when we write or speak about long-term past situations:
> *In the 1950s, people **didn't use to drive** to work – most people **walked** or **cycled**.*

154

7A Comparatives and superlatives

a Complete the sentences about three brothers, Alex, Eric and Jack.

1 Alex is good at tennis but ...   Eric is _____ *better* _____ than Alex.   Jack is _____ *the best* _____ tennis player.
2 Alex is very fit but ...   Eric is _____ than Alex.   Jack is _____
3 Alex has travelled quite far but ...   Eric has travelled _____ Alex.   Jack has travelled _____
4 Alex is very friendly but ...   Eric is _____ Alex.   Jack _____
5 Alex drives carefully but ...   Eric _____   Jack _____
6 Alex works fast but ...   _____   Jack _____
7 Alex is fashionable but ...   _____   Jack _____

b Look at each group of sentences. Which sentence (a, b, or c) has a different meaning?

1 a I run faster than him.
   b He doesn't run as fast as me.
   c I run as fast as him.

2 a Her English is better than mine.
   b Her English isn't as good as mine.
   c She doesn't speak English as well as me.

3 a It's the most boring book I've ever read.
   b It's the least interesting book I've ever read.
   c I've never read a more interesting book.

c Correct the mistakes in the sentences.

1 He drives worse as me.
2 This is best movie I've ever seen.
3 She isn't friendly as her sister.
4 I'm a good runner but Tom's the faster in the school.
5 The weather is not as cold than it was.
6 The island was the more beautiful place I've ever visited.
7 This book is least interesting than the last one.
8 I don't speak French as well that she does.

d ▶ Now go back to p.68

7B used to

a All of the sentences about the past are false. Change them so that they are true.

500 years ago ...
1 People used to work in IT. *People didn't use to work in IT.*
2 People didn't use to work on farms.
3 People used to live as long as they do now.
4 Children's education used to be free.
5 Cities didn't use to be smaller than today.
6 People didn't use to travel by horse.
7 People used to use microwaves to cook food.

10 years ago   *Today*

b Rewrite the sentences. Change the <u>underlined</u> verbs from the past simple to *used to*.

1 I <u>ate</u> a lot of chocolate when I was younger.
   I used to eat a lot of chocolate when I was younger.
2 People <u>wrote</u> a lot of letters in the days before email.
3 Where <u>did you live</u> when you were a child?
4 She <u>was</u> a manager before she stopped working.
5 <u>Did</u> your parents <u>read</u> you stories when you were young?
6 I <u>didn't like</u> vegetables when I was a child.
7 <u>Were</u> you a good student at school?
8 We <u>weren't</u> as fit as we are today.

c Look at the pictures of Mary and Jeff ten years ago and today. Write sentences about how they have changed. Use *used to / didn't use to* and the words in brackets.

1 _____ (Mary / have long hair)
2 _____ (Jeff / be thinner)
3 _____ (Jeff / wear suits)
4 _____ (They / look after the garden)
5 _____ (They / ride a motorbike)
6 _____ (They / own a car)

d ▶ Now go back to p.71

8A The passive: present and past simple

Active:

Most verbs in English are active – the **doer** of the verb comes before the verb.

Francis Ford Coppola *made* The Godfather *in 1972.*
He *also made ...* (We are talking about the person.)

Passive:

In passive verb forms the **object** comes before the verb.

The Godfather *was made in 1972 by Francis Ford Coppola.*
It *was filmed in ...* (We are talking about the film.)

We use passive verb forms when the main thing we are talking about is the **object** of the verb.

Some common uses of the passive are:

* when the doer isn't important:
  This house **was built** *in the 1960s.*
  (It doesn't matter who built it – the date is more interesting.)
  130,000 copies of Thriller **are sold** *every year.*
  (It doesn't matter who sells them.)

* when we don't know who did something:
  The picture **was stolen** *last night.* (We don't know who stole it.)
  This photo **was taken** *in Barcelona.* (I don't remember who took it.)

We form the passive with **be + past participle**. **be** shows the tense of the verb, e.g. present simple.

 2.59

	Present simple	Past simple
+	*I* **am chosen** *for the school football team every year.*	*Three* Godfather *films* **were made** *altogether.*
–	*This car* **isn't sold** *in the US or Canada.*	Harry Potter **wasn't written** *for adults.*
Y/N?	**Am** *I* **invited** *to your party?* Yes, you **are**. / No, you**'re not**.	**Was** The Hobbit **written** *for children?* Yes, it **was**. / No, it **wasn't**.

(See p.176 for a list of irregular past participles.)

We use *by* to introduce the doer after the verb:
The Godfather was made **by Francis Ford Coppola.**
This house was built **by my grandfather.**

8B Present perfect with *for* and *since*

We can use the present perfect with *for* and *since* to describe a situation that started in the past and continues now.

In positive statements, we use the present perfect with *for* and *since* with particular verbs which describe things that are often true for a long time: *live, work, know, have, be, like, love, hate, enjoy, own,* etc.

 2.66

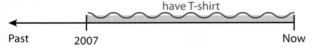
have T-shirt

Past   2007   Now

We use *since* to say when something started:
*I'****ve had** this T-shirt **since** 2007.*

We often use a verb in the past simple after *since*:
*I'****ve loved** tennis **since** I was a child.* (I was a child when I started liking tennis, and I still like it now.)

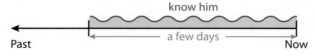
know him
a few days

Past   Now

We use *for* to describe the length of time:
*I'****ve known** him **for** a few days.* (I met him a few days ago.)

We often use *How long ...?* questions with the present perfect to ask about a period of time:
A ***How long have** you **lived** here?*
B *Since I was a child. / For about ten years.*

We form the present perfect with *have* + past participle.
See Grammar reference 3A for the full form.

> 💬 **Tip**
>
> We can also use *always* or *all my / your life*:
> *I'****ve always hated** cheese. / I'****ve hated** cheese **all my life**.*

> 💬 **Tip**
>
> * Don't use the present simple to talk about periods of time up to now. Use the present perfect instead:
>   *How long* **have you known** *each other?*
>   NOT ~~How long **do you know** each other?~~
> * Don't use the present perfect for periods of time which are finished. Use the past simple (with *for, from ... to*) instead:
>   *I* **lived** *there for two years / from* **2009 to 2011**.
>   NOT ~~I**'ve lived** there from 2009 to 2011.~~

He's **been** a member of the team **since** 1975.
He's faster than anyone!

8A The passive: present and past simple

a Rewrite these sentences in the passive, using the highlighted words as the subject of the sentence. Don't include the doer.

1 Somebody wrote the story 200 years ago.
The story was written 200 years ago.

2 A company made my car in Germany.
_____

3 Bookshops don't sell that book in your country.
_____

4 People eat sushi all over the world.
_____

5 In the UK, DJs play the number 1 song on the radio every hour.
_____

6 Somebody broke a window in the night.
_____

7 The journalist didn't describe India very well in the article.
_____

The Godfather was made in 1972 by...

Shhhhhh. Let's watch the film!

b Rewrite these sentences in the passive. Include the doer in the new sentence.

1 Frank Gehry designed The Guggenheim, Bilbao.
The Guggenheim, Bilbao was designed by Frank Gehry.

2 Marilyn Monroe wore Chanel No. 5 perfume.
_____

3 Every year, 3 million people visit the Taj Mahal.
_____

4 A fire destroyed many parts of London in 1666.
_____

5 Clyde Tombaugh discovered Pluto in 1930.
_____

c Put the words in the correct order to make questions in the passive.

1 made / was / the / where / film
Where was the film made?

2 was / the book / written / when
_____

3 made / cheese / is / how
_____

4 your bike / was / when / stolen
_____

5 the statue / was / in France / made
_____

6 who / her wedding dress / was / designed by
_____

d ▶ Now go back to p.79

8B Present perfect with _for_ and _since_

a Write _for_ or _since_.

1 _since_ last week
2 _____ a week
3 _____ a long time
4 _____ last weekend
5 _____ five minutes
6 _____ I was a child
7 _____ July
8 _____ 1,000 years
9 _____ yesterday
10 _____ months
11 _____ ten days
12 _____ I last saw you

b Rewrite the sentences with the present perfect and _for_ or _since_.

1 I work here.   I've worked here since January.
2 I live here.   three months.
3 He holds the record.   the last Olympics.
4 She owns that car.   2011.
5 They are married.   two days.
6 I don't listen to pop music.   a long time.
7 We are not friends.   we had a fight.
8 I don't have a TV in my home. a few years.
9 He doesn't eat meat.   New Year's Day.

c Complete the questions in the present perfect.

1 How long _____ (you / study) English?
2 How long _____ (she / live) in this area?
3 How long _____ (Mr Bell / teach) at this school?
4 How long _____ (we / have) our passports?
5 How long _____ (he / be) a football fan?

d Complete the sentences. Use past simple or present perfect.

1 _____ (she / work) here for ten months.
2 _____ (she / start) work last July.
3 When _____ (you / buy) your car?
4 How long _____ (you / have) this car?
5 _____ (we / not see) him since last summer.
6 _____ (we / not see) him in October.
7 _____ (I / love) animals when I was a child.
8 _____ (I / love) animals all my life.

e ▶ Now go back to p.81

9A First conditional

We use the first conditional to talk about a possible future situation and the result of that situation:

(possible future situation) **If** the weather **is** good at the weekend, (result) we**'ll go** to the park.
(possible future situation) **If** I **get** a good grade, (result) I**'ll be** very happy.

There are two clauses in a conditional sentence: the *if* clause and the main clause.
The *if* clause can go before or after the main clause.

If I **pass** my exams, I**'ll** get into university.   I**'ll** get into university **if** I **pass** my exams.
    if clause   **main clause**   **main clause**   **if clause**

To talk about a possible future situation, use the present simple in the *if* clause.

> 💬 **Tip** Never use *will / might* in an *if* clause.
> If **I go** to London ... NOT ~~If I will go to London ...~~

To talk about the result of the situation, use a suitable future form, e.g. *will, might, be going to*, present continuous.

If I **pass** the entrance exam, I'**m going to study** maths at the best university in the country.

 3.7

Statements
I**'ll get** a good degree **if** I **work** hard this year.
If he **works** hard, he **won't fail**.
If they **don't work** hard this year, they **won't get** good degrees.
Her teacher **might ask** her to repeat the year if she **doesn't work** hard.

Questions and short answers
What **will** you **do if** you **pass**?
If she **doesn't work** hard, what **will happen**?
If you **don't get** in to university, **will** you **look** for a job? Yes, I **will**. / No, I **won't**.
Are his parents **going to** buy him a car **if he works** hard? Yes, they **are**. / No, they**'re not**.

> 💬 **Tip**
> - The word order in the *if* clause doesn't change in questions.
>   *What will you do if it rains?*
>   NOT ~~What will you do if does it rain?~~
> - We can make short questions with *What if ... ?*:
>   **What if** it rains?

9B Verb patterns

 3.10

Some verbs are often followed by another verb. The two most common patterns are:

- verb + *to* + infinitive:
  I **hope to see** you soon.
- verb + verb + *-ing*:
  I **don't mind reading** about famous people.

Sometimes both forms are possible with no change of meaning:
He started **talking**. / He started **to talk**.
I prefer **talking** to my friends. / I prefer **to talk** to my friends.

To make a negative on the second verb in both verb patterns, *not* goes before the verb:
I decided **not to go** to the party.
I hate **not going** to work.

> 💬 **Tip**
> We can make negatives with either the first verb or the second verb. This sometimes changes the meaning:
> I **didn't choose** to go to the party.
> (I went to the party but only because I had to.)
> I chose **not to go** to the party. (I didn't go to the party.)

verb + *to* + infinitive	verb + verb + *-ing*	Both
choose decide, want would like, promise expect, need plan learn offer hope	describe discuss enjoy finish not mind stop keep think of	begin start, continue prefer* like* love* hate*

> 💬 **Tip**
> *I **love going** to parties. ✓ I **love to go** to parties. ✓
> But remember, after **would** like / love / hate / prefer you must always use *to* + infinitive:
> I **would love to come** to the party.
> NOT ~~I would love coming to the party.~~

When a verb comes after a preposition (e.g. *on, by, from, about* etc.), it is always in the *-ing* form:
You shouldn't **worry about talking** to strangers.
I'm **thinking of studying** history.

I **enjoy reading** about the lives of famous people.

9A First conditional

a Match the sentence halves.

1 [g] If you study hard, …
2 ☐ If you don't take a coat, …
3 ☐ You won't be late …
4 ☐ It'll be hard to get a good job …
5 ☐ If you drive too fast, …
6 ☐ If I get a place at medical school, …
7 ☐ He's going to travel around the world …
8 ☐ We might go to the beach tomorrow …

a if you don't go to university.
b if he has enough money.
c you'll get cold.
d I'm going to become a doctor.
e if you set off now.
f if the weather is nice.
g you'll get good grades.
h you might have an accident.

b Choose the correct options. All the sentences are about the future.

1 If you *pay / will pay* the bill, *I pay / I'll pay* you back next week.
2 If I *don't / won't* do some exercise, *I / I'll* put on weight.
3 She *isn't going to / doesn't* catch her plane if she *doesn't / isn't going to* leave soon.
4 What *do / will* you do if *there is / there'll be* a traffic jam?
5 If we *like / might like* the hotel, we *might stay / stay* a few more days.
6 They *won't / don't* enjoy the journey if they *won't / don't* get a seat.
7 *Are you going to / Do you* cook if I *get / might get* home late?

c Complete the conversations with the correct form of the verbs in brackets. Use *will / 'll* or the present simple. All the sentences are about the future.

A I've just bought an old car for £500.
B What [1] _____ (you / do) if [2] _____ (it / break) down?
A [3] _____ (I / ask) for my money back.

C If [4] _____ (it / be) sunny tomorrow, [5] _____ (I / take) the children to the park.
D That's nice. If [6] _____ (I / have) time, [7] _____ (I / make) a picnic for you.
C Brilliant, thanks! But, if [8] _____ (you / not do), don't worry, [9] _____ (we / be) OK.

E [10] _____ (I / not finish) this essay tonight, if [11] _____ (the cat / not get) off my laptop.
F Just push him off.
E If [12] _____ (I / push) him off, [13] _____ (he / jump) back up again.
F I'll put him outside.

d ▶ Now go back to p.89

9B Verb patterns

a Choose the correct option.

1 They want (*to leave*) / *leaving*.
2 I enjoy *to play / playing* football.
3 Do you mind *to work / working* late?
4 We discussed *to start / starting* a business.
5 We hope *to visit / visiting* you soon.
6 Why did you choose *to live / living* in the city?
7 Please stop *to talk / talking* now and open your book.
8 They've offered *to help / helping* us.
9 We really need *to go / going* very soon.
10 You should plan *to save / saving* more money.

b Cross out the verb forms which are NOT possible in these sentences. Remember, after some verbs both verb forms are possible.

1 He began *to act / acting* when he was a child.
2 He chose *not to do / not doing* his homework.
3 He worries about *making / to make* mistakes.
4 I prefer *not to be / not being* late.
5 Do you mind *to start / starting* without me?
6 We're thinking of *to become / becoming* vegetarians.
7 The children continued *to be / being* noisy.
8 I like *to cook / cooking* for other people.
9 Would you like *to have / having* dinner with me?
10 We hate *to think / thinking* about money when we're on holiday.

c Complete the sentences with the correct form of the verbs.

1 I don't expect _____ the exam. (pass)
2 She promised _____ late. (not be)
3 We don't mind _____ up early. (get)
4 I enjoy _____ on a uniform every morning. (not put)
5 They learned _____ English very quickly. (speak)
6 He couldn't concentrate on _____ his work. (do)
7 Which cities are you planning _____? (visit)
8 Did he choose _____ in the match? (not play)

d Complete the text with the verbs in the box.

| ~~hates~~ hated started discussed didn't expect |
| thinks of preferred continued needed |

My friend says he [1] _____hates_____ speaking in public. He told me that when he [2] _____ getting up in front of a crowd, he feels terrified. I'm very surprised. I thought I knew everything about my friend and I [3] _____ to hear this. He said that he [4] _____ feeling embarrassed around big groups of people when he was about 11 years old. He [5] _____ standing up in front of the class at school and [6] _____ to feel this way as an adult, when he [7] _____ to speak at meetings at work. We [8] _____ getting professional help for his problem, but he said he [9] _____ talking to friends about it.

e ▶ Now go back to p.91

10A Second conditional

We use the second conditional when we imagine a situation in the present or future. The situation is unreal, unlikely, or impossible.

We describe the unreal situation in the *if* clause. We talk about the result of that situation in the main clause.
(unlikely future situation) **If** I **stole** from work, (result) I'd feel bad.
(result) I'd take a holiday from work (impossible present situation) **if** I **had** more money.

Use the past simple (and/or past continuous) in the *if* clause. We can use *would* + infinitive or *could* + infinitive to talk about the result.
If it **was raining** and I **saw** a hitchhiker, **I'd stop.**
I **could go** on more holidays **if** I **had** more money. (*could* = it would be possible)

▶ 3.22

Statements
If she **crashed** my car, **I'd be** very angry. He **wouldn't stop** to help **if** he **saw** an accident. **If** you **didn't have** a job, you **couldn't pay** the rent. Hollywood **wouldn't stop** making films **if** people **didn't go** to the cinema. **I'd give** more money to charity **if** I **were** rich.

Questions and short answers
What **would** you **do if** you **lost** your job? **If** you **didn't know** the answers, **would** you **cheat**? Yes, I **would**. / No, I **wouldn't**. **Would** you **buy** your child a motorbike? Yes, I **would**. / No, I **wouldn't**.

> ### 💬 Tip
> - When we talk about impossible present situations with *be*, we usually use *If I were*, not *If I was*:
>   **If I were** taller, I'd be better at basketball.
> - We can also use the second conditional to give advice, with the phrase *If I were you* (NOT ~~If I was you~~):
>   **If I were you**, I wouldn't park there. (I'm imagining the situation where I'm you.)

10B Quantifiers; too / not enough

Quantifiers

We use quantifiers before countable and uncountable nouns to describe the amount of something.

Countable nouns are things that we can count:
one book, five books.
Uncountable nouns are things that we don't usually count:
water NOT ~~one water, five waters.~~

▶ 3.24

	Countable	Uncountable
Large quantity	There are **a lot of** books.	There's **a lot of** water.
No particular quantity	There are **some** books.	There's **some** water.
Small quantity	There are **a few** books. There are**n't many** books.	There's **a bit of** water. There is**n't much** water.
Zero quantity	There are **no** books. There are**n't any** books.	There's **no** water. There is**n't any** water.
Question	Are there **any** books? **How many** books are there?	Is there **any** water? **How much** water is there?

> ### 💬 Tip
> Be careful with the nouns *money, fruit* and *furniture*. They're all uncountable in English. We can say *five euros, ten apples* and *six chairs*, but NOT ~~five moneys, ten fruits~~ and ~~six furnitures.~~

too / not enough

We use *too* to say something is more than the right amount:
*There are **too** many people. There's **too** much noise.*
We use *not enough* to say something is less than the right amount:
*There is**n't enough** food for everyone.*

▶ 3.25

		More than the right amount	Less than the right amount
Nouns	C	There are **too many** people.	There are**n't enough** people.
	U	I eat **too much** cheese.	There is**n't enough** cheese.
Verbs		He **talks too much**.	He doesn't **talk enough**.
Adjectives		It's **too hot**.	It is**n't hot enough**.
Adverbs		She eats **too quickly**.	She doesn't eat **quickly enough**.

very

We use *very* before adjectives and adverbs. There is an important difference between *very* and *too*:
*It's **too** small. / He's driving **too** slowly.*
(= I'm complaining about problems.)
*It's **very** small. / He's driving **very** slowly.*
(= I'm describing situations, not complaining.)
We use *very much* with verbs:
*I like it **very much**.* NOT ~~I very like it.~~

10A Second conditional

a Match the sentence halves.

1 [e] If you saw a celebrity in the street,
2 [ ] Would you help a stranger with their bags
3 [ ] If I didn't like my job,
4 [ ] If I saw an accident,
5 [ ] I could sell my motorbike
6 [ ] Where would you go for help
7 [ ] If we got a huge phone bill,
8 [ ] Could she deal with the stress,

a I'd look for a new one.
b if you were lost?
c my father would be annoyed.
d if she were a nurse?
e would you try to talk to them?
f if we needed some money.
g I'd try to help.
h if you were in a hurry?

b Choose the correct verb forms in each sentence.

1 If I *would be / were* rich, *I'd give / I gave* up work.
2 The film *would be / was* better if it *wasn't / wouldn't be* three hours long.
3 If *I'd have / I had* time, *I'd read / I read* more books.
4 What *would / did* you do if *you'd see / you saw* a snake in your room?
5 If you *wouldn't / didn't* smoke, *you'd save / you saved* a lot of money.
6 I *wouldn't / didn't* spend time with him if I *wouldn't / didn't* like him!
7 If you *would find / found* a lost phone, *would you / did you* keep it?

c Complete the conversation with the second conditional forms of the verbs in brackets.

A If ¹_____ (I / be) you, ²_____ (I / not eat) those grapes.
B It's a supermarket. Nobody cares. If ³_____ (I / not eat) them, ⁴_____ (they / throw) them away.
A What ⁵_____ (you / do) if ⁶_____ (a shop assistant / see) you?
B ⁷_____ (I / promise) to pay for them at the till.
A What if ⁸_____ (they / not believe) you and ⁹_____ (they / call) the police? ¹⁰_____ (you / go) to prison for stealing grapes!
B You're being very silly! If ¹¹_____ (the police / come) ¹²_____ (they / not send) me to prison. But, ¹³_____ , (it / be) embarrassing.

d ▶ Now go back to p.99

10B Quantifiers; *too / not enough*

a Choose the best quantifier to complete each sentence.

1 Hurry up! We haven't got _____ time!
a some b no ©much d many
2 Just _____ chips, please. I'm not very hungry.
a a few b any c a bit of d much
3 Can I have _____ milk in my coffee, please? Not much.
a a few b no c a lot of d a bit of
4 You don't need to take _____ money with you. I'll pay for everything.
a any b no c a few d many
5 When I moved here I had _____ friends. But now I've got lots.
a a bit of b much c no d any
6 I bought _____ books last week, but I haven't read them yet.
a any b no c much d some

b Tick ✓ the sentences which are correct.

1 There aren't much people here in the winter.
2 We saw a lot of hitchhikers on the motorway.
3 Are there many empty seats in the cinema?
4 A bit of the vegetables were not enough soft.
5 I'd like a bit of bread with my soup.
6 I love too hot weather.
7 I don't earn enough money.
8 Was the test too much difficult?

c Correct the mistakes you found in the sentences in **b**.

d Write a sentence about each picture using the words in brackets and *too / not enough*.

(people / on the beach)

(soup / hot)

(she / tall / to reach the top shelf)

(waiter / spoke / quickly)

(service / here / slow)

(Sorry, I / have / money)

e ▶ Now go back to p.100

11A Defining relative clauses

We use defining relative clauses to define a noun. A relative clause explains what kind of thing, or which particular thing, we are talking about.

The film *is about an android.* ✗ (not specific enough – you don't know which film)

The film that is on TV tonight *is about an android.* ✓ (more specific – you know which film I'm talking about).

*A vet is **a doctor**.* ✗ (not enough information for a clear definition)

*A vet is **a doctor that looks after animals**.* ✓ (more specific – you know what kind of doctor)

To add a defining relative clause after a noun, we use a relative pronoun (e.g. *who, which, that*) or a relative adverb (e.g. *where*).

▶ 3.35

Use *who* or *that* when the noun is a person:
*It's about a man **who / that** travels through time.*
Use *which* or *that* when the noun is a thing:
*There's an art gallery **which / that** stays open 24 hours a day.*
Use *where* when the noun is a place:
*'The Matrix' is about a world **where** computers control everything.*

who, which, where and *that* replace other words in the clause:
*It's about a person ~~he~~ **who** travels through time.*
*There's an art gallery ~~it~~ **which** stays open 24 hours a day.*
*'The Matrix' is about a world **where** computers control everything ~~there~~.*

11B Articles

		Things in general	Specific things	
		Ø = no article	first mention	know which one
C	Singular		*a man, an egg*	*the man, an egg*
	Plural	*Ø scientists*	*some scientists*	*the scientists*
U		*Ø chocolate*	*some chocolate*	*the chocolate*

▶ 3.37

When we talk about things in general, we usually use no article:
Ø Tourists sometimes have Ø accidents when they are climbing Ø mountains.

When we talk about specific things for the first time, we usually use *a/an* for singular nouns:
*I met **a scientist**. She was wearing **a** white **coat**.*
*We found **an underground cave**.*

We don't use an article for plural and uncountable nouns. We often use words like *some, any, much, many,* etc., or a number:
*He put **some popcorn** in a bowl.*
*They found **8,000 soldiers**.*
When we talk about specific things that we have already mentioned, we usually use *the*:
The popcorn *popped.*
The soldiers *were all different.*

We sometimes use *the* when we mention a specific thing for the first time:
- with a defining relative clause:
  The film that I saw last night *was brilliant.*
- with a superlative adjective:
  *Usain Bolt is **the fastest runner** in the world.*
- when there is only one of something:
  *He was **the only / first foreigner** in the village.*
  The sun *was low in **the sky**.*
- when we expect the reader / listener to know what we are talking about:
  *Where's **the car**?* (= my / your / our car)
  *He got a taxi from **the airport** to **the hotel**.* (= the airport that he arrived at, the hotel he was staying at)
  *They saw a man in **the ice**.* (= the ice on the mountain)

We don't use articles for the names of most places, including countries (e.g. *Vietnam, China, Austria*) or cities (e.g. *Vienna, Xian, New Orleans*) and other places (e.g. *Mount Everest, Lake Winnipeg*).
But there are exceptions: *the USA, the UK, the Alps, the Nile, the Golden Gate Bridge.*

> 💬 **Tip**
>
> There are some phrases where you can't change the articles. You just have to learn the phrase:
> *by accident / by chance / on purpose;*
> *in bed / at home / at work;*
> *by car / by plane / on foot*

11A Defining relative clauses

a Write the correct word, *who, which* or *where*, to complete the sentences.

1 A dictionary is a book _____ contains words and definitions.
2 An architect is someone _____ designs buildings.
3 That's the cinema _____ they show films at midnight.
4 She's the girl _____ lives next door.
5 What do you call a machine _____ cuts paper?
6 The restaurant _____ we met was very quiet.
7 The shop _____ sold nice cards has closed down.
8 The chef _____ works on Fridays isn't here today.

b Cross out the relative pronouns which are NOT possible.

1 The car *who / which / where / that* won the race was a Ferrari.
2 The area *who / which / where / that* he lives is very nice.
3 I've got a friend *who / which / where / that* loves science fiction.
4 That's the office *who / which / where / that* I used to work.
5 I read about some scientists *who / which / where / that* are studying time travel.
6 The film's about a planet *who / which / where / that* it's dark all the time.
7 He made the discovery *who / which / where / that* won the Nobel Prize.

c Correct one mistake in each sentence.

1 The actor he played the doctor was very good.
2 Where are the shoes what were under the stairs?
3 Is there a shop which I can buy DVDs near here?
4 A smoke alarm is a device tells you when there is a fire.
5 A man who fixed my dishwasher says he knows you.
6 Our wedding pictures were in the camera it broke.

d ▶ Now go back to p.109

11B Articles

a For each noun, decide which article (*a, an, the* or *Ø*) is NOT possible. Cross out **one** wrong article.

1 *A / Ø / The* books are expensive.
2 We went to *a / Ø / the* shop.
3 They come from *Ø / the* India.
4 *A / Ø / The* tourists often used to come here.
5 *An / Ø / The* ice is dangerous – you can fall over easily.
6 We found it by *a / Ø* chance.
7 They made *a / Ø / the* clothes in that factory.
8 I need to go to *an / Ø / the* airport.
9 She's at *Ø / the* work at the moment.
10 *An / Ø / The* Indian food is delicious.

b Decide if the underlined words are the same thing or two different things. Write *S* or *D*.

1 He didn't find the book that he was looking for. But he found a really interesting book in the cupboard. __D__

2 He put some popcorn into a bowl, and it popped. Then he put some chocolate into a bowl and it melted. ____

3 Two climbers were going up a mountain. Far ahead, they could see somebody on top of the mountain. ____

4 He took a photograph of his son and entered it in a competition. He was very surprised to see the picture on TV. ____

5 I saw a girl at the station. She looked like the girl that lives next door, but she has black hair. ____

6 **A** I sent you a message about school. Did you get it?
   B No, I don't think so. Maybe you sent the message to somebody else? ____

c Complete the story with the correct articles: *a, an, the* or *Ø*.

In 1738, some engineers near ¹_Ø_ Naples in ²___ Italy wanted to build ³___ palace for ⁴___ King of Naples, so they started digging ⁵___ hole.

They found ⁶___ wall under the ground. ⁷___ wall had ⁸___ beautiful paintings on it. After more digging, they found ⁹___ whole city.

¹⁰___ city was Pompeii, which was destroyed by ¹¹___ volcano nearly 2,000 years ago. The discovery showed ¹²___ world exactly how ¹³___ people lived 2,000 years ago.

d ▶ Now go back to p.111

12A Past perfect

When I got home my goldfish **had disappeared**.

Past ← disappear ✗ get home ✗ → Now

The past perfect shows that something happened before a particular point in the past:
*In 2008, I **had left** London and I **had moved** to Cambridge.* (I did this before 2008.) *I **got** a job ...* (I did this in 2008.)

We form the past perfect with *had* + past participle. It is the same for all persons.

▶ 3.50

	I / You / We / They / He / She / It
+	I'd **left** before he arrived.
-	He **hadn't arrived** when I left.
Y/N?	**Had** you **seen** him? Yes, we **had**. / No, we **hadn't**.

(See p.176 for a list of irregular past participles.)

The past perfect is often used with the past simple. The two clauses are often joined with *when*, *because* or *so*.

when + past simple, past perfect
When I **got** home, my goldfish **had disappeared**.

past simple, *because* + past perfect
*I **was** late **because** my car **had broken** down.*

past perfect, *so* + past simple
*We'd never **been** to a concert before, **so** we **were** very excited.*

12B Reported speech

When we talk about what someone said in the past, we often use reported speech:
I don't know what happened. (direct speech)
→ *She **said** she **didn't know** what **had happened**.* (reported speech)

We usually use the verbs *say* and *tell* in the past simple. After *tell* you must include the person who was spoken to:
*My sister **said (that)** ...*
*My sister **told me (that)** ...*
We can also include *that* before the reported words – however, it's not necessary.

We change the verb forms in the reported words by shifting them back one tense.

My sister **told** me she **didn't know** what **had happened** to my best shoes. But I didn't believe her.

Direct speech		Reported speech	▶ 3.55		
present simple	→	past simple	I **don't like** this book.	→	He said he **didn't like** the book.
can	→	could	You **can** start eating.	→	He said we **could** start eating.
will	→	would	She'**ll** be angry.	→	I told him she'**d** be angry.
present continuous	→	past continuous	I'**m watching** TV.	→	He said he **was watching** TV.
am / is / are going to	→	was / were going to	I'**m not going to** sleep.	→	He said he **wasn't going** to sleep.
past simple	→	past perfect	I **saw** you break it.	→	She said she'**d seen** me break it.
present perfect	→	past perfect	I'**ve** never **been** to London.	→	I told them I'**d** never **been** to London.

> 💬 **Tip**
> Don't forget to change the pronouns (e.g. *I, you, she*) and possessives (e.g. *my, her, your*) in reported speech, depending on who you are talking to.
> *'I like **your** trousers!' she said.* → *She said she liked **my** trousers.*

12A Past perfect

a Complete the text with the past perfect form of the verbs in brackets.

S taff at a supermarket were surprised to find a tiger in their shop on Monday morning. The tiger ¹ _had gone_ (go) into the supermarket because it was hungry. It ²_____ (break) the door to get in, but the alarm ³_____ (not go) off because the shop manager ⁴_____ (forget) to put it on. The tiger ⁵_____ (make) a terrible mess in the shop. It ⁶_____ (find) the meat section and it ⁷_____ (eat) a lot of the meat from the fridges. The police gave the tiger some more meat with a drug in it. When the tiger ⁸_____ (finish) eating the drugged meat, it fell asleep. Then the police took the tiger back to the zoo. The tiger ⁹_____ (escape) from the zoo the previous night, after a zoo worker ¹⁰_____ (leave) a cage open.

b Match the sentence halves.

1 [f] When she turned on the TV …
2 [ ] Yesterday I found some old pictures …
3 [ ] When I checked my emails after my holiday, …
4 [ ] When I started my meal, …
5 [ ] The flat was dark when we got home …
6 [ ] They didn't know what to do …

a everybody else had already finished.
b I saw that I'd received over 200!
c because they hadn't listened to the instructions.
d because we'd forgotten to leave the light on.
e which I'd drawn when I was a child.
f the programme had already started.

c Complete the sentences with one past simple and one past perfect form of the verbs in brackets.

1 Nobody ___came___ (come) to the meeting because Jed
   had forgotten (forget) to send the invitations.
2 Zofia _____ (arrive) late because her bus _____ (break) down.
3 My parents _____ (not go) to Rome before, so they _____ (be) really excited.
4 Fred _____ (not do) his homework when the teacher _____ (ask) for it.
5 By the time I _____ (find) the website, they _____ (sell) all the tickets.
6 The kitchen _____ (be) very messy because I _____ (not have) time to clean up.
7 I _____ (never fly) before so I _____ (feel) very nervous.
8 _____ (the match / finished) when you _____ (get) there?

d ▶ Now go back to p.119

12B Reported speech

a Choose the correct option in the reported speech on the right.

1 I can swim 12 km.   He said he _could_ / would swim 12 km.
2 He isn't going to go to the party.   She said he _wouldn't going_ / wasn't going to go to the party.
3 We'll phone you when we get there.   They said they _were_ / would phone him when they _got_ / get there.
4 We saw you steal the laptop.   We said _we'd seen_ / we've seen him steal the laptop.
5 I'll go and get the car from the garage. She said _she'll go_ / she'd go and get the car from the garage.
6 We like flying.   We _told them_ / said them we _would like_ / liked flying.
7 They can come to the party.   They said they _will come_ / could come to the party.
8 I have been to New York a few times.   I said I _went_ / had been to New York a few times.

b Complete the reported sentences with the correct pronouns and possessive adjectives.

1 I don't want to see you tonight.   She told me _she_ didn't want to see _me_ tonight.
2 All of my friends are going to the cinema.   He said all of _____ friends were going to the cinema.
3 You can't go out until you finish your homework.   He told us _____ couldn't go out until _____ finished _____ homework.
4 I've left my book on the train.   She told me _____ had left _____ book on the train.
5 You'll catch a cold if you don't wear your coats.   I said they would catch a cold if _____ didn't wear _____ coats.
6 You can't tell me what I can and can't do!   I told my parents _____ couldn't tell _____ what _____ could and couldn't do.

c ▶ Now go back to p.120

Unit 1

▶ **1.2**

1 A It's a nice day today.
 B Yes, it's a perfect day for a birthday party. It's great that so many people are here.
 A So, how do you know Ana?
 B We were at university together. We did the same course.
 A Oh right. What did you study?
 B English Literature. And you? How do *you* know Ana?
 A I'm her neighbour. I live in the house next door.
 B Really? It's a lovely street.
 A I think so. So did you come …

2 C How's the food?
 D It's great. The pizza is delicious. It's always nice to get good food at a party … Err … So, do you live near here?
 C Yeah, I live down by the river. You know those flats …
 D Oh yeah! The new ones. They're expensive! How much rent do you pay?
 C Err … not much. It's not so … expensive … err …
 D So what do you do?
 C I work for a bank.
 D So, how much do you earn?
 C Erm, is that … er … over there … Sorry, I just have to speak to my friend, because …

3 E What do you think of the party?
 F Yeah, it's great. It's really nice to meet all of Ana's friends. You?
 E It's alright, but the music is a bit boring.
 F Mmm.
 E I like your T-shirt. Is it for a football team?
 F No! At least I don't think so!
 E So, do you play any sports?
 F No, not really. I don't really like sport.
 E Well, what do you like then?
 F I prefer reading, or watching films.
 E Oh.
 F Yeah, so I might go to the cinema after the party. There's a new film about a man who goes to Peru to visit his brother and …
 E Yeah, I saw that last week.
 F Oh. What was it like?
 E Oh, it's an awful film. Really boring.
 F OK, well, I'd like to see it anyway. Perhaps I'll like it.
 E No, I don't think so. It's a really strange story. And in the end, the man can't find his brother and he just goes home again.
 F Oh, thanks a lot!

▶ **1.10**

TARA Last year, my ex-boyfriend told me he didn't want to see me any more … by text message! What kind of person does that? It was horrible. I called him for days, but he didn't answer. It made me feel like I wasn't important to him at all. I think he just wanted me to go away. What an idiot.
MAGDA When I want to plan something, I generally just send a text. It's the same when I cancel plans – a text message is easier. You don't need to give a long explanation, you know, a lot of reasons. Or have a difficult conversation. It's better for everyone.
CHRIS Birthdays are different now. I hardly ever get cards or presents from friends, or even my brother, and no one calls. Everyone just writes 'happy birthday' on my wall on Facebook. It's not very friendly, in my opinion.
MIKE My daughter is travelling around South America at the moment. She's writing a blog so we know what she's doing. But she rarely calls. And I'd love to get a postcard or a letter sometimes. Just to know she's thinking about the family.

▶ **1.15** **PART 1**

RACHEL Annie?
ANNIE Rachel!
 R Long time no see! How are you?

 A I'm great. What a lovely surprise! Great to see you!
 R Yeah! You too.
 A When did we last see each other?
 R Oh, I think it was about … six years ago! So … where are you living these days?
 A Oh, not far from here. I live on Hampton Street. Do you know it?
 R Yes, I do. That's really close to the centre.
 A Mmm. How about you?
 R We live on Compton Road.
 A Oh – how nice!
MARK My name's Mark, by the way.
 A Hi. Nice to meet you.
 M Nice to meet you, too.
 R Sorry, yes – Mark's my husband!
 A Husband – wow! That's fantastic news. When did you get married?
 R Six months ago.
 M Eight months ago.
 R It was six, Mark.
 A Well, congratulations! I want to know all the details! Look – I'm going to the café down the street now to meet Leo, my boyfriend. Would you both like to come?
 R Yeah, that sounds good.
 A Brilliant! Let's go.

▶ **1.20** **PART 2**

MARK Do you play much sport?
LEO Not really. I occasionally watch the rugby on TV, but I'm not a big sports fan.
 M Did you see the match at the weekend?
RACHEL Oh, not sport again!
ANNIE So, have you got any exciting plans for next week?
 M Well, er …
 R No, not really. Just work. I've got a lot to do in the shop this week, because we're going to a wedding next weekend.
 A Oh, the shop? What do you do?
 R I'm a florist.
 A What a great job! Where's the shop?
 R Not far from here. I'll show you some time.
 A That would be great! And are you the manager, or …
 R Well, not really – it's my shop.
 A Wow. That's amazing! So you're a businesswoman! Do you work on your own?
 R No, I have someone to help. Tina. She comes in for a few hours every day.
 A Oh, that's good.
 R How about you? What do you do?
 A Oh, marketing. Boring!
 R Same as Mark. He works in marketing.
 A Oh, I'm sorry. I find it boring.
 R Do you have any plans for the weekend?
 A Actually, yes. I'm going to visit my brother, Dan.
 R Oh, I remember Dan. How is he?
 A He's fine. He's married now. To Martina.
 R Anyway, we really must go. I need to get back to the shop.
 A Yeah, of course.
 M It was really nice to meet you.
 A Yeah, you too.
 L Nice to meet you, Mark.
 R It was great to see you again, Annie.
 A Yeah! We must meet up soon!
 R Definitely!
 A Actually, it's Leo's birthday in a couple of weeks. Perhaps we could meet then.
 R OK, great. I'll give you a call. And say hello to Dan for me!

▶ **1.22**

CHRIS So, are you good about keeping in touch with people?
NINA Er, not really. I always plan to write to people, but then I forget. I send emails to my parents sometimes, about once a month, but more often I get emails from them saying 'Are you OK? We haven't heard from you for a long time.' Then I always send them a quick email and tell them what I'm doing. How about you?

 C Oh, I like keeping in touch. I think it's important to keep in touch with your family. I write emails to my parents sometimes, but I also phone or Skype. I phone my mother every weekend.
 N Every weekend!
 C Yes, she gets worried about me and she wants to know what I'm doing.
 N I hardly ever phone my parents. I wait until I go and see them, and talk to them then.
 C Don't you ever phone them to have a chat?
 N No, I only phone if it's something important. You don't have to be in touch with people all the time.
 C What about friends? Surely you keep in touch with friends?
 N Not very much, maybe I should do. I send texts or messages sometimes, but that's about all. I always think if you have good friends you can talk about everything when you meet. It's more fun to tell people your news when you can have a real conversation.
 C Oh well, I often send messages to people so they know I'm thinking about them. And sometimes, when I have a particularly good photo, I send it to everyone by email. I think it's a nice thing to do …

Unit 2

▶ **1.23**

DAY THREE
So, the next morning, we started with some water skiing practice on the beach. First, they showed us how to stand up on the skis … and then how to fall off safely. The lesson took about an hour, and then we were ready to go out to sea. There were five other people in my group, who were all very excited. But not me – I was really worried. The instructor looked at me and said, "Do you want to go first?" and then everyone looked at me. I felt sick but I said, "Yes" …

Ten seconds after I started, I fell over. I tried again. And I fell over again. Then the third time, something amazing suddenly happened. I didn't fall over. And I found out that I love water skiing. The ten minutes in the water passed very quickly and I didn't want to stop!

When we got back to the hotel, the receptionist asked me, "So, did you enjoy the water skiing course?" I said, "Yes" which, for the first time, was the truth.

And then later on that evening I had a drink in the bar with the other water skiers. I felt really happy. And that was when I realised I was enjoying being a 'Yes Man' after all.

▶ **1.24**

DAY SEVEN
On the last day of the holiday, I couldn't wait for midnight. At 12 o'clock I could stop answering 'yes' to every question. The week had been fun but I wanted some control of my life again! That evening I went for one last dinner with some of my new friends. "So, did you have a good week?" one of them asked me. "Yes," I said. "What was your favourite thing?" she asked.

And do you know what? I couldn't really answer her. There were so many things I'd enjoyed. I worked as a waiter for a day – I didn't get any money for it, but I made friends with some interesting people who came to eat at the restaurant. I also spent a day fishing with five Greek fishermen and caught several fish. I stayed at a beach party until six in the morning. Oh, and I won a dancing competition!

Of course, some of my experiences weren't very good. I took the same boat trip three times … I went swimming at midnight – actually, I liked the swimming, but I didn't like the mosquitoes that bit me when I got out of the sea. And I spent over 200 euros on souvenirs that I hate!

It was great to try new things. But I was glad the week was nearly finished. I wanted to get back home and relax for a day before I started work again on Monday. But Day 7 wasn't finished yet! Without thinking, I asked my new friends what they planned to do next. They were all smiling at me. One of them said, "We're flying to Thailand tomorrow. Do you want to come with us? You'd love it!"

I looked at my watch. It was 11.55.

1.33

Well, I was in a rush that morning and I suppose I set off a bit late. It was raining when I left the house and there was a lot of traffic on the roads. I got to the airport just before the desk closed.

When I boarded the plane, all the other passengers were waiting for me. It was a bit embarrassing, but we took off OK. I had a seat in the middle of the plane and for the first couple of hours it was fine.

So I was reading my book when one of the flight attendants came over and spoke to me. She said that there was something wrong with *her* seat and that she needed to take mine. I was the last passenger to check in, so they chose me.

I asked the flight attendant where I should sit and she told me that the only place was the toilet. At first, I thought it was a joke, but then I realised that she was serious.

So I was sitting on the toilet when the turbulence started. It was quite frightening because of course there was no seatbelt in the toilet. I almost fell off a few times. After the turbulence stopped, I opened the door. About five passengers were waiting outside to use the toilet. I just closed the door again.

And then to top it all, when we landed at Istanbul there was a delay of an hour before we could get off the plane because of a problem in the airport.

I still can't believe they told me to stay in the toilet for two hours. It was terrible. You just can't treat customers like that.

1.38 PART 1

ANNIE Excuse me … Excuse me!
EMPLOYEE Yes, how can I help you?
A I'm going to Birmingham to visit my brother.
E OK. Erm, which train are you taking?
A Oh, I don't know. What time's the next train?
E The next one leaves in … four minutes.
A How often do the trains leave?
E Every … 30 minutes. So the next one after that is at 15.32.
A OK, great. And er, which platform does it leave from?
E That train leaves from … platform 12. So, it's just over there.
A Sorry, just one more thing.
E Yes, of course.
A Could you tell me where the ticket office is?
E It's over there. But it looks quite busy – there's a long queue. I can sell you a ticket.
A Oh, brilliant! How much is a ticket?
E Well, when do you want to come back?
A Oh, I don't know. Probably tomorrow evening. But on Sunday it's going to be sunny I think and my brother's going to have a party and so maybe I'll stay until Monday.
E The ticket prices change. Sunday is cheaper than Monday.
A Oh, Sunday then. His parties are never very good.
E OK, you want a return to Birmingham. Coming back on … Sunday?
A Yes, that's right.
E So, that's £26.30.
A Can I pay by card?
E Yes, sure … OK, so here's your card, and your ticket. Is there anything else I can help you with?
A Actually, there is one more thing. Where can I buy a magazine? Is there a newsagent's here?
E Yes, look – there's one just over there.
A Great. Thanks so much.
E No problem. Have a good journey.

1.45 PART 2

ANNIE He doesn't live in Birmingham any more! He doesn't live in Birmingham any more! He doesn't live in Birmingham any more!
EMPLOYEE Sorry?
A My brother. He moved. He doesn't live in Birmingham any more. He lives in Stratford now! Can I change my ticket …?

1.46

TIM So, when I get to Jakarta, what should I do?
KAREN I'm not really sure. I mean, I left Indonesia about ten years ago and … well … it's probably all changed now.
T So, yeah, I think we'll just get a taxi from the airport to the hostel.
K You could, but if you want to save money, I think there's probably a bus service.
T I suppose so. Is that what you did?
K Well, I was going to Jakarta to work, so someone met us with a car and drove us into the centre of town.
T So what was it like when you arrived?
K It's something I'll never forget. You know, this was the first time I went somewhere that was completely different, the other side of the world. I remember we had a pretty bad flight, there was a long delay at the airport because there was something wrong with the plane. And we had quite a lot of turbulence – and as we were landing I remember thinking 'Is this all a big mistake?'. But no … as soon as we got off the plane and I felt how lovely and warm it was, I began to feel much happier. I loved it there, I'm sure you will too.
T And, so, once you were away from the airport, what did you see?
K Well, the first thing I saw was a traffic jam!
T Oh no.
K Yes, and a traffic jam that was much noisier and longer than in this country. And a storm!
T Oh no! Really?
K Yes, quite often in the spring, the rainy season, there's suddenly a storm with heavy rain and lightning. And you just have to run for the nearest building! For me, it was exciting though. I expect you'll love it, too.
T You must have so many memories of your time there.
K Yeah … yeah I do.
T Did you write them down? You know, do a blog or something.
K No … I didn't have an internet connection in my apartment.
T Or a diary or something like that?
K No, I never did.
T That's a pity. But you seem to remember it pretty well!

Unit 3

1.49

After leaving his job, Philip Wollen opened up the Kindness Trust, an organisation that finds small charities in countries where a little bit of money can make a big difference. Wollen then surprises these charities with a gift to continue their good work. So far, he has given money to between 400–500 different charities in 40 countries. His money has built schools, children's homes, and homes for animals.

A special charity for Wollen is the Morning Star orphanage in Bangalore. The orphanage started when, 20 years ago, a man called John Samson found a hungry baby boy in the street. He gave him a home and then he looked for more homeless children to help. Today the orphanage looks after 60 children. With money from the Kindness Trust, John has made the Morning Star bigger and opened a new learning centre. Wollen went to India to open the centre, meet the children and hear about their lives. One little girl has won a place at a famous women's college, another child is an excellent chess player and another wants to be a doctor. The little boy that John Samson found in the street has now become a chemist.

And it is not just people that Philip Wollen has helped. He has also given money to a large number of animal charities, such as Edgar's Mission in Australia, a charity that cares for old farm animals and finds new homes for them. The charity also tries to teach people how to look after animals, so they are healthy and happy.

Wollen thinks everyone can help to make the world a better place for other people and animals. He says, 'One man can make a difference and every man should try.'

1.51

PRESENTER So, in these difficult times, how are people spending their money? Are people still borrowing from the banks? I came to Norwich to talk to shoppers.
Excuse me, sir, do you mind if I ask you a few questions about your spending habits?
SPEAKER 1 Err, OK.
P Can I ask what you've got in your bags?
1 I've just bought my food for the week. They had some special offers on cheese! I think I've got enough for a month.
P Are you saving up for anything at the moment?
1 Yes actually, I'm saving for a car. My girlfriend is moving away to Leeds to study and I want to visit her at weekends. The train is really expensive so in the end, it's cheaper to drive.
P Why didn't you borrow the money for the car?
1 Well, I don't want to owe money to a bank. I generally don't like borrowing. I've got three credit cards and I've never used any of them. I've only got them, because of the free stuff you get – travel insurance, cinema tickets, that kind of thing.
PRESENTER And what have you just bought?
SPEAKER 2 Not much! It was all too expensive. But I found a good price on some suntan lotion. So I bought a lot.
P Are you saving up for anything at the moment?
2 Well, I'm always saving, but there isn't really anything I actually want to buy. I've already got everything I need. Why should I spend my money on new things when the things I have are perfectly OK? Everyone should save for when they're older. I don't want to be working when I'm an old man.
P So, I suppose you don't need to borrow?
2 No, not yet! And I hope I never do. When I can't afford something, I don't buy it. Simple. And I never lend money to other people. Never. You give them money, and you never get it back. Then you lose a friend.
PRESENTER Have you bought anything nice today?
SPEAKER 3 Some perfume … and a small necklace. The necklace was quite expensive … well, very expensive … but I need a new one to go with a dress I've just bought.
P Lovely! And are you saving up for anything at the moment?
3 No, not really. I don't really save up for things, to be honest. If I need something, I just buy it. I've got credit cards. I've already spent my salary this month, but that's life. Life's too short to worry about money.
P So you don't mind borrowing money?
3 I don't borrow money. Well, I use my credit cards, but that's not really borrowing, is it? Oh! And I got a small loan last year. I haven't paid it back yet.

1.56 PART 1

RACHEL OK, what's next? Oh, we need to buy a present for Leo.
MARK Really? Why?
R It's his birthday, remember. Annie told us last week.
M Well, we don't know him very well.
R Oh, come on. We need to buy him something. Oh, look – how about this shop? I'm sure we can find something in here.
M Hmm.

▶ 1.57 PART 2

MARK This place is great! I could stay here all day!

RACHEL Well, we're only here for Leo, remember.

SHOP ASSISTANT Hi, can I help you?

R Er, yes. We're looking for a present for a friend. It's his birthday.

SA OK. Are you looking for anything in particular?

R Umm, I don't know …

M Something fun!

SA OK. What sort of thing does he like? Is he a sports fan?

M Yeah.

R Is he? Does he like sport?

M Yeah, I'm sure.

SA OK … How about this? 'Football in a tin'. Perfect for a birthday present.

R What is it exactly?

SA It's a football game. Look, you put the boots on your fingers, there's a ball …

M This looks perfect! He loves football.

R Does he? I'm not sure. What else do you have?

SA What about this? A weather station.

M Oh – what does it do?

SA Well, it tells you the weather now, and the next day. It's also an alarm clock.

M Do you have anything cheaper?

SA Well … well, this is a great product. A book money bank.

R A book money bank?

SA Well, you open it here and there's a place to put your money. To keep it safe.

R Oh, that's quite nice.

M Yeah, I suppose he might like that.

R OK, we've decided.

SA Great …

M On second thoughts, I really think we should get something sporty. Could you show us something else?

SA Oh, I know. What about this? A football clock.

M Brilliant! Let's get that!

R Well, if you really think he likes football.

M Yeah, of course. He was talking about football last time we saw him. We'll take it.

R Was he? I don't remember that.

▶ 1.61 PART 3

SHOP ASSISTANT 2 Who's next, please?

MARK Oh, yes. Just this, please.

SA2 How would you like to pay?

M Cash.

SA2 OK.

M Actually, I think I'll put it on my credit card.

SA2 OK. Can you put your card in, please? … And can you enter your PIN, please? … Thank you. OK, here's your receipt, and here's the clock.

M Thanks a lot.

▶ 1.62

SHONA I support Oxfam. You see, I had a really happy childhood myself and I think it's important to help other people in poorer countries have happy childhoods. I haven't got a lot of spare money, but I try and help them in other ways. For example, last year I ran a marathon and people sponsored me, you know, gave me money for doing the run. I made just over a hundred pounds. And then, once a month, I make cakes and take them to my office. I sell pieces of cake to my colleagues for morning tea and give the money to Oxfam.

JACK Well, giving to charity is quite easy really. You can go online and pay with your credit card. I've given money to Greenpeace that way a few times recently. And once a year, I sell their calendars – mostly to friends and the people I work with. I think that helping to save our natural world is the most important thing you can do. I think I should do something now – so that my children and my children's children can enjoy the kind of world that I live in.

JESSICA Of course, I think it's important to … well, that people give money to charities. But actually, I haven't got a lot of money myself. I owe money to my parents and I have to pay back the government for my university study and … In fact, I've never given any money to a charity. I can't really afford it.

WILLIAM Our history is really important and we need to protect it. When I think of all the old buildings that we've already lost, it's terrible. So, once every six months I go around my neighbourhood and collect money door to door for the National Trust. I tell people about local places the National Trust want to protect and they are usually very generous.

Unit 4

▶ 1.65

INTERVIEWER So Marta, what exactly is a May Ball?

MARTA Well, it's a huge party at our college. They have it every summer after we finish our exams because we need to celebrate after all that stress. Everyone gets dressed up, and there's food and drink and entertainment. There are eight different stages and over 70 bands. This year one of my favourite DJs is playing. I really can't wait.

I What are you going to wear?

M I've just bought the dress I'm going to wear – it's dark blue and I feel really good in it. I'm going to wear it with high heels and some nice jewellery!

I Is there anything else you need to do?

M Get ready and sleep! I need to look my best … I'm going to the hairdresser's tomorrow. And a beautician is doing our make-up. Apart from that, I'm not going to leave the house on Saturday. I'm going to get as much sleep as possible!

I What time are you leaving?

M The ball doesn't start until 9 pm but I'm meeting the others at 7 pm so we can start queuing. Everyone says it takes a really long time to get in … but then we're going to stay the whole night – until 6 am, when they serve breakfast!

CRAIG So, hi, everyone – welcome to today's audio blog. Well, today is the fourth day of my wedding. Everyone's going to be back here again in a few hours. There's going to be more dancing and food, of course. And today they're going to make a special cream from a spice called turmeric and rub it on my face and arms. The idea is that it cleans your skin and makes you ready for marriage. I hope it doesn't hurt …

Then tomorrow is the wedding day. It starts at 9 am, so quite early. But it finishes in the afternoon, after lunch. My friends are arriving early tomorrow to help me get ready and take me there. I'm going to wear a traditional Indian suit called a 'kurta pajama'. It's actually really comfortable.

I'm really excited now. I'm looking forward to seeing all my friends and relatives, and, of course, my new wife! But I need to be patient … the first part of an Indian wedding is breakfast with all the guests. The bride eats in a separate room with some of her friends. So, I'm not going to see Monisha until the ceremony actually begins, later in the morning.

▶ 1.68 PART 1

HARRY Hello?

MIKE Hi, Harry! It's me! I'm here! I've just arrived at my hotel.

H Welcome to Tokyo! Did you have a good journey?

M Yeah, it was fine. I was so lucky to get a stopover in Japan!

H And lucky that I'm here to show you around! I've already got a few ideas about what we can do.

M OK, but I really don't want to go where all the tourists go. I want to see the real Tokyo.

H OK, so we won't go to Disneyland then! And I won't take you to the Imperial Palace, either.

M OK.

H I mean, the palace is nice but it's so crowded. It's really just a place for tourists.

M Fine.

H So … shall we start with something to eat?

M OK.

H There's a great noodle restaurant I know. The noodles are delicious, some of the best in Tokyo. And it's also really simple. You just eat quickly and then you leave. So we won't waste any time!

M Brilliant.

H After that, I'll take you to Yoyogi Park. It's a huge park and it'll be really busy at the moment because everyone's going to see the cherry blossom.

M The cherry blossom?

H Yeah, it's beautiful. You see young people, businessmen in suits, families – everyone goes to look at the pretty flowers. There are also lots of musicians there, and the teenagers doing 'cosplay' …

M Who?

H Well, basically they're people who dress up as characters from computer games and cartoons. That kind of thing. They just do it for fun but they spend a lot of time and money on it so they look incredible.

M Wow – I think I've seen pictures of them before. I'd love to see them in real life. And after that?

H Well, do you want to do any shopping?

M Actually, yeah – I want to look for a new camera.

H Excellent. I'll take you to Akihabara, then. There are lots of electronics shops there. And they often have special offers.

M Perfect. And what are we doing in the evening?

H I've already booked a room for karaoke.

M Really? I don't really like karaoke that much. I'm a terrible singer.

H Yeah, but you haven't tried karaoke Japanese-style! I've booked a private room for six people. So, you, me and four of my friends. You'll love them – they're really good fun. Anyway, I've booked it till 2 am.

M 2 am?! Remember my flight leaves at 7 am tomorrow!

H Don't worry – you won't miss your flight! I promise. Anyway, we won't be finished at two. After that we're going to the Tsukiji fish market!

M A fish market? In the middle of the night?

H Yeah, it's the best time to go. They bring in all the fish they've just caught. Trust me, it's an amazing sight.

M OK. This is going to be an interesting day …

H So, shall I come to your hotel in about an hour?

M OK, see you in a bit.

H Bye!

▶ 1.75 PART 2

HARRY Airport, please.

TAXI DRIVER OK.

M Ooof!

H Tired?

M Yes, and I'm a bit worried about my flight. It leaves in two hours …

H Don't worry – you'll be fine. It only takes half an hour to get there. We've got plenty of time.

M Hmm.

H So, what was your favourite part of the day?

M Difficult question. I liked all of it. The food was great. The fish market … well, I've never seen anything like that.

H Yep!

M But I think I liked the karaoke best. It's such good fun in a private room. I hate it in England, when you do it in front of 50 strangers.

H Yeah, absolutely.

▶ 1.76 PART 3

MIKE Can you ask the taxi driver to go a bit faster? I really am worried about this flight.

HARRY Yeah, he is a bit slow. Can you go a bit faster?

M This is a nightmare now! The flight leaves in an hour!

H Yeah, I'm really sorry about this. We stayed too long at the fish market. And I didn't know there'd be so much traffic.

M Mmm.

H Look – I've got an idea. You enjoyed your day, right?

M Definitely. Well, until now anyway.

H Well, change your flight and stay another day. I'll take the day off work. There are lots more places in Tokyo I want to show you.

M I don't know … what about the flight?
H You can change the flight! Come on, it'll be great!
M Yeah, but …
H Come on … shall I tell the taxi driver to turn round?
M Well …

▶ 1.77 PART 1

RACHEL Hello, Fantastic Flowers.
ANNIE Oh, hi. Rachel?
R Yes?
A It's Annie.
R Oh, hi Annie! How are you?
A I'm OK, thanks. You?
R I'm great.
A Listen – you know it's Leo's birthday this week?
R Of course!
A Well, are you doing anything on Wednesday? Would you like to come round for a meal?
R Oh, that sounds nice. I'll just check. No, we can't do Wednesday. Sorry. We're meeting some friends.
A Oh, OK. How about Thursday? Is that OK for you?
R Thursday … hang on a minute … oh, no, sorry. I'm working on Thursday evening.
A Oh.
R This week's really busy for us. Next week?
A OK. What are you doing on … Monday?
R Just a moment … Nothing! We can do Monday – perfect.
A Great!
R What time shall we come round?
A Let's say … seven o'clock.
R OK – and would you like us to bring anything?
A No, nothing! See you on Monday then!
R Great! See you then.
A Bye!

▶ 1.81 PART 2

MARK That was great!
RACHEL Yeah, thanks, Annie. You're a great cook.
ANNIE Thanks! I'm glad you enjoyed it.
M Enjoyed it? I don't think I can move!
A Excuse me for a moment.
M I think I need to go for a run tomorrow.
R I always tell you not to eat so much.
A Rachel, can you come here for a second? I need you to help me carry something.
R I'll send Mark. He needs the exercise! Go on.
LEO I think I need to get some exercise as well!
R Mark said you're a big sports fan.
L No, not really. I mean – I like to keep fit, so I go to the gym. But I don't really like sport. It's a bit boring. And I can't stand football.
R Oh.
A Happy birthday, Leo!
M & R Happy birthday!
L Thanks, everyone. What an amazing cake!
M Oh … we've got this for you, Leo.
R Yes, happy birthday!
L Oh, you really didn't need to! . . . Ha, thanks . . . Wow, that's great. I love it! That's very kind of you.
M I knew you'd like it! Actually, Leo, I was thinking … since you're a sports fan, maybe we could do something together some time. Maybe go to a football match?
L Well … sure, or how about a workout? I like going to the gym. How about that? Do you want to come with me some time?
M Oh, OK. Why not? The gym sounds great.
L When are you free? I normally go in the evening.
M Well, are you going next Tuesday? I'm free then.
L I can't Tuesday. How about Thursday?
M OK. Sounds great!

▶ 1.85

SUSANNA I don't really like having a party at home to celebrate. It's too much work. I think it's better to go out together and find a nice place where you can celebrate. Then you can all have a good time together.
This weekend, it's my 21st birthday and we're going to book a function room at a hotel and have a big party there. All my friends are coming and we're going to have a band and a DJ. Everyone's going to look their best – all the men are going to wear suits and I'm going to buy a new dress. I'm really excited about it!

BARBARA I like inviting friends to my home, but I'm not a very good cook. I always get very stressed if I have to cook meals for people. Everyone else is having a nice time, but I'm just worrying if the food's OK. So, I don't really enjoy it. What I do like is if we all cook something together, then you don't get bored – like going to the cinema or bowling maybe, or going out somewhere nice together.
We're doing that on Saturday. We're having a barbecue, but I'm just making some salads and I'm going to ask everyone to bring something for the barbecue. I'm looking forward to it.
SVEN I sometimes enjoy parties, but they're all the same really: you just sit around and talk to people about all the usual stuff until it's time to go home. With friends, I think it's better to do something together, then you don't get bored – like going to the cinema or bowling maybe, or going out somewhere nice together.
This weekend, I'm going to the countryside with some old friends I haven't seen for a long time. We're going to a lake to swim and have a picnic together, and maybe we'll play volleyball. That'll be fun.

Unit 5

▶ 2.5

ALISHA I love my job … working with people and helping them … but it's often stressful. I have to work long hours including weekends, and sometimes deal with very serious problems. These days, to become a nurse you have to do well at school – especially in maths, science and English. Then you have to do a nursing degree before you can get a job. You also need to be good at making decisions and working in a team. There are lots of rules to remember. You can't enter a room without washing your hands. You can't lift a patient on your own. When you work with people who are very sick, every decision you make is so important.
JOHN For my job, you need to do two or three years training – usually while you are working with a company. You can't go to people's houses on your own and start fixing things without a qualification. Now I have my own company, I usually work about 45 to 50 hours a week. It can be tiring. And, of course, you have to be careful, especially when you're tired. There are a lot of health and safety rules … for example, you always have to switch off the mains power. I heard of one guy who forgot and nearly died. Anyway … there are good things, too – you don't have to wear a suit or go to many meetings and I enjoy being my own boss.
MIRIAM I'm in investment banking … and to get in I needed a good university degree, and, also, to be a good communicator. You have to enjoy working really hard … I work very long hours, a hundred hours or more a week … And, well … I have to deal with a lot of stress … I look after millions of pounds of other people's money. You also can't relax because if something goes wrong, you lose money – other people's money. I suppose I also like that – it's exciting. But it's not an easy job and sometimes I feel that what I do isn't really that useful.

▶ 2.9

INTERVIEWER Are you enjoying the careers fair?
SARA It's not bad. It's good to meet people from different companies.
I Are you looking for work at the moment?
S Yes. But it won't be easy to find a job I'll enjoy. There just aren't enough jobs – you have to take what you can find. I applied for a job this week but I don't think I'll get an interview. They won't be interested in me, because I don't have any experience.
I Are you enjoying the fair today?
MARCO Yeah, it's great. I'm sure I'll make some really useful contacts. There are people from some really interesting companies here.
I And are you applying for jobs at the moment?
M Yes. I don't think it'll take long to find work. You never know … I might get a job today! I know someone who found a job at an event like this last year.
I Are you enjoying it today?
KATE Yes, it's good. It's useful because I'm not sure what kinds of jobs I'm interested in.
I So are you looking for work at the moment?

K Not yet. I'm still studying and then I'll try to get some work experience when I finish my course. After that, I can start looking for a job. I might not get my perfect job, because not many people do, straight out of university.
I And how do you feel about that?
K Well … I just need to pay the bills, you know. I'm sure I'll find some kind of work because I'm happy to do anything they'll pay me for. I can work my way up. I've got time!

▶ 2.15 PART 1

RACHEL Oh dear.
TINA Is everything OK?
R I'm not sure really. I've just got a text message from my friend Annie. Do you remember her?
T Yeah, of course.
R Yeah, well she says she's had some bad news and she needs to talk to me.
T Oh dear. I hope she's OK.
R Hmm, I'd better give her a ring. Or maybe I should go and see her.
T Yeah, maybe you should. I'll finish things here, if you want.
R But I can't leave you here on your own.
T I'll be fine! Don't worry about it.
R But we've still got so much to do.
T Oh, it doesn't matter. Honestly, I'll be OK.
R I don't want to leave you with too much work. It doesn't seem very fair. It means you won't be able to leave early today.
T Oh, never mind. Look, why don't you tell me what we still need to do? And I'll write a list. Then you can go and see Annie.
R OK, well if you're sure.
T Of course. It's no problem.
R Well, …

▶ 2.17 PART 2

RACHEL Right, and after that …
TINA Shall I finish off those flowers? The ones you were doing?
R OK. That would be great.
T And would you like me to prepare some of the orders for tomorrow?
R Yeah. You could start with that order for Mrs Thompson, because she's picking it up early.
T OK.
R And then maybe you should start on the order for that big birthday party.
T OK.
R Actually, no – we can do that tomorrow morning – we'll have time.
T Yeah, fine.
R OK, I think that's everything. Oh, when you leave, you'll need to put the alarm on. I'll write down the code for you.
T OK. Oh – do you want me to take out the rubbish when I leave?
R Er, no, don't worry. The bag's not full yet. I'll do it tomorrow.
T OK, fine.
R OK, great. I'll text Annie to say I'm coming.
T Oh, how about taking her some flowers? That'll cheer her up.
R Good idea … Oh, hello. How can I help?
CUSTOMER Hi, yeah. Er, I just wanted to make an order for some flowers.
R Of course. What would you like?
C Well, actually, it's for my daughter's wedding. So … er … some red roses …
R Yep.
C Some white roses …
R Hmmhmm.
C Some lilies …
T Rachel – why don't I deal with this?
R Are you sure?
T Yes! Just go!
R OK – bye!
C Oh, bye.
T So, that was some red roses …
C Three dozen, please.
T Three dozen …
C Er, white roses, three dozen.
T OK.

2.20

PENNY Are you working this summer?

JOHN Yeah, I've got a job in a café, same as last year. How about you?

P I don't know. I usually work in a supermarket, but I don't like it much. It's so tiring and you have to start really early in the morning. I might look for a different job this summer. What's working in a café like?

J Oh, it's good. It gets quite busy, so you need to be good at working really fast. But I like that.

P Well, that's the same as a supermarket.

J Yeah. But it's good fun, too. You're working in a team and you meet lots of people. It's great!

P Is the pay good?

J Not bad and you can sometimes make quite a lot from tips.

P Really? How much do you make in tips?

J It depends. I can sometimes make £20 in one day!

P Wow! That sounds good.

J It's not always that much though. Listen, why don't you apply for a job? I'm sure they'll give you one. They're always looking for new people.

P Yeah, I don't know. I've never worked in a café. I don't know anything about it.

J Oh, that doesn't matter; they'll give you training. You don't need to know anything.

P Really?

J No, you just have to smile a lot and be nice to people. It's easy.

P Hmm, OK. What are they called?

J Cuba Coffee Company, they've got a website.

P OK thanks, I'll have a look tomorrow, update my CV and apply!

J Great – good luck!

Unit 6

2.28

INTERVIEWER So what did you do?

CAROLINE Well, I was really confused. I thought I was going to die. I didn't really know what to do – I just wanted to get out of the water. But then I saw a shark; then another, and another. And suddenly I stopped feeling frightened. I forgot about dying, and watched those amazing fish moving through the water. Seeing those sharks probably saved my life, because they made me feel relaxed. I started breathing better and – very slowly – I made my way to the top.

I And how did you feel when you got back to the surface?

C Well, once we were back on the fishing boat, I felt a lot of different things. I was happy to be alive, but I was also embarrassed because I used most of my air. And I was shocked and angry with my instructor for taking me down to 40 metres and then disappearing.

I And how has the whole experience changed you?

C After that experience, every time I tried to dive, I got really worried. In the end, I stopped scuba diving. I still love sharks, but I'll never go that deep again to see them.

2.31

INTERVIEWER So, Aaron, your story is pretty amazing. What happened to you?

AARON Well, I think I'm very lucky to be alive today. I was pulled along under a plane when we were flying at a height of 6,000 metres.

I Wow! That's unbelievable! How did it happen?

A So, there were three people in the plane that day. Me, and two other jumpers, Monica and Ben. I wasn't an experienced parachute jumper at the time. I had only done about 15 jumps.

I So, what went wrong?

A Well … Monica told me I should go first … I stood up and put my foot outside the plane door, but then the wind pushed me to the side. I was stuck, flat against the side of the plane. I tried to push myself away, but it didn't work. Then, part of my parachute got stuck on the plane, I couldn't move my leg so I couldn't fall. I was hanging under the plane, hanging from my parachute, and there was nothing

I could do. The others couldn't see me. The plane was just pulling me along in the sky and nobody knew I was there.

I That sounds terrifying! How did you feel?

A Obviously, I was very frightened. I knew how dangerous it was. I knew I could die if I hit the back of the plane.

I So, did the others help you?

A At first, they didn't know I was there. But when Monica was getting ready to jump, she saw me and shouted 'Aaron's under the plane!' The pilot slowed the plane down and they freed my parachute. When I started to fall, I felt better, but when I landed I was shocked to think about what had happened.

I Did that experience stop you from jumping?

A No, but I realised how serious it was. Because I jumped first, Monica saw me and saved me, but if I had been the last one to jump, I would have died. Because the pilot couldn't have saved me while he was flying the plane.

2.32 PART 1

RACHEL Hi, Annie.

ANNIE Oh, hi Rachel. Thanks for coming.

R That's OK. Here, I brought you some flowers.

A Oh, thank you. They're lovely.

R Oh, that's OK. What's happened?

A It's work. My boss asked to see me this afternoon. And she told me I'm going to lose my job.

R Oh, how awful! I'm really sorry to hear that. Did she say why?

A She just said the company's having problems.

R That's terrible.

A Yeah … anyway, I'll make some tea.

2.34 PART 2

RACHEL So, what happened when you talked to your boss? Did you ask when you're going to lose your job? Or if it's completely certain?

ANNIE No, I didn't say much. I was too upset.

R Of course you were.

A I didn't really ask anything. What do you think I should do?

R OK, well, I'd get all the details first.

A Right.

R So I think you should speak to your boss again. Maybe there'll be other jobs there.

A I don't think that's a good idea. I don't know if I want to stay. Lots of people are unhappy there. And I don't think there are any other jobs anyway.

R OK, but I think it's a good idea to ask. You don't know what she'll say.

A I suppose so.

R And why don't you speak to some of the people you work with? Ask them what they're doing?

A Mmm, I don't think I should do that. My boss told me not to talk to anyone else. Because other people are going to lose their jobs too.

R Mmm. You work in marketing, right?

A Yeah.

R Well, Mark works in marketing, too. His company's often looking for new people.

A Really? Do you think I should speak to him about it?

R Definitely. I'll speak to him, too.

A OK. Great.

R And I wouldn't worry too much – changing jobs could be a good thing. You'll have the chance to do something new.

A Yeah – you're right.

2.38 PART 3

RACHEL Is that everything, Annie? Has something else happened?

ANNIE No, it's stupid …

R Come on – you can tell me.

A Well, it's just – I called Leo to talk about my job but he didn't answer the phone. I sent him a text but he still hasn't replied.

R Don't worry. I'm sure he'll call you soon.

A Yeah. Maybe he's not interested in me any more. Oh, I don't know.

R Oh, you shouldn't worry. He's probably just busy at work!

A You're right, you're right.

R Everything will be fine. Call Mark tomorrow. I'll tell him what's happened when he comes home tonight.

A OK.

R And I'm sure Leo will ring you soon!

A Thanks, Rachel … for your help.

R That's OK! That's what friends are for!

2.39

CHLOE The problem is that I think about my job even in my free time. I'm so busy during the day I don't have time to think and then when I get home I spend all my time thinking and worrying. You see, my old boss had to leave in a hurry – a family problem – and they gave me his job. But I haven't had any training and I don't feel ready to be a manager and make decisions. Friends tell me I should do something relaxing after work, like go for a walk on the beach. But I still can't stop thinking about meetings I've been to or meetings I'll have to go to the next day. And all the reports I have to write! There's so much to do and I just feel so stressed.

BOB At first, I was excited about doing something new. I've never done anything like this before. Well, I'm sorry to say I've stopped feeling excited, I'm just generally confused. I don't feel like I'm improving at all. The thing is my wife is Polish and I want to be able to speak to people in her family when we go to Poland. I wasn't very good at languages at school. I mean, I learnt a little bit of French and that was quite hard. But I find Polish really difficult. My wife says 'don't worry – when we go to Poland you'll really start to learn'. But, to be honest, I'm not so sure. I don't think I'm the kind of person who can just listen to a language and learn it.

MARISA I feel really tired, because I haven't been sleeping well for the past week. I stay up late most nights and drink coffee to stay awake. I read the books on my booklist and the notes I've made during the year again and again. And I test myself all the time to help me remember information. My parents tell me I should take more breaks. They forget that I didn't do very well in my exams last year and I was very disappointed with my results. I really want to do well this year, so I need to do all this work. So, I think I'm just going to have to continue like this until I'm sure that I can remember everything.

Unit 7

2.42

RIVALDO

The subject of this week's one-minute inspiration is Brazilian footballer, Rivaldo. Rivaldo came from a very poor family. They didn't have enough to eat and so, growing up, he had some serious health problems. As a teenager, he spent his days on the beach, he sold souvenirs to tourists in the morning and played football in the evening.

Rivaldo got on very well with his father, who was sure that one of his three sons would become a professional footballer. But when Rivaldo was only 16, his father died in a car crash. Rivaldo wanted to give up football and didn't play for a month, but his mother told him he should make his father's dream come true.

Later that year, he got an offer to join Paulistano, a small football club in his home town. He didn't get paid much and he sometimes had to walk 15 kilometres to go to training, because he did not have enough money for the bus. He worked very hard at the club but, because of his health problems, his coach did not believe he could get fit enough to be a star.

But Rivaldo proved the coach wrong and became one of the best footballers in the world. He played for Brazil, and helped them to win the 2002 World Cup. He also played for Barcelona, who paid a 26-million-dollar transfer fee for him. Rivaldo dedicates his success to his father who he says was always with him.

SYLVESTER STALLONE

One-minute inspiration this week comes straight from Hollywood. Sylvester Stallone grew up in a poor neighbourhood in New York. He had a difficult childhood and, after his parents got divorced, he got into trouble at school. When he left school, he managed to get a degree before looking for work in films.

But Stallone couldn't get regular work as an actor. In 1975, he was at his poorest. He had got married and his wife was going to have a baby. He got a job at a cinema and another at a zoo to pay the bills, but he didn't even have enough money to feed his dog. Instead, he sold his dog for $50 to a man outside a shop and walked away crying.

Two weeks later, he was watching a boxing match and he had an idea. In just 20 hours he wrote the script for *Rocky*. Then he tried to sell it. Amazingly, he got an offer of $325,000 from a film studio but he said no! He told the studio he wanted to play Rocky in the movie, but the studio didn't think the film would be successful if he did.

In the end, the studio agreed to let him star, but they only paid him $35,000 for the script. As soon as he got paid, Stallone went to see the man he sold his dog to and gave him $3,000 to get it back!

The rest is movie history. *Rocky* was a big hit. It was nominated for ten Oscars and Stallone got rich and became a star.

▶ 2.49 PART 1

RECEPTIONIST Mr Seymour?
LEO Yes.
R Dr Evans is ready to see you.
L Thank you.
DOCTOR Come in … Please, take a seat. So, what's the problem?
L Well, my back hurts. It's very painful. And I can't get to sleep.
D I see. And when did this problem start?
L About three or four days ago.
D Hmm. And where does it hurt? Could you show me?
L Here. This area.
D Can I have a look?
L Sure.
D So, does it hurt here? And here?
L Yes. Not so much.
D And here?
L Yes!
D And here?
L Yes!
D OK. You can sit down again. Have you had any accidents recently?
L No.
D And you haven't hurt your back in any way. Playing sport, that kind of thing.
L No, no. Nothing.
D OK.
L I'm quite worried about it. It hurts all the time – when I walk, when I sit down. I've spent the last few days in bed and I feel exhausted.
D OK. Well, I don't think it's anything to worry about.
L Phew. That's good to hear.

▶ 2.51 PART 2

DOCTOR OK. Well, I don't think it's anything to worry about.
LEO Phew. That's good to hear.
D But you shouldn't stay in bed – that's not going to help.
L Oh dear. Really?
D No – try to do all the things you normally do, but gently. And don't stay in the same position for a long time. Maybe go for a short walk.
L OK. That sounds fine.
D Do you do any exercise?
L Well, I usually go to the gym, but I haven't been recently. I'm very busy at work at the moment and I just don't have the time.
D I see. And do you spend a lot of time sitting down at work?
L Yes, I do. I work in an office, so I spend a lot of time at my computer.

D Right. It's really important, if you spend a lot of time at a desk in an office, to take regular breaks. And you'll need to start doing exercise again. When you feel ready.
L OK. Breaks, exercise. Fine.
D Are you taking anything for the pain?
L Yes, I've taken some aspirin.
D OK, good. And do you have any allergies?
L No, I don't think so.
D Good. Well, I'll give you a prescription for something a bit stronger.
L OK, that's great.
D Take these, but only when you need them, after food. No more than two every four hours.
L Right.
D And don't take any more than eight in a 24-hour period.
L Fine.
D And come back again in a week's time if it doesn't improve. I expect you'll feel a lot better by then anyway.
L OK, thanks very much.
D I really don't think it's anything to worry about.
L What a relief! Bye.
D Bye now.

▶ 2.56

PRESENTER My name's Jenny Jackson and today we're talking about how to change your life. In the studio with us today, we have three people who have made changes in their lives: Jeff, Silvia and Lucas. Hi guys, welcome to the show.
GUESTS Hi.
P So first of all, Jeff. Can you tell us what your problem was? Why did you need to make a change?
JEFF Well … one day I suddenly realised that if I wanted to buy a new car or my own apartment, I needed to save some money.
P I see. Why didn't you have any money?
J Well. I used to spend a lot of money on things that I didn't really need. So, for example, I used to go out for dinner at a restaurant at least four times a week. I loved getting new things – like, you know, the latest phone, clothes … One weekend I sat down and added up the money I had spent in a month … I was shocked.
P I can imagine. So, what have you changed?
J Well, now I eat at home most of the time. And I think 'do I need this?' before I buy something new. I've saved almost £5,000. I'm really pleased with myself.
P Cool. That's great. Next up we have Silvia. Silvia, tell us about your change.
SILVIA Hi, Jenny. Well, my story began when one day I had to walk up a hill. When I got to the top, it was difficult to breathe. I was so unfit! The problem is I really hate most kinds of exercise – you know, running, cycling, swimming … Then this friend said, 'why don't you come to a dance class?' The first time was so hard, I had to sit down and rest. But … but I enjoyed it … So I went back again … and again. And very slowly I'm getting fitter and losing weight. I climbed that hill again last week – easy!
P That's great, Silvia. I really need to get fit myself! Anyhow, last up we have Lucas. Hi, Lucas.
LUCAS Hi.
P So, Lucas, what did you need to change?
L Well, about six months ago I realised that I had a very small number of friends. But if I thought back … well, seven, eight years ago I used to have a lot of friends. And I asked myself, why is that? Well, some of them got married and had children and their lives sort of went in another direction. And a couple of friends got job offers overseas. But when I thought about it a bit more, well, another answer was I'm a bit lazy – lazy about keeping in touch with people.
P I see. So, what did you do about it?
L So, I started to get in touch with my old friends. And then, after that, I had to stay in contact and arrange to meet them again. Now I find that people call me! And the great thing is we still enjoy the things that we used to.
P Well, thanks so much, guys, for sharing your story with us. It just shows that we can all make that change if we decide to do it!

Unit 8

▶ 2.60

Number one is false. Only four of the songs on *Thriller* were written by Michael Jackson. Number two is true. The performance wasn't very successful. The orchestra made a mistake. It was also a very cold day and the audience was cold and tired at the end of the performance. Number three is false. The *Mona Lisa* was painted by Leonardo Da Vinci. Number four is true. *The Dark Knight Rises* contains many of the ideas in *A Tale of Two Cities*. Number five is false. Morgan Freeman is in the film, but the main character is played by Tim Robbins. Number six is false. *Game of Thrones* is directed by many different people, but not Peter Jackson. Number seven is true … although, of course, none of the magical places are real places. Number eight is false. The building was designed by Antoni Gaudi.

▶ 2.61

HOST Welcome to *I can't believe it!* Today's topic is famous world record breakers, and, as usual, we have three players: Michael, Alice and Neil. Each player is going to talk about one record breaker. While they're talking, they'll tell two lies. The other players are going to guess which information is not true. Michael. We'll start with you … Who are you going to talk about today?
MICHAEL Yes. I'm going to talk about …

▶ 2.62

H Michael. We'll start with you … Who are you going to talk about today?
M Yes. I'm going to talk about the fastest man in the world – Usain Bolt from Jamaica. Well, Bolt has been in the Jamaican Olympic team since 2004. He was only 17 when he was chosen. He's 1.95 metres tall – that's a lot taller than most runners. And because of this, his team mates call him 'Giraffe'. Runners as tall as Usain don't usually win races. So it's amazing that he's held both the 100 metres and 200 metres world records since 2008. And we all know that, in 2012, he became the first person ever to win those races in two Olympics. In the 100 metres in 2012 he forgot to tie his shoes and he also slowed down at the end of the race. But amazingly he still won!
H Thank you, Michael. Alice and Neil, can you guess what Michael's lies were?

▶ 2.63

H Thank you, Michael. Alice and Neil, can you guess what Michael's lies were?
ALICE I don't think it's true that he slowed down at the end of the race.
H Michael – is that true?
M It is true, actually!
H Bad luck, Alice! Neil …
NEIL Well, I don't think he forgot to tie his shoes.
M You're right. He did run with one shoe untied, but it was in 2008 not in 2012!
H Well done on that one, Neil. What was lie number 2?
N Hmmm. Is it true that tall runners don't usually win races?
M Yes, that one's also true.
H So, what was the lie, Michael?
M Well, he is very tall but his team mates don't call him 'Giraffe'.

H Alice – what are you going to talk about?
A Well, I'm going to talk about Konishiki Yasokichi, the sumo wrestler. He's actually from Hawaii, but he's lived in Japan for most of his life. He is famous, because he was the heaviest professional sumo wrestler ever. He weighed an incredible 287 kilos. Konishiki used his huge weight to help him win fights – he usually sat on people until he won. As Konishiki got older he started to lose against smaller, faster wrestlers. But in Japan, sumo wrestlers are as famous as film stars and the Japanese people loved him even when he lost, because he was so big. He has been really successful since he stopped fighting. He's a musician, he's acted in films and he's had his own radio show for many years now. He even had his own TV cookery show for a while – he showed people how to cook sumo meals.
H And finally, let's hear from Neil.
N Thank you. I'm going to talk about a captain in the US Air Force, Joseph Kittinger. In 1960, he broke three world records when he jumped to earth from the stratosphere – that's the edge of space, 31 kilometres above the earth. He travelled up there by balloon and when he jumped he broke the record for the highest jump ever. He fell for more than four minutes – the longest free fall ever. He fell at a speed of 988 kilometres per hour, and got the record for travelling through the air faster than any other human. He actually fell faster than the speed of sound. He later wrote a song about the experience, called 'Jump into Space', which is quite good!
But Kittinger's story doesn't end there. In 2012, a man called Felix Baumgartner tried to break his three records. Kittinger helped him because he was the only person who had ever jumped from space before. But Baumgartner didn't break all of Kittinger's records, he only broke two. He opened his parachute early and so Kittinger has held his amazing record of longest free fall for over 50 years!

H Thank you, Alice. Right – Neil and Michael. What do you think the lies were about Konishiki Yasokichi?
N Hmm. I don't know … I don't think he sat on people in his fights. That sounds too dangerous.
H Alice?
A You're right. That isn't true. He won his fights by pushing the other man out of the ring, not by sitting on him.
H Well done, Neil! Anything else?
N Hmm. I don't think he acted in films.
A No, that was true. He was in a couple of films.
H How about you, Michael?
M I don't think he's originally from Hawaii.
A Sorry, that's true.
H Tell us the lie then, Alice.
A The lie was the cookery show. He didn't have one.

H Interesting story about Captain Kittinger, Neil. What do you think, Michael and Alice?
M What about the balloon? Was that really how he got up there?
N Yes, it was. Sorry.
H Alice?
A Well, I'm not sure he was the person who helped Felix Baumgartner.
N Actually, he was. And he was there on the ground when Baumgartner landed.
H So, what were the lies?
N Well, he didn't fall faster than the speed of sound. And he didn't write a song about his parachute jump. He wrote a book about it.
H Well done, Neil! Alice and Michael believed both of your lies! You're today's winner on *I can't believe it!*

LEO Hi, Annie.
ANNIE Oh, hi.
L Are you busy? Can I come in?
A Er, yeah – come in … Do you want anything to drink? A coffee?

L No, no, I'm fine.
A So, how are you?
L I'm … well, I'm OK. Look, I'm really sorry I haven't called you.
A It doesn't matter.
L No, look – let me explain. I couldn't call or send you a message. I've had a really bad back. I was in bed for days.
A What do you mean, you couldn't call? Did your arms stop working? How hard is it to call someone?
L No, no – you don't understand. I was going to call you, but I couldn't find my mobile.
A I don't know, Leo. How can I believe you?
L It's true!
A I thought you were avoiding me.
L No, of course not.
A So, what happened? Did you have an accident?
L No, nothing. I just woke up one day and it was hurting. And then every day it got worse.
A Oh.
L So, in the end, I went to the doctor.
A And what did the doctor say?
L Well, he said it was because I'm always behind my desk, in the office.
A I was worried, you know?
L I'm sorry. I didn't mean to make you worry. And then I meant to call you after I went to the doctor, but I was working so much.
A Well, it's not your fault. But why were you working so much?
L Well, because I missed so much work. Because of my back.
A Leo, the doctor said you had a bad back because of your work. And then you work even more?
L I know, I know. I had to work that much. I didn't have a choice.
A Oh, Leo.
L I'm sorry, Annie.
A Don't worry about it.
L No, there's no excuse.
A No really, it's fine. Are you sure you don't want that coffee?
L Oh, that would be great – thanks.

ANNIE Oh, is it hurting now?
LEO A bit.
A Did the doctor give you anything?
L Yeah, he gave me some pills. They're helping, but not much.
A Ooh, I know! Lie down and I'll walk on your back.
L What?
A I saw it on a TV programme! It'll help.
L Annie, I don't really think that's for serious back problems.
A No, of course not – sorry.
L No, it's fine – it's just, you know – I think I should do what the doctor says.
A Well, you could come to my yoga class! I think yoga's really good for your back.
L Hmm, yoga … I'm not sure.
A Come on – you'll love it!
L Do any other men go?
A Well, no, but you could be the first.
L It's not really my kind of thing.
A They do water aerobics too … in the swimming pool …
L Annie, that sounds worse than yoga.
A Well, what about the gym? I know … you can go with Mark! He asked you, remember? You should call him! What do you think?
L Yeah, I suppose.
A Call him! It'll be fun!
L OK, OK – I will. I promise.

1 I'm reading a book called *Two Lives*. I've had this book for about a year, but I only started reading it last week. It's about a man and a woman who fall in love, but then something happens in the family and the man has to leave. He goes abroad and lives there, but then he comes back and they meet again years later. The man still loves her, but of course he's been away for years and now she's found another man and she's going to marry him. I don't know what's going to happen, but I hope they'll be

happy in the end! I'm really enjoying it. I usually read it on the way to work.
2 I'm reading a very good book at the moment. It's fiction, but I think it's based on a true story. It's called *Eye of the Storm*, and it's about a hurricane – a very strong storm – which is coming towards the coast of Florida, in the USA. The main characters in the story are a man and his daughter, and her friend. And the man is out in his fishing boat and he hasn't heard about the hurricane. So, his daughter and her friend have to go out to sea and try to tell him before it's too late. It's very exciting. I can't stop reading it!
3 I'm not reading anything at the moment, but I've just finished a book called *A Puzzle for Logan*. It's a crime story and it happens in Edinburgh, in Scotland. It's a murder mystery. The police have found a woman who was murdered, and at the same time a man has just escaped from prison. He's been in prison for six years and he knows the woman, so of course everyone thinks that he murdered her. But the police officer, Inspector Logan, doesn't believe it. So, he tries to find out who really murdered the woman. It's a good story, I liked it.

Unit 9

A I'm writing an essay at the moment. But I'm a bit worried, because I only started today and I have to hand it in on Friday. I really need to speak to my lecturer. I might fail the year if she doesn't give me more time.
B I can't believe it's all over – the last exam was yesterday. Now I just have to wait for the results. I studied hard, so I'm quite confident. If I pass, I'm going to have a big party! If I don't, well … I'm not going to think about that …
C So I've got my results and … I'm really happy with my marks. All those hours in the library paid off! The problem now is that I have to choose which course to do at which university. I've got three places to choose from and they're all really good, but they're slightly different. I have to be quick – if I don't decide soon, I'll miss the deadline.
D Well, my exams start next week, so I'm revising a lot at the moment. I really want to do an economics degree but it won't be easy to get a place – there are a lot of people who want one. But I'm sure I'll get the grades I need if I work hard.
E The exam's in a couple of hours. I'm not really ready, because I went to a few parties this week and I haven't had time to revise. If the questions aren't too hard, I might be OK. But this lecturer normally gives us difficult exam papers, so I think I'm in trouble!

PRESENTER So, let's have a look at another story in the news today. A study reported in the newspapers this week has found that 50% of people in the USA say they are shy. And also that this is an increase, and shyness is becoming more common. Well, here to talk about this is Dr Lamb from the University of South London. Dr Lamb, good morning.
DR LAMB Good morning. Thanks for inviting me here.
P Let's talk first about shyness in general. Obviously we all feel shy sometimes. When does it become a problem?
L Well, it becomes a problem when it stops you doing what you want to do. Shy people normally want to communicate with other people. They don't want to be on their own. But they find it difficult when they need to talk to other people. Or when people talk to them.
P OK, and is it true that people are becoming shyer? Is shyness becoming more common in the world?
L That's a difficult question to answer. But some people say that modern technology is making us shyer.
P Yes, in fact the study mentions technology. What is the relationship between technology and shyness?
L Yes, well, the idea is basically that we speak to other people much less now … because of

technology. The Internet has changed things a lot. We maybe use email or Facebook more than we talk on the phone or meet our friends. We check our bank account online. We don't go to the bank much any more and speak to someone. We book our holidays online, not at a travel agent's. So, there are all of these things. We just speak to other people less than in the past. So, when we do speak to someone, it's more difficult for us.

P So tell us – what makes shy people feel the way they do? What's going on in a shy person's head?

L Well, first it's important to say – everyone is different so there's no single answer. But in general, shy people worry a lot and they expect things to go wrong. Let's imagine a shy person wants to go to a party. He or she will probably make lots of predictions about the party, normally bad ones. So, they'll say, 'If I go to the party, I won't know anyone and it will be difficult. I won't enjoy it.' And so on. Or often they imagine terrible situations – 'Everyone will laugh when I speak', 'Everyone will hate me', that kind of thing.

P These are, I think, the kinds of feelings we all get sometimes. But you're saying that very shy people get more of them.

L Yes, yes – absolutely.

P And what can you do to help shy people?

L Well, when I work with shy people, I ask them to talk about these feelings. I tell them to make a list of all the things they worry about. Then I can ask, 'Well, do you think these things will really happen?' At the beginning they say 'yes'. But I work with them and I hope in the end they'll realise the things probably won't happen. That's important. And after this training, I ask the shy person to go out and speak to people, to see what happens. And normally nothing bad happens. Then they can compare this real experience they've had to the list of fears they wrote on Day 1. There's normally a big difference and this really helps them to deal with their shyness.

P OK, Dr Lamb, we have to finish there. Thanks for coming to speak to us.

L Thank you.

▶ **3.12 PART 1**

RECEPTIONIST Good morning, Turner and Collins.

ANNIE Oh, good morning. Is it possible to speak to Mark Riley in Marketing?

R I'll just put you through.

COLLEAGUE Hello, Mark Riley's phone?

A Oh, hello. Is Mark there?

C I'm afraid he's not available – he's in a meeting. Can I take a message?

A Umm, can you just tell him that I called?

C And who's calling, please?

A This is Annie Morton speaking.

C OK. And shall I ask him to call you back?

A Ah, yes please.

C Did you say your name was Annie Morgan?

A No, sorry, Annie Morton. That's M-O-R-T-O-N.

C OK. And has he got your number?

A Yes, he has.

C Fine, I'll ask him to call you.

A Thanks very much.

C No problem. Bye.

A Goodbye.

▶ **3.14 PART 2**

RACHEL So, how are you doing? Are you feeling better about finding a new job?

ANNIE Yeah, definitely. I'm sure I'll find something.

R Good … thank you, Tina.

A And I called Mark this morning. He wasn't there, but I left a message for him.

R Great. And did you speak to your boss? Did you ask about other jobs at your company?

A Yeah, I did. But she said there won't be anything else there.

R Oh dear. Well, it was still a good idea to ask.

A Yes, definitely. It was good to get everything clear. I understand the situation now.

R Exactly. And what happened with Leo in the end? Is everything OK?

A I met him just now for lunch actually. But yeah, everything's fine. He wasn't very well – that was all.

R Oh dear.

A Anyway, what about you? How are things here at the shop?

R Fine. Actually, it's been quite quiet this week.

A Oh, this could be Mark now.

R Answer it!

A Hello?

MARK Hi, is that Annie?

A Yes?

M Hi, it's Mark here.

A Oh hi, Mark!

M Is now a good time?

A Yeah, it's fine.

M Well, I got your message. And Rachel explained you're looking for a new job.

A Sorry, Mark, I didn't catch that.

M Yeah, I was just saying, Rachel explained you're looking for a job.

A Yes, that's right.

M Well, look, why don't you come in to the office some time? We're always looking for new people here. Come in and we can have a chat.

A OK, that sounds great. How about two thirty tomorrow?

M Sorry, was that three thirty tomorrow?

A No, two thirty.

M Er … OK, that's fine.

A Great. Well, see you tomorrow then. Oh, I'm with Rachel and she wants to speak to you.

R Hi, Mark.

M Yep.

R Yes, I just wanted to ask you if you could buy a few things on your way home.

M Er …

R We need some milk, some orange juice …

M Sorry, can I call you back? I've got a meeting now, so I've got to go.

R OK …

M I'll call you in about an hour.

R All right. Speak to you soon. Bye.

M Bye.

▶ **3.19**

ROBERTA Hi, Janina. What are you reading?

JANINA I'm just looking at the course information for next year.

R Oh, OK.

J It says that one of the psychology courses I have to do is going to be online.

R That's good.

J You think so? I've never done an online course.

R I did one this year – it was great. I wouldn't mind doing my whole degree online.

J Really, Roberta? What's so good about it?

R Well, we only had about two classes on the whole course. And they recorded them and put them online anyway. I was free to study whenever I wanted. Good for people like me who are always late for classes!

J Yeah, I don't have a problem with that but it sounds good.

R I mean, you still have to write essays and hand things in on time and all that kind of thing.

J Of course.

R And I got good grades on that course.

J But did you … I mean, didn't you miss asking your teachers questions? And what about meeting other students?

R Well, we could go and meet the teachers if we wanted to … you know, make an appointment and ask about something one-to-one. And at the beginning of the course, we had to write an online profile. We had students from all round the world in our class, so the profiles were really interesting.

J How many international students were there?

R About 15, I think. And from all kinds of different places – Colombia, China, Morocco, Turkey, Oman – all over the place.

J And did they talk about their countries a lot?

R Yeah, that's what I really enjoyed.

J The only thing I'm not sure of … well, you know that my IT skills aren't very good. Like, I'm OK making documents and using the Internet. But this could be a bit more … I don't know … difficult?

R Not really. You don't need any special skills. It's quite easy. And there's an introduction course you can do.

J Yeah, I was just reading about that. At least it's free.

R Yeah, you should do it, Janina. It's only two weeks long and you can do it any time. It really helped me.

J OK – sounds like a good idea.

Unit 10

▶ **3.20**

PRESENTER Downloading is in the news again, with the news that more people downloaded the hit show *Game of Thrones* than actually watched it on TV. We're often told that downloading illegally from the Internet is the same as stealing from a shop. But do people really believe this? We asked the people of Camden Town: *If you wanted to watch a TV programme but it wasn't available in your country, would you download it illegally?*

1 Ah … maybe. I don't know … Yeah, if the programme wasn't available, I'd download it!

P What if it *was* on TV in your country, but not for another month?

1 Yeah, I would still download it. What's the difference? Downloading doesn't hurt anyone and no one ever gets into trouble. It would just mean I didn't need to wait a month!

2 Maybe it depends who made the programme. I don't think the big companies that make these TV programmes are poor. All the actors are rich enough … But if it was a film made by a small company, it would be a bit different. I'd prefer to pay a company like that because they need the money.

3 No, I wouldn't. I just watch what's on TV. No need to download things.

P And how about a book? Would you download a book?

3 Well, no. It would be illegal, I think.

P But what if it was a book that you knew was in your local library. But you didn't have time to go to the library.

3 Well … I suppose … if it was in the library … but, no. It's illegal. I wouldn't do it.

4 A TV programme? Of course, why not? It's easy. Everyone does it!

P And what about music? Would you download an album?

4 An album … ? Yeah, maybe. But I'm one of those strange people who still buys CDs. So if I liked the album, I'd buy it afterwards – because I like to own something I can hold in my hands.

P And what if it was a charity album? Would you download that?

4 No, I wouldn't download an album if it was for charity. That wouldn't be right.

5 I'd have no idea how to download a TV programme! But I'd ask my granddaughter to download it for me if I really wanted to see it. Although, I'd probably be worried about the police knocking at my door the next day.

▶ **3.26**

PRESENTER Now, a new survey has shown the countries in the world where people complain the most. And to discuss the results we've got two guests, Clara Gomes from Brazil, which is in the top ten of countries that like to complain, and Zhang Feng, from China, from the bottom ten on the list.

CLARA Good morning.

FENG Good morning.

P So let's start with you, Clara – what do you think of the survey results?

C Well, I'm surprised that we are in the top ten, but I'm not shocked because things are slowly changing in Brazil. Many Brazilians have got more money these days. So they buy more and also expect better quality – if something's not good enough, they'll complain. And another thing is education. I think people know more now about the law than they used to. They know what the companies have to do, like replace things if they break easily, or giving customers their money back if the bill is wrong … so they're asking companies to play by the rules.

P OK, and what about China, Feng? You're very low down the list. Do you think that's surprising?

F Not really, not these days. In China, people don't really believe everything a company says. Because of this, they always like to check the products carefully before they pay for them. When you buy something online in China, you can contact the company first to check all the details of the product – it's very quick and easy to do. And then, you don't have to pay when you order, you don't even have to pay when the product arrives – you *only* pay if *you* think the product is the same as the product that the company promised. So in the end, there isn't much to complain about.

▶ **3.27**

PRESENTER Right, well we're also joined by John Sutherland, a journalist from the magazine *What Product*. Let's talk about the UK, then. It seems like it's quite important to know how to complain in the UK, since we're top of the list.

JOHN Yes, I think so!

P So, what advice do you have for someone who has to make a complaint?

J Well, the first thing is that you should be quick. Complain as soon as the problem happens – the same day if possible. And also, be polite, so choose your words carefully and don't shout.

P OK.

J Another thing is to be clear – give a good description of the problem. And ... you should also always give a date – tell the company *when* you want them to do something by. So, you can say you want a decision in no more than ten days, something like that.

P Right.

J Also – don't be afraid to go to the top. Ask to speak to the manager or write to the director of the company. It can be the best way to get things done.

P And what's best – a phone call or a letter?

J I think letters are usually the best way to complain. You can explain the problem in detail and avoid getting too angry. But remember though, you should always tell them how you felt. Say how the problem spoiled your enjoyment or made your life difficult. This makes your complaint stronger.

P OK, well we have to leave it there. Thanks very much to all our guests.

▶ **3.29** **PART 1**

LEO Hi. Could you help me, please?

SALES ASSISTANT Yes, of course. How can I help?

L Er, I'd like to return this clock, please.

SA Would you like to exchange it for something?

L No. I'd like a refund, please.

SA Do you have a receipt?

L No, I don't. It was a present, you see.

SA Well, I'm terribly sorry, but we can't give you a refund without a receipt.

L But ... it came from this shop. Look – you've got the same clock there.

SA Yes, but without a receipt I can't give you a refund. I'm very sorry. Is there anything wrong with it?

L No. It was a present, but I don't really like it.

SA Well, I'm sorry, but there's nothing I can do then.

L Right. Could I speak to the manager, please?

SA Of course.

MANAGER Hello. What seems to be the problem?

L Yes, I'd like to make a complaint.

▶ **3.31** **PART 2**

MANAGER What seems to be the problem?

LEO Yes, I'd like to make a complaint. I have this clock. It was bought in this shop. Your sales assistant hasn't been very helpful. She won't give me a refund.

SALES ASSISTANT He doesn't have a receipt.

L No, I don't have a receipt.

M Well, I'm sorry, but we don't do refunds without a receipt.

L Yes, that's what she said. OK, then. Can I exchange it for something else?

M Is there anything wrong with it?

L No, there's nothing wrong with it.

M Can I just ask – why do you want a refund if it works OK?

L Well, I just ... It was a present and I'm not a big football fan. And it's a bit ugly. Well, not ugly but it's not very ... adult. You know, it's more for children.

SA I have one. I love it!

M Look, as it was a present, I'll let you exchange it for something else in the shop. But normally we wouldn't do this.

L That's very kind.

SA So, what would you like to exchange it for?

L Actually, I've decided that I'll keep it. It might be useful.

M Well, OK then, if that's what you prefer.

L Yes, yes, it's fine. Thanks very much for your help.

M Thank you.

L Bye.

M Goodbye.

SA Bye.

▶ **3.33**

TIM I went to buy a new pair of jeans the other day. I was the only customer in the shop and there were two shop assistants. They were chatting about what they did at the weekend, and when I asked for assistance, they just carried on talking. It was so rude. All I wanted to know was the price of some jeans. In the end, I decided to just leave the shop. I don't think they even noticed I was there. I felt like writing an email to the shop manager to complain, but then I forgot to.

VICKI One thing that I think is rude is when shops or companies don't reply when someone makes a complaint. I remember once I bought an MP3 player online. It took ages to arrive – like, about a month. So, I wrote an email to complain, but I didn't hear anything from them. I mean, is it too hard just to send an email saying sorry? If I were the manager of a company, I'd make sure I replied to every customer. I know it's not easy to run a business. But if you want to keep your customers happy, you should answer their emails. Well, I won't use that company again. I'll go to a local shop instead.

REBECCA Look, if I invited you to my party, you'd let me know if you could come or not, wouldn't you? You'd think so. But last month I had a party and invited about 40 people and about half of them didn't say if they were coming or not. Most of them didn't come in the end and, in my invitation, I did ask them to let me know. I think that kind of behaviour is incredibly rude, don't you? I mean, I needed to know how many people were coming, so I had enough food and drink. But then I made too much food and it was embarrassing. All they needed to do was send a text or email – which is not very difficult. There are some people I invited to that party who I'll never get in touch with again.

Unit 11

▶ **3.34**

There aren't any road signs in the sky yet, but just like in *Back to the Future II*, flying cars are real. The *Terrafugia Transition* is a car which can fly for 800 kilometres at a speed of 185 kilometres an hour. It has two seats and wings that fold up, so it can be driven on a road, too. But it isn't cheap – it costs about €220,000. And to fly the *Terrafugia*, you have to have a pilot's licence.

...

People who have seen *AI* might be happy to hear that no one can make robots that love their human owner yet. But scientists are trying to make friendly robots: one example is *Kirobo* – a Japanese robot that was designed as a friend for astronauts. Kirobo goes with the astronauts into space. It recognises their faces and says "hello" in Japanese when it sees them. It also gives them messages from people on Earth.

...

You might not know it, but there are already many cyborgs – doctors give people robotic hands and arms every week. And, these days, *'Iron Man'* suits are also available ... well, almost. In Japan, *Cyberdyne* have created a suit which allows people who can't use their legs to stand, walk and climb

stairs. The suit also makes the person who wears it five to ten times stronger. At the moment, the suit is produced for use in hospitals, but *Cyberdyne* also want it to be used by rescue workers, to lift heavy objects and get to injured or trapped people more quickly after an accident or disaster.

...

In the United States, the Memphis Police Department is trying to predict the future, just like in the film *'Minority Report'*. They don't have psychics, but they do have a computer program called *Blue CRUSH*. The program can't tell the police exactly who will break the law, but it can tell the police where it might happen and even what kind of crime it might be. Crime has gone down by 30% since they started using the program in 2006.

...

The Japanese company *NEC* has invented billboards which are similar to the ones in *'Minority Report'*. The billboards know how old you are and if you are male or female. And when you look at one, it chooses an advert for something it thinks you will like. It also records how long you look at the advert and how close you stand. This measures your interest in the advert. The billboards are already used in train stations in Tokyo.

▶ **3.40** **PART 1**

ANNIE Excuse me. Can you tell me where the reception is?

PERSON It's over there, by the trees. Can you see the doors? And the sign that says reception?

A Oh, yes. Thanks very much.

P You're welcome.

RECEPTIONIST Good afternoon.

A Hello. I'm here to see Mark Riley.

R What's your name, please?

A It's Annie Morton.

R OK, I'll let him know you're here. Oh, hello Mark, it's Sandra here at reception. I've got Annie Morton here to see you. OK, thanks. Bye. Yes, he's expecting you. He said you can go up and see him. Have you been to his office before?

A No.

R OK. It's on the first floor. So, go up the stairs and turn left. Go through the door and turn right. Then go down the corridor and it's the first door on the right.

A Fine. Thank you.

▶ **3.43** **PART 2**

ANNIE Sorry, I got lost. Could you tell me where the office is again, please?

RECEPTIONIST Yes, of course. So, first go up the stairs to the first floor and turn left. Then go through the door and turn right.

A So go up the stairs to the first floor and turn left. Then go through the door and turn right.

R Yes. Then go down the corridor and it's the first office on the right.

A Sorry, the fourth office?

R No, the first.

A Right, I think I've got that.

R Good.

A So can I just check? Go up the stairs and turn right ...

R No, turn left.

A Left! Then go through the door and turn left ... no ... right.

R That's it.

A Thanks very much.

▶ **3.45** **PART 3**

MARK Obviously, I can't promise anything. But I think you've a really good chance of getting a job here.

ANNIE Thanks, Mark! That's great. You've helped me so much.

M Not at all. You've got a really good CV and lots of experience. I'm sure my boss will be very impressed.

A I hope so! Anyway, I'll let you get back to your work now.

M OK.

A Oh, and have fun at the gym with Leo tomorrow!
M Thanks. I'm sure it'll be good. Do you want me to walk down with you or … ?
A No, it's OK – I know the way out. Thanks again.
M Not a problem. See you soon.
A Bye.
M Bye.

▶ **3.48**

HOST Hi, welcome to the show. Today we're looking at great inventions for the future. What really useful inventions do you think we need? People have called in to the show to tell us their ideas. First up we have Amir. Hi, Amir.
AMIR Hi.
H So Amir, tell us about what invention you'd like to see.
A I think the most important invention we need is a new kind of car engine that doesn't need petrol. There are too many cars in the world already, and as countries become richer, more and more people will want a car. That will be terrible news for the environment. But imagine a world with clean cars and no more pollution to worry about! I'm sure it will be invented soon. We already have electric cars, but I think it will be something different, maybe something like a car that runs on air. I'm sure someone will invent something to solve the problem. I hope so, anyway.
H Thanks, Amir. That's a great invention. Next on the line we have Utta. Utta, tell us about your invention.
UTTA Hi, well, one really useful invention would be artificial meat that's cheap and tastes good and which doesn't need cows, sheep or chickens to produce it. It sounds like science fiction, but in fact they've already invented it in a way. Amazingly, they've produced beef in a laboratory, but it cost thousands of pounds to make. But that's the same with all new inventions; they're always expensive at the start. So, I think it will happen and it'll be really good, because all the fields we use to grow food for cows could be used for something else – to grow vegetables or plant trees, for example.
H Thanks, Utta. Artificial meat! Wow, that sounds scary … Anyhow, last up we have Pierre. Hi, Pierre.
PIERRE Hi.
H So Pierre, tell us about your idea for a great invention.
P Well, a really useful invention I read about was a device that you could put in your ear and it would translate languages for you. You wouldn't need to study for hours and hours to learn a foreign language. You could just put it in your ear when you went on holiday to foreign countries and you'd understand everything everyone was saying to you. It would help people to communicate and would be very useful for business people or … or for politicians. But it wouldn't be very good news for teachers. Fortunately, for them, it's probably impossible to make such a device, or at least it will take many years.
H Cool. I'd love that invention! Thanks for those great ideas. Who knows which of them will happen! We can only wait and see.

Unit 12

▶ **3.53**

A parrot in Denver, USA, became a hero when it helped to save the life of a two-year-old girl. Megan Howard – the parrot's owner – was looking after two-year-old Hannah. It was morning and Hannah was eating her breakfast on her own, because Megan had gone to the bathroom.

While Megan was in the bathroom, the parrot, Willie, started to make a very strange noise. Megan realised something bad had happened. Willie started screaming the words "Mama! Baby!" again and again. Megan said she had never heard the parrot scream like that before.

She came out of the bathroom to see what was happening. And when she looked at Hannah, she saw that her face had gone blue. Some of Hannah's breakfast had got stuck in her throat. She couldn't breathe because the food was still there.

Luckily for Hannah, Megan had learned what to do in this situation. She immediately ran over to her and performed the Heimlich manoeuvre.

Hannah started to breathe again normally. And once Willie saw that Hannah was OK, he stopped screaming.

Willie the parrot was given a prize by the Red Cross for his actions. He was named 'animal hero of the year' and they gave him a box of cereal with his picture on it.

Hannah's mum thanked both Megan and Willie and said she thought they had both saved Hannah.

▶ **3.54**

CLAIRE My little sister and I have always had our fights. I think the funniest time was when I made her ride a cow. We lived in a house with a field of cows on one side and I told my sister that they were horses. I went into the field and stood behind the cows making horse noises. When the cows were right next to our garden fence, I said she could ride one of the horses … just like a cowboy! I still can't believe she listened to me! She just jumped off the fence onto a cow's back! The cow was very surprised. It ran away with my sister holding onto its back. I couldn't stop laughing. In the end, my sister fell off. Her clothes were really dirty and she was crying. Then, I felt bad and helped her back home. When we got back, I told my mum my sister had tried to ride a cow and I had saved her. She believed me … I still feel guilty.
JEREMY I often used to play with my younger brother, but we did fight a lot, too. I remember one time when I was really mean to him. That day my parents had burnt some leaves in the garden and the fire was still a bit hot. So I had an idea for a joke to play on my brother. We had an old kettle in the garden. It was really dirty. I told my brother I was going to make 'grass soup'. So I took some grass and put it in the dirty old kettle with some water. I put it on the fire for a minute. Then I poured some into a cup and gave it to my brother. It was a horrible brown-orange colour with green bits of grass in it. He didn't look very sure about drinking it, so I put the cup near my mouth and told him I had drunk some and it was delicious. I hadn't even tasted it, of course. I gave him the cup and he drank all of it. Later that evening, my brother said he wasn't feeling very well. My parents wanted to know why … so, really, I had to tell them about my 'soup'.
TANYA My sister's a year and a half older than me and we always got on well. When we were little, we were very similar and did everything together. But then she started to read a lot, and she was very strong for her age. I didn't mind, but I didn't like the attention she got from my parents. One day, some of my parents' friends came to visit us. My dad told them he was very proud of my sister, because she could read so well. I got really angry, so I went to the bookcase in the hall and chose five of the biggest, thickest books I could see. Then I went back to my parents and their friends and said I had just finished reading the books. My dad asked me to describe the stories. I had no idea, so I just looked at the front of the books and guessed. So I talked about a happy king with lots of rings – that was *Lord of the Rings* – and also lots of stories about people with names beginning with *N*. That was volume 12 of an encyclopaedia. I could hear my sister laughing in the other room the whole time …

▶ **3.59** **PART 1**

MARK So, any plans for the rest of the week?
LEO No, not really. Oh, tomorrow I've got to take the car to the garage. It's making a strange noise – must be the engine.
M Oh, what a pain! What kind of car have you got?
L It's a Nissan. It's strange. Normally these Japanese cars are very reliable.
M That's true – Japanese cars are normally reliable.
L Yeah.
M But I'm afraid Nissan is actually Korean.
L Er … I don't think so … I'm pretty sure it's Japanese.
M I'm sorry, but it's definitely Korean. I remember reading an article about the factories in South Korea.
L Well, maybe Nissan have factories in Korea, but that doesn't mean it's a Korean company. I think they just make some of them in Korea.
M Maybe you're thinking of Toyota? That's a Japanese company.
L That's right. Toyota is the biggest Japanese car company.
M Exactly.
L Yes, but the second biggest is Nissan, then Honda, probably. Or maybe Suzuki.
M Oh, I'm sorry but firstly, Nissan isn't a Japanese company – like I said. And then, Mazda is a much bigger company than Suzuki or Honda.
L I'm not sure about that. I think they're all a very similar size. And Nissan *is* Japanese.
M No, I really think …
L Oh, never mind. It's not important.
M Maybe you're thinking of Mitsubishi? They're a big Japanese company.
L No, I have a Nissan. That's what I'm talking about.
M In Korea, there's Kia, and I'm sure Nissan.
L Mark …
M Or … maybe I was thinking of Hyundai.
L Mark!
M Oh, sorry!

▶ **3.60** **PART 2**

RACHEL So, when do you start the new job?
ANNIE Next month. I'm a bit nervous, actually …
R Oh, don't worry, you'll be fine. Just remember …
MARK Maybe you were right. I don't know now … but no, I'm sure it's not Japanese.
LEO Really, it doesn't matter.
M I know – I can check on my phone!
L Hi.
M Or Chinese? Maybe it's Chinese.
A What's he talking about?
M Do they make cars in China? I think they do.
R Mark … be quiet.

▶ **3.64**

When I was a child we went to live in an old house in the country with a big garden. And at the end of the garden there was a summer house, it was a little house with just one room and windows, and my sister and I often played in this summer house. When I was about five – my sister was eight – we were playing one day in the summer house, and suddenly I looked up and I saw an old lady in black. She was wearing a hat and she was reading a book. I said to my sister, 'Who's that old lady?' and my sister said, 'What old lady?' She couldn't see her. So we ran back to the house and I told my mother that I'd seen this old lady, but, of course, she didn't believe me.

Then, a few months later, my mother was talking to the neighbours and they told her about the person who had lived in the house before us. They told her that a rather strange old lady had lived there. She had always worn black clothes and a hat – and she had died in the summer house.

Phonemic Symbols

Vowel sounds

Short

/ə/ teacher	/æ/ man	/ʊ/ put	/ɒ/ got
/ɪ/ chip	/i/ happy	/e/ men	/ʌ/ but

Long

/ɜ:/ shirt	/ɑ:/ part	/u:/ who	/ɔ:/ walk	/i:/ cheap

Diphthongs (two vowel sounds)

/eə/ hair	/ɪə/ near	/ʊə/ tour	/ɔɪ/ boy	/aɪ/ fine	/eɪ/ late	/əʊ/ coat	/aʊ/ now

Consonants

/p/ picnic	/b/ book	/f/ face	/v/ very	/t/ time	/d/ dog	/k/ cold	/g/ go	/θ/ think	/ð/ the	/tʃ/ chair	/dʒ/ job
/s/ sea	/z/ zoo	/ʃ/ shoe	/ʒ/ television	/m/ me	/n/ now	/ŋ/ sing	/h/ hot	/l/ late	/r/ red	/w/ went	/j/ yes

Irregular verbs

Infinitive	Past simple	Past participle
be	was /wɒz/ / were /wɜː/	been
become	became	become
begin	began	begun
blow	blew /bluː/	blown /bləʊn/
break /breɪk/	broke /brəʊk/	broken /'brəʊkən/
bring /brɪŋ/	brought /brɔːt/	brought /brɔːt/
build /bɪld/	built /bɪlt/	built /bɪlt/
buy /baɪ/	bought /bɔːt/	bought /bɔːt/
catch /kætʃ/	caught /kɔːt/	caught /kɔːt/
choose /tʃuːz/	chose /tʃəʊz/	chosen /'tʃəʊzən/
come	came	come
cost	cost	cost
cut	cut	cut
deal /dɪəl/	dealt /delt/	dealt /delt/
do	did	done /dʌn/
draw /drɔː/	drew /druː/	drawn /drɔːn/
drink	drank	drunk
drive /draɪv/	drove /drəʊv/	driven /'drɪvən/
eat /iːt/	ate /et/	eaten /'iːtən/
fall	fell	fallen
feel	felt	felt
find /faɪnd/	found /faʊnd/	found /faʊnd/
fly /flaɪ/	flew /fluː/	flown /fləʊn/
forget	forgot	forgotten
get	got	got
give /gɪv/	gave /geɪv/	given /'gɪvən/
go	went	gone /gɒn/
grow /grəʊ/	grew /gruː/	grown /grəʊn/
have /hæv/	had /hæd/	had /hæd/
hear /hɪə/	heard /hɜːd/	heard /hɜːd/
hit	hit	hit
hold /həʊld/	held	held
keep	kept	kept
know /nəʊ/	knew /njuː/	known /nəʊn/

Infinitive	Past simple	Past participle
leave /liːv/	left	left
lend	lent	lent
let	let	let
lose /luːz/	lost	lost
make	made	made
meet	met	met
pay /peɪ/	paid /peɪd/	paid /peɪd/
put	put	put
read /riːd/	read /red/	read /red/
ride /raɪd/	rode /rəʊd/	ridden /'rɪdən/
ring	rang	rung
run	ran	run
sit	sat	sat
say /seɪ/	said /sed/	said /sed/
see	saw /sɔː/	seen
sell	sold /səʊld/	sold /səʊld/
send	sent	sent
set	set	set
sing	sang	sung
sleep	slept	slept
speak /spiːk/	spoke /spəʊk/	spoken /'spəʊkən/
spend	spent	spent
stand	stood /stʊd/	stood /stʊd/
steal /stiːl/	stole /stəʊl/	stolen /'stəʊlən/
swim /swɪm/	swam /swæm/	swum /swʌm/
take /teɪk/	took /tʊk/	taken /'teɪkən/
teach /tiːtʃ/	taught /tɔːt/	taught /tɔːt/
tell	told /təʊld/	told /təʊld/
think	thought /θɔːt/	thought /θɔːt/
throw /θrəʊ/	threw /θruː/	thrown /θrəʊn/
understand	understood /ʌndə'stʊd/	understood /ʌndə'stʊd/
wake /weɪk/	woke /wəʊk/	woken /'wəʊkən/
wear /weə/	wore /wɔː/	worn /wɔːn/
win	won	won
write /raɪt/	wrote /rəʊt/	written /'rɪtən/